Organizational Reputation Management

Organizational Reputation Management

A Strategic Public Relations Perspective

Alexander V. Laskin
Quinnipiac University

WILEY Blackwell

Library of Congress Cataloging-in-Publication Data
Names: Laskin, Alexander V., author.
Title: Organizational reputation management : a strategic public relations
  perspective / Alexander V. Laskin, Quinnipiac University, CT, US.
Description: Hoboken, New Jersey : Wiley-Blackwell, [2024] | Includes
  index.
Identifiers: LCCN 2024002855 (print) | LCCN 2024002856 (ebook) | ISBN
  9781394180332 (paperback) | ISBN 9781394180349 (adobe pdf) | ISBN
  9781394180356 (epub)
Subjects: LCSH: Public relations–Management. | Organization.
Classification: LCC HD59 .L375 2024 (print) | LCC HD59 (ebook) | DDC
  659.2–dc23/eng/20240304
LC record available at https://lccn.loc.gov/2024002855
LC ebook record available at https://lccn.loc.gov/2024002856

Cover Design: Wiley
Cover Image: © erhui1979/Getty Images

Set in 9.5/12pt STIXTwoText by Straive, Pondicherry, India
SKY10071665_040424

Dedicated to My Family

Contents

Preface

Strategic approaches to public relations have been standard in public relations education for years. Public relations is taught as a strategic management function of building and maintaining relationships with key organizational publics such as customers, investors, employees, government agencies, local communities, and so on. Yet, in the "real world" public relations is commonly treated as nothing more than media relations and a marketing support function – in other words, the focus is on a few public relations tactics instead of public relations as a whole strategic function.

Public Relations Society of America (PRSA), the largest professional association for public relations, proposed that one of the reasons behind this gap may be the lack of education about the strategic role of public relations in such programs as business administration and management. As a result, future organizational leaders are simply not educated about public relations as a strategic function of managing reputations of organizations.

As a result, PRSA proposed PRSA MBA/Business Program Initiative. The Initiative's goal is to "provide MBA candidates with a better appreciation of public relations' strategic value and help them to understand and apply the associated knowledge required for organizational and leadership success in the future" (PRSA, 2023).

The program was supported by several leading business schools in the United States. In fact, business schools have long recognized the importance of training future leaders in public relations – year after year, business school leaders talk about the importance of training their students in strategic communication. The first example of the program was led by Professor Paul Argenti at the Tuck School of Business at Dartmouth University. Among other pioneers of the program were Northwestern University, Syracuse University, Virginia Tech University, University of Maryland, and others.

I have been teaching such a course for the MBA program at Quinnipiac University for over 10 years as well. Over multiple surveys that I conducted with students taking this course I learned about the importance of understanding the public relations concepts for business students. Unfortunately, I was not able to find a textbook that would meet my needs in teaching this course. Dedicated public relations textbooks focus too much on the insides of the public relations industry and present the topic from the standpoint of somebody who wants to have a job in strategic communication – not the case for most of my MBA students. Business textbooks do not teach public relations concepts at all – either treating public relations as a very technical function of marketing support or even labeling the whole public relations industry as a bad and unethical practice. No wonder business students have no appreciation or understanding of public relations!

Thus, I decided that I would have to write such a textbook myself. This book presents public relations as a strategic function of managing relationships with various organizational publics. It actually has dedicated chapters for some of the most important publics for various organizations: Chapter 6, employees and other internal publics; Chapter 7, investors and shareholders; Chapter 8, customers and subscribers; Chapter 9, governments and regulators; and Chapter 10, media and influencers. In addition to the chapters on each of these publics, the book also presents case studies focused on a specific example of managing relations with each of these publics.

The core part of the book teaches the actual concepts of public relations and strategic communications that future organizational leaders should understand. This knowledge will enable them to demand strategic contributions from their public relations employees and utilize their expertise to advance the mission of the organization they are managing. It starts with defining public relations as a strategic function and compares various academic definitions with the PRSA's official definition. The book teaches about the public relations process (what PRSA calls RPIE process); talks about communications goals and objectives, strategies, and tactics; and introduces important practical concepts such as Gantt chart, PESO, SWOT, and codes of professional conduct. A stand-alone chapter is dedicated to the measurement and evaluation where Barcelona Principles are discussed, along with the importance of a multilevel approach in evaluating public relations activities, outputs, and outcomes; effects on awareness, attitude, and behavior; and, of course, overall organizational results.

The main claim of this book is the focus of public relations on building and maintaining organizational reputation. While talking about such terms as identity, image, and reputation, the book defines reputation as the product of relationships that various publics have with the organization. In fact, the book claims that there is no reputation outside of the relationship and, as a result, public relations as a relationship management function is actually the reputation managing function! Armed with this knowledge, future managers will be able to rely on strategic public relations to build and maintain reputations no matter what kind of organization they lead – corporate reputations, nonprofit reputations, and government reputations.

I started working on this book over 10 years ago, right after I finished teaching my first class as part of the PRSA MBA Initiative - MBA650/STC519, Strategic Public Relations and Reputation Management. It was obvious to me that the class really needed a dedicated textbook. It took me significantly longer than I expected to actually write such a book and complete this project, but it is not important how long the book took to write; it is more important how much use it can have and how helpful it can be for students and other instructors teaching public relations and strategic communications to future organizational leaders at different levels – undergraduate and graduate – and in various business programs, management programs, public policy programs, or nonprofit management programs. I welcome feedback from students and instructors – please let me know what works and what does not!

I am truly appreciative of all the students who took this class with me. The MBA650/STC519 class at Quinnipiac University had hundreds of students over the years. In fact, most case studies featured in the book were first developed and analyzed as part of this class. I would like to thank all the students involved and especially

Christopher Benson, Joshua Boos, Mark Costonguay, Ellsworth Evarts IV, Aaron Falzon, Erin Fennell, Symone Foster, Heather Hayes, Autumn Hirsch, Katherine Kandiew, Madison Isherwood, Michael Lovello, Katie O'Dell, Ryan Pettinheo, Kelsey Reynolds, Caitlin Taddeo, and Varvara Vandysh for their contributions. I would also like to thank all the members of the PRSA MBA/Business Program Initiative and the early instructors for advancing this important work and especially Paul Argenti, Kathy Fitzpatrick, and Tricia Hansen-Horn.

Reference

PRSA (2023). MBA/Business School. https://www.prsa.org/about/mba-business-school

1

Organizational Reputation: Defining the Indefinable

LEARNING OBJECTIVES

1. *After reading this chapter, students will be able to define key reputational concepts: reputation, identity, image, and relationship.*
2. *After reading this chapter, students will be able to analyze reputations of the organizations they are familiar with.*
3. *After reading this chapter, students will be able to apply the reputational concepts to their own personal reputations and reputations of their classmates.*

Have you ever thought about your personal reputation? What do people think when they hear your name? What about the reputation of a restaurant you are planning on going to? What do you know about it? What do others think about it? What does it even mean for a restaurant to have a good reputation? And do you think it matters at all what kind of reputation a restaurant may have?

Let us think about it. Would you go to a restaurant known for giving people food poisoning? I think most people would avoid going to a restaurant known for poisoning its customers – even if the food looks good, the building is clean and welcoming, and the staff is smiling (see Figure 1.1). Thus, reputation in that case would mean a difference between getting customers' business and not getting it. In other words, it would be a very important factor for the restaurant's success and even survival.

The same may also be true for cars, phones, clothes, hotels, universities, sports teams, political parties, and even countries. Take for example a case when the Dominican Republic experienced a decline in bookings and an increase in cancellations of already-booked reservations in 2019. A *Washington Post* story reported only 30 people on a private beach at one of the most luxurious Dominican Republic hotels of more than 400 rooms and suites (Krygler, 2019). The story concluded that the country's reputation had a potentially devastating problem after the shooting of David Ortiz, a famous baseball player, and the death of several U.S. tourists. In fact, the reputational impacts were so severe that the country launched a #BeFairWithDR social media campaign in order to restore its reputation as a safe and enjoyable tourist destination. But why did a few negative cases overshadow millions of tourists who traveled

Organizational Reputation Management: A Strategic Public Relations Perspective,
First Edition. Alexander V. Laskin.
© 2024 John Wiley & Sons, Inc. Published 2024 by John Wiley & Sons, Inc.

Figure 1.1   Food in a Restaurant. *Source:* GoodLifeStudio/Getty Images.

to the Dominican Republic over the years and had amazing experiences? To answer that question one must seriously consider how reputations are built and maintained, and what can harm reputations.

Most often reputation research focuses on corporations, and study after study concludes that reputation is among a corporation's most valuable assets (Gomez-Mejia & Balkin, 2002). In fact, customers of corporations with positive reputations will become loyal to their products and services, employees of corporations with positive reputations will be more likely to stay in their jobs longer and be more productive, and even investors will be more likely to invest in corporations with positive reputations (Goldberg and Hartwig, 1990; Laskin, 2013; Raithel and Schwaiger, 2015; Rao, Agarwal & Dahlhoff, 2004; Roberts and Dowling, 2002; Shapiro, 1983).

Thus, reputation becomes an important concept to study and define. When it comes to defining reputation, it seems like everyone knows what it is. Indeed, we use the term reputation in our casual conversations without much hesitation. Yet, reputation is one of those words that are easy to use but hard to define. In addition, there is a plethora of terms that seem similar to reputation and sometimes even used interchangeably with reputation. See, for example, if you can differentiate reputation from organizational identity or an organization's image. This chapter reviews definitions of reputation and compares reputation with similar terms.

Identity

Identity is the starting point when defining a reputation. It is also what organizations have the most control over. Simply speaking, identity is how you want to be perceived. For example, Walmart may want everyone to think of it as a place where you can find

Figure 1.2 Shopping at Walmart. *Source:* PJiiiJane / Shutterstock.

the best prices on everything, the best place for a bargain, while Neiman Marcus, instead, may want to be perceived as an exclusive shopping venue for exclusive few customers – pricey but with a great shopping experience (see Figures 1.2 and 1.3).

Does it mean that customers would feel exactly how the organization wants them to feel? Not necessarily. A person may go to Neiman Marcus to find a bargain, while another person may go to Walmart because they enjoy the shopping experience there without even looking at prices. In other words, identity is the story the organization tells about itself, whether others would agree with it or not. Identity is not limited to organizations – this can be extrapolated to products (product identity), brands (brand identity), people (personal identity), and so on.

How do organizations build their identities? It starts with the goals, values, and mission of the organization. Neiman Marcus's mission statement, for example, declares, "we have continually transformed and elevated the luxury shopping experience, offering the finest in fashion, shoes, handbags, jewelry, beauty and decorative items for the home." Compare it with Walmart's mission statement, "to save people money so they can live better." If these statements were the starting points for two organizations, no wonder they needed to make very different choices about the types of their stores, products they sell, people they hire, and pretty much everything else.

It may be an interesting exercise to compare mission statements of several organizations working in the same industry and then analyze how the different visions of the organizations' mission lead to different results. For example, Table 1.1 lists mission statements of several automakers producing very different brands of cars.

Figure 1.3 Shopping at Neiman Marcus. *Source:* Dfwcre8tive / Wikimedia Commans / CC-BY 3.0.

The mission statements and other essential statements are not the only documents shaping an organization's identity. Every communication from the organization makes a statement about what that organization stands for. Annual reports, CEO press conferences, appearances on national and local news, emails to employees, and all other communications project the organization's identity. That's why it is important for all communications to be guided overall by the organization's mission and be done in coordination with each other. Sometimes organizations have different divisions responsible for different types of communications – the investor relations department may produce annual reports, the marketing department may work on advertisements, the public relations department may write news releases, and the social media team may manage Facebook and Twitter activities. Without close coordination between these teams, their communications may pull an organization's identity in different directions, harming the efforts of each other instead of complementing and enhancing each other's work.

The organization's identity is built on not only what it says but also what it does. In fact, a proverb states that actions speak louder than words! This means actions of an organization may have a stronger effect on its identity than its released statements, advertisements, and social media posts. Imagine a Neiman Marcus store with unfriendly employees, dirty floors, and clothes lying around in unorganized piles. It is unlikely that such a store would be projecting an identity of an exclusive and luxury shopping experience no matter what its managers say. Or, imagine Walmart selling items with significantly higher prices than other local retailers. It may seriously threaten the store's identity despite all the communications to the contrary. Thus, it is very

Table 1.1 Mission Statements of Select Car Manufacturing Companies.

BMW
BMW creates driving pleasure from the perfect combination of dynamic, sporty performance; ground-breaking innovations; and breathtaking design.

Ferrari
Born of the spirit of racing, Ferrari epitomizes the power of a lifelong passion and the beauty of limitless human achievement, creating timeless icons for a changing world.

Ford
To help build a better world, where every person is free to move and pursue their dreams.

Honda
At Honda, The Power of Dreams drives us to create intelligent products that enhance mobility and increase the joy in people's lives.

Kia
Respecting people and practicing environmental management to maximize value creation and pursue balanced and shared growth with stakeholders.

Lucid
We're proud to be an American electric vehicle company, owned and operated in the United States. Inspired by the spirit of California, we're moved to think beyond mobility and design for a world where life is the most important journey we'll ever take. To look beyond tomorrow, and shape a future where we no longer have to choose between doing great things – and doing the right thing.

McLaren
McLaren exists to create breathtaking performance road cars. And deliver the most thrilling driving experiences imaginable.

Mercedes-Benz
We have been moving people and goods for more than 130 years. Building outstanding, fascinating vehicles is what we do best, and by doing so we inspire our customers, both today and tomorrow.

Nissan
As a company worthy of trust, Nissan provides unique and innovative automotive products and services that deliver superior measurable values to all stakeholders.

Rivian
Rivian is on a mission to keep the world adventurous forever. This goes for the emissions-free Electric Adventure Vehicles we build, and the curious, courageous souls we seek to attract.

Rolls-Royce
Inspiring Greatness. Pushing boundaries and creating new realities both within and beyond automotive design for over 100 years.

Subaru
More than just a company that makes cars, aircraft, and related technologies,
Subaru aims to be a company that "makes our customers smile."

Tesla
To accelerate the advent of sustainable transport by bringing compelling mass market electric cars to market as soon as possible.

Toyota
To attract and attain customers with high-valued products and services and the most satisfying ownership experience in America.

Volkswagen
Our goal is to be an industry leader in providing unmatched quality automotive products and services.

---

important for an organization to weigh all its decision against its mission statement and other key principles to make sure every action is aligned with the company's vision of itself and with what it wants to project to the outside the world.

Many studies analyzed identities of organizations and, as a result, researchers developed a classification of components of the organizational identity. One of the key components of the organizational identity is its industry and corporate strategy – in other words, how the organization differentiates itself from all other organizations and what place it wants to secure for itself among all the competitors within the industry. We can think back to our example of Walmart and Neiman Marcus – both are retail companies but they have very different strategies and unique approaches to selling stuff. Another component is corporate communication – how an organization communicates and represents itself. For example, McDonald's and Wendy's seem to be in the same industry with pretty similar strategy, but their communications are miles apart. In fact, Wendy's marketing leader explained that for Wendy's social media presence the main goal is not to sell products but to entertain anyone who visits their page. End result: Wendy's has been recognized as the best fast-food company on social media (McKinnon, 2023).

Identity is also shaped by the organizational design – its logo, color scheme, other visual elements. In fact, companies spend millions of dollars developing and updating their logos. For example, in March 2023, Pepsi unveiled its new logo, the seventh one in its corporate history from 1899 to 2023. The reason for the change – to make the logo reflect the company's identity better and showcase that Pepsi is "a bold and confident brand" according to Pepsi's chief marketing officer (Wiener-Bronner, 2023, p. 1).

Another element shaping the organizational identity is its corporate culture, including the mission statement, values, history, and even the location where the organization is from. Indeed, country of origin may have a strong effect, especially on consumers not familiar with the product directly (Al-Sulaiti & Baker, 1998). When people are choosing a bottle of wine they may lean toward Italian or Spanish brands even without knowing how that specific bottle of wine would taste. Country of origin may have a negative effect as well – staying with the same example of wines, an amazing wine from Moldova may have more difficulty in persuading customers to give it a try than a mediocre wine from France.

And, of course, as mentioned above the actual behavior of the organization – the actual actions the organization takes – has a very strong influence on its identity. Research suggests, however, that organizational identity is affected by more than just official actions of organizations – it is also what its employees do and how they behave. From the CEO to an intern, the organization's employees constantly shape organizational identity. People in communities surrounding an organization's headquarters may find it upsetting if employees park on the streets blocking the road or throw garbage out of their windows. All of these actions – intentional or not – are reflected by the people in the local community and can affect how the organization is perceived.

Image

An image of an organization is a reflection of the organization's identity in the eyes of a particular public or stakeholder. If identity is how the organization wants to be seen, an image is how the organization is actually seen. An image can be compared with a mirror that somebody pointed at an organization – the reflection in that mirror is the organization's image.

As a result, an organization's image has a very strong connection to the organization's identity. Organizations that focus on great customer service make sure it is central to their identity and, as a result, invest significant resources in perfecting customer experiences, which are reflected in the images customers have about such organizations. What organizations project to the world through their identity – all their actions and communications – are often reflected in their image.

The reflection in the mirror, however, is not always a perfect match with the object it is reflecting. Mirrors can distort the image; the lighting and other details of the surrounding environment can distort the reflection as well; mirrors can reflect only a certain part of an object, completely missing everything else. The same is true with an image. The organization's image may fail to perfectly match with an identity the organization wants to project. Take, for example, Neiman Marcus again. A person can go to a Neiman Marcus store while being in a bad mood – maybe a person had a fight with their significant other on the way to the store. No matter what the store employees are doing, the customer remains angry and unhappy. The mirror's own peculiarities are affecting how the organization's identity is being reflected and the resultant image fails to create in the customer's mind what the organization is trying to project. Or imagine a customer shopping at Walmart takes out their smartphone and starts comparison-shopping online, finding better bargains on different websites – changes in the technological environment influence the image of Walmart as a low-price merchant.

Some audiences may not even care about the shopping experience. For example, investors may care only about the share price and may want their shopping experience to be a bit less luxurious, as long as it means cutting costs and improving profits. Or people who live on the same road where Walmart is located may care about only the constant traffic going in and out of the store, thus lowering the prices on goods that can potentially lead to more traffic going to the Walmart store will be a negative event for these local residents rather than positive. Different groups of people may care only about a very specific issue or a very specific part of the organization and completely disregard what the organization itself thinks is important.

And, of course, both Neiman Marcus and Walmart, retailers operating multiple locations worldwide, may be faced with inconsistent images based on varying experiences from only one or two outlying stores (see Figure 1.4). It is difficult to persuade a customer who just had a bad experience in a store that most other stores of the same brand are significantly different and would provide a better experience. As a result, one negative experience may potentially destroy years of good work organizations invest in building and maintaining their identities. On the other hand, it is also possible that years of good work would protect an organization from one or two bad experiences.

One of the key challenges in managing organizational reputations is identifying gaps and misalignments between organizational identity and its image. Imagine a situation where consumers, for whatever reason, completely miss the mark on what the company's products are about. For example, Toyota's identity focuses on building high-quality cars that lead to satisfying ownership experience (in fact, according to Toyota's mission statement "the most satisfying ownership experience") (2023). Its identity is not about building fast cars or flashy cars. Compare it with Ferrari that starts

Figure 1.4 Shopping at Walmart Supermarket in China Provides Different Experience Than Shopping at Walmart in the United States. *Source:* pcruciatti / Shutterstock.

describing its identity with this: "Born of the spirit of racing . . ." (2023). Ferrari describes its cars with such words as power, passion, beauty, and timeless icons. Both of these car manufacturers have very different identities, which should be reflected in their images.

As a result, if for some reason Toyota cars start experiencing poor reliability and Toyota's image as a manufacturer of reliable car starts suffering, it is a real threat to the company, as reliability is at the center of its identity. The organizational image will be drifting away from the organizational identity, creating a gap that may lead to confusion and bewilderment on the part of consumers. Eventually, this misalignment may affect other audiences important to the organization and even threaten the organizational existence. On the other hand, if Ferrari cars develop an image of poor reliability, it is unlikely to cause significant misalignment between the organization's identity and image. In fact, Ferrari cars are somewhat famous for their poor reliability already – some of the car rankings even place them as the most unreliable cars ever (Warrantywise, 2023). It does not hurt their sales or their customers because the organization does not focus on reliability – it is not central to its identity. Even the principal of Ferrari's Formula 1 team, Mattia Binotto, in response to poor reliability of cars on track, responded that he would rather have fast cars than reliable cars (Cooper, 2022). Having slow but reliable cars, however, would be a pretty disastrous scenario for Ferrari, while it would be quite a success for Toyota. Table 1.1 lists some of car manufacturers' identity statements.

In managing organizational reputation, it is important to understand the connection between identity and image and act accordingly in order to keep the two aligned. When in 2002, for example, Toyota decided to join Formula 1 to race with such competitors as Ferrari, McLaren, or Williams, it had very little to gain, as winning in Formula 1 would not reinforce its identity. In fact, Toyota had to work extra hard to simply avoid embarrassment in the sport. Despite having the largest budget among all F1 teams, Toyota never managed to win a single F1 Grand Prix race, and withdrew from the sport after eight years (Collantine, 2008). On the plus side, this failure in F1 did not affect Toyota much, as its customers did not necessarily care about racing results as it was not central to what makes Toyota Toyota. In fact, Toyota international sales almost doubled during the time it was failing to perform in F1 (Toyota, 2012).

As a result, it is important for organizations to understand their true identity and make sure the image of the organization is a true reflection of such identity. In fact, identity can be compared with human DNA – this is who we actually are. However, our friends or colleagues will not recognize us if they looked at scans of our DNA. Instead, they would recognize us if they looked at our photos. There is a connection between our DNA and how we look – DNA determines how our hair, eyes, and nose look. However, we can color our hair and we can wear contact lenses to change our eye color. The same is true for organizations – while identity shapes the organizational image, organizations have the power to adjust and modify their perceptions.

Nevertheless, there is another variable that comes into play that can affect the alignment between organizational identity and image – the relationship between an organization and its various stakeholders.

Relationship

Relationship is an interpersonal concept, but it can also be applied to relations between people and organizations and even between organizations. Imagine, for example, a grocery store that for years has been buying produce from a local farm. We can say that they established a good business relationship. In fact, if the farm consistently provides good quality produce, delivery after delivery, at fair prices and in a timely manner, the store is more likely to overlook an occasional error or mistake or a rotten case of tomatoes. The established relationship allows for a mistake. The reverse is also true. If that local farm is happy with their long-term relationship with the grocery story, they may say no to another company that wants to buy their produce even if they offer a higher price. The farm may prefer to keep and maintain this long-term relationship over a short-term profit.

These relationships become the context in which identity is being projected and reflected into an image. Relationships affect both parts of this equation – the projection and the reflection. Organizations have many relationships and those relationships have different levels of prominence and significance. Think of your personal relationships, for example. You may have several relationships of high importance in your life – parents, siblings, children, significant others. You may have relationships that are also important but maybe not to the same degree – you may put your friends or your roommates in this category. You may also have relationships that are less relevant – you colleagues or your neighbors. Finally, you may have relationships that you do not even think of and do not even know about. For example, a person driving next to you on a highway. But this insignificant relationship can change into one of the most important relationships in your life if that person swerves into your lane forcing you to crash and sending you to the ER. In other words, the relationships and their importance can change. Sometimes this change is slow and gradual, but sometimes it can be fast and unexpected. As a result, it is important to monitor and try to predict how your relationships with the outside world can develop and change. This concept is known as environmental scanning – scanning your environment for changes in the relationships you have.

The same is true for organizations. Organizations also have many different relationships of various importance (see Figure 1.5). Corporations tend to focus on their relationship with customers, making it one of their most important relationships. But corporations cannot exist without employees – as a result, employee relationships are also among the most important for organizations. Publicly traded corporations spend significant resources managing their relationship with their shareholders and investors. Universities care about student relationships. For many organizations, government relationships are important to monitor and manage, as a small change in laws and regulations may mean a difference between losses and profits. It is also true that even a seemingly unimportant relationship may change into one of the most important for the organization. Nike probably could not imagine back in 2005 that one student-led group, United Students Against Sweatshops, would generate so much publicity and protest that Nike would have to take responsibility over the way it produced its clothes, shoes, and sporting equipment in Southeast Asia. Although many years have passed since 2005, Nike is still connected with that sweatshop scandal, and its reputation even today suffers from this connection.

As a result, relationship becomes a key part of understanding and managing organizational reputation – it's the context in which reputations live. Mary Ann Ferguson was among the first to highlight the importance of relationship leading to what today

Figure 1.5 People and Organizations Have Many Relationships. *Source:* sodafish visuals / Adobe Stock.

is known as *OPR Theory, Organization-Public Relations Theory*. Advocating for the importance of studying relationships, Ferguson explains (1984):

> By putting the research focus on the relationship rather than on the organiza-tion or on the public, we can come to better understandings of what it is that is important about these relationships, both to the public and to the organization. A model that focuses on either the organization or the public assumes that if and when changes occur either the organization and/or the public must change. A relationship-centric model has the assumption that the relationship is the prime issue of concern, not the parties. (p. 19)

This paradigm shift in public relations from *what organizations do* to *the relationship organizations have* with various publics became an important step in understanding the concept of organizational reputation. Indeed, if an organization decides to improve its reputation, it may do a lot of things and invest a lot of money but still produce zero effect on its reputation or, worse, make its reputation score decrease. Thus, looking at the organization by itself is not sufficient to understand its reputation. And this brings us to the definition of the reputation.

Reputation

Reputation, in most simple terms, is the sum of all the images and relationships the company has over time. In many definitions of reputations we would typically find words like overall perception, collective judgment, combined stakeholders, long-term, and similar (Abdullah and Abdul Aziz, 2013; Barnett, Jermier, & Lafferty, 2006; Pomering and Johnson, 2009). In other words, reputation is a summative and long-standing concept. One way to understand reputation is to compare it with climate. Climate of a given location is the sum of all weather experienced in that location over time. For example, we know that climate in Miami is warmer and wetter than in New York City. Miami has 61.9 inches of rain on average a year, while New York gets 46.23 inches. The average temperature in New York City in its hottest month, July, is 77° Fahrenheit, and the average July temperature in Miami is 83° Fahrenheit. This is climate – long-term averages. However, on any given day two cities may experience different weather: it may rain in New York while it may be absolutely dry in Miami. A day in July may be hotter in New York City than in Miami as well. This is daily weather. Even when the weather is colder in Miami than in New York (it does happen!), it still does not change the fact that Miami's climate is warmer overall.

The same is true for reputation. Reputation is defined through these long-term aver-ages – and, as a result, is slow to change. At the same time, an image can be changing all the time. A company may have a good quarter of sales, posting record profits – it would have a very positive affect on the company's image among investors. But next quarter the company may fail to meet its profit targets – its image among investors would suffer, as a result. But none of these events alter the long-standing reputation of a company's stock as a reliable investment.

This long-term nature of reputation is one of the reasons Reputation Dividend, an organization that measures and evaluates reputations of corporations, has similar companies at the top of its reputation list year after year. Reputations are slow to change and may not always react to daily changes in operations as stock markets tend to do, for example. In fact, Cole's (2019) report on global reputation notes that while stock markets declined 0.4%, the value of reputation increased 2.1%. The value of reputation of all corporations comprising 15 equity market indices equates to $16.77 trillion, which represents 35.3% of the overall market capitalization. This truly makes reputation the most valuable asset!

Reputation is also stable across different relationships as it is a sum of all images and relationships organizations have. In fact, changes in an investor's perception of an organization may influence an organization's customers and employees. It is impossible to silo an organization's reputation. When students started protesting Nike's sweatshops, the information spilled over to customers, investors, employees, and even government agencies – in other words, it did not just affect Nike's image among students: over time it affected Nike's overall reputation.

Although reputation is based on the products the company makes, profits the company posts, and the salaries it pays to its employees, reputation is more than any of these singular components. One way to think of a company's reputation is to imagine it in an environment completely out of its usual business. For example, imagine if Nike opened a hotel. What hotel would it be, how would it look, what amenities would it have? Nike's overall reputation would guide your imagination. Or imagine if Hilton would start making shoes. What kind of shoes would they make? What you think about Hilton's reputation would help you envision what kind of shoes they would make.

As a result, we can conclude that reputation is a long-term belief that sums up the images about the organization from various publics based on their relationships with the organization. Thus, it becomes important to understand who the publics are and how to manage relationships with them.

Chapter Summary

All organizations have their *identities* – same way as people have DNAs. These identities affect how the organization appears to all different publics the organization interacts with – consumers, investors, suppliers, employees, and others. However, the same way as people are not judged simply based on their DNA, the perceptions of organizations may differ from their internal identities. This perception is known as the organizational *image*. The image is strongly affected by the relationships between the organization and various publics – consumers' perceptions of an organization are shaped based on their shopping experience, but employees' perceptions are affected by their work experience. Thus, the context in which identity is perceived by various publics and translated into an image is shaped by the *organization-public relationship*. When we add it all up – identity, image, and relationships across various publics the organization deals with – we arrive at reputation. As a result, we define *reputation* as a long-term belief that sums up the images about the organization from various publics based on their relationships with the organization.

Five Key Terms to Remember

Identity
Image
Reputation
OPR Theory
Mission statement

Discussion Questions and Activities

1 Explain the relationship between identity, image, relationships, and reputation.
2 Based on the key characteristics of reputation described in this chapter, propose your own definition of reputation.
3 Find a recent ranking of organizational reputations. Review the companies at the top of the list. Discuss why, in your opinion, these companies have the best reputations. What is different about these companies in comparison with their peers?
4 Pick any industry and select three to five companies working in that industry. Find their mission statements and compare and contrast them. Discuss the differences and similarities.
5 Take any large company making consumer products. It can be Apple, BMW, Nautica, or anything else. Pretend this company opens a chain of hotels. Based on the company reputation, propose what kind of hotels this company would have. What would be unique features and amenities of these hotels and why?

References

Abdullah, Z., & Abdul Aziz, Y. (2013). Institutionalizing corporate social responsibility: Effects on corporate reputation, culture, and legitimacy in Malaysia. *Social Responsibility Journal*, *9*(3), 344–361. https://doi.org/10.1108/SRJ-05-2011-0110

Al-Sulaiti, K. I., & Baker, M. J. (1998). Country of origin effects: A literature review. *Marketing Intelligence & Planning*, *16*(3), 150–199. https://doi.org/10.1108/02634509810217309

Barnett, M. L., Jermier, J. M., & Lafferty, B. A. (2006). Corporate reputation: The definitional landscape. *Corporate Reputation Review*, *9*(1), 26–38.

Cole, S. (2019). What price reputation? *AMO Strategic Advisors*. https://www.reputationdividend.com/files/6415/6215/6989/RD_AMO_GLOBAL_REP_VALUE_030719.pdf

Collantine, K. (2008, September 22). Toyota has 445.6m F1 budget. *Race Fans*. https://www.racefans.net/2008/09/22/toyota-has-biggest-f1-budget-4456m

Cooper, A. (2022, June 13). Ferrari prefers fast unreliable F1 car rather than other way around. Motorsport.com. https://us.motorsport.com/f1/news/ferrari-prefers-fast-unreliable-f1-car-rather-than-other-way-around/10321645

Ferguson, M. A. (1984). Building theory in public relations: Interorganizational relationships as a public relations paradigm. Paper presented at AEJMC Conference, Gainesville, FL (1984, August).

Ferrari (2023). About us. https://www.ferrari.com/en-EN/corporate/about-us

Goldberg, M. E., & Hartwig, J. (1990). The effects of advertiser reputation and extremity of advertising claim on advertising effectiveness. *Journal of Consumer Research, 17*(2), 172–179.

Gomez-Mejia, L. R., & Balkin, D. B. (2002). *Management.* McGraw-Hill.

Krygler, R. (2019, June 12). For the Dominican Republic, seven U.S. tourist deaths, the shooting of David Ortiz and a new image problem. *Washington Post.* https://www.washingtonpost.com/world/the_americas/for-the-dominican-republic-six-us-tourist-deaths-the-shooting-of-a-beloved-ballplayer-and-a-new-image-problem/2019/06/11/8e31af1a-8c4a-11e9-b6f4-033356502dce_story.html?noredirect=on&utm_term=.d9223722ceeb

Laskin, A. V. (2013). Financial performance and reputation. In C. Carroll, Ed., *The handbook of communication and corporate reputation* (pp. 376–387). Malden, MA: Wiley.

McKinnon, T. (2023, February 4). Wendy's brilliant Twitter strategy & its top 22 best tweets. *Indigo9Digital.* https://www.indigo9digital.com/blog/wendystwitterstrategy

Pomering, A., & Johnson, L. W. (2009). Constructing a corporate social responsibility reputation using corporate image advertising. *Australasian Marketing Journal, 17*(2), 106–114. https://doi.org/10.1016/j.ausmj.2009.05.006

Raithel, S., & Schwaiger, M. (2015). The effects of corporate reputation perceptions of the general public on shareholder value. *Strategic Management Journal, 36*(6), 945–956 https://doi.org/10.1002/smj.2248

Rao, V. R., Agarwal, M. K., & Dahlhoff, D. (2004). How is manifest branding strategy related to the intangible value of a corporation? *Journal of Marketing, 68*(4), 126–141 https://doi.org/10.1509/jmkg.68.4.126.42735

Roberts, P. W., & Dowling, G. R. (2002). Corporate reputation and sustained superior financial performance. *Strategic Management Journal, 23*(12), 1077–1093 https://doi.org/10.1002/smj.274

Shapiro, C. (1983). Premiums for high quality products as returns to reputations. *Quarterly Journal of Economics, 98*(4), 659–679 https://doi.org/10.2307/1881782

Toyota (2012). Sales of passenger cars, trucks and buses. https://www.toyota-global.com/company/history_of_toyota/75years/data/automotive_business/sales/sales_volume/overseas/index.html

Toyota (2023). What are Toyota's mission and vision statements? https://support.toyota.com/s/article/What-are-Toyotas-Miss-7654?language=en_US

Warrantywise (2023). Top 10 least reliable used car makes and models www.warrantywise.co.uk/blog/top-10-least-reliable-car-makes-and-models

Wiener-Bronner, D. (2023, March 28). Pepsi has a new logo. *CNN.* https://www.cnn.com/2023/03/28/business/pepsi-new-logo/index.html

2

Publics and Relationships: The True Job of Public Relations

LEARNING OBJECTIVES

1. *After reading this chapter, students will be able to define public relations.*
2. *After reading this chapter, students will be able to identify different publics.*
3. *After reading this chapter, students will be able to apply the concept of public prioritization for various organizations.*

An organization's reputation depends upon the relations it has with its key constituencies and the images these constituents have about this organization. If customers are not happy about the organization and do not find value in their interactions with the organization, it will have a negative effect on this organization's reputation. If employees do not value their relationship with the organization, such organization is not likely to have a good reputation.

Publics

These constituencies are called *publics*. Publics are groups of people connected with a common interest or a common belief or a common connection to an organization (Kelleher, 2018). For example, employees of an organization represent one of the publics that organizations should focus on – their unique relationship with the organization makes them into a distinct and easily recognizable group. Another example can be volunteers at a local animal shelter – they also have a unique relationship with the animal shelter distinct from the relationships that customers or employees would have. See Figure 2.1 for examples of organizational publics.

At the same time, employees, as one of the organization's publics, do not necessarily share common demographics. In fact, it is quite common for organizations to have people of different ages, genders, races, national origins, educations, and so on among their employees. The same is true for volunteers – they may be made up of a variety of people. This makes the concept of publics different from a similar concept of audiences or markets. In fact, target audiences and target markets are concepts that

Organizational Reputation Management: A Strategic Public Relations Perspective,
First Edition. Alexander V. Laskin.
© 2024 John Wiley & Sons, Inc. Published 2024 by John Wiley & Sons, Inc.

Figure 2.1 Organizational Publics.

primarily focus on consumers and usually group them together based on some demographic and, more recently, psychographic characteristics (Ferrell and Hartline, 2005). In the case of publics, however, it is quite possible that they would have very different demographic and psychographic types.

Stakeholders

Another similar concept is a *stakeholder*. Stakeholder is a common term in management that describes a party that has a stake, or an interest, in the organization (Center et al., 2008). Some common examples are shareholders, but employees also clearly have a stake in the organization, same as customers, and so on. In fact, it is quite common to use the terms publics and stakeholders interchangeably. However, there is a certain difference. What stake did the student protesters have in Nike when they organized demonstrations against the sweatshops? Some of them maybe were customers and purchased Nike products. Some maybe were shareholders and owned Nike stock. Maybe some were employees or interns at Nike. And many probably had no connection to Nike at all. In other words, they were not connected by a common stake they had in Nike. Instead, they were united by a common idea and a common issue. Perhaps they did not even care about the company itself – they cared about the issue of sweatshops and Nike simply served as an example for this issue. As a result, although both terms – publics and stakeholders – are often used interchangeably, it is possible to draw a distinction between the two and, as a result, in this book we will primarily focus on the term "publics" as more relevant for the concept of reputation.

Public Relations

The function of managing relationships between an organization and its various publics is known as *public relations*. The largest professional association in public relations, Public Relations Society of America (PRSA), conducted a crowdsourcing campaign among practitioners to define what public relations is. The result became the official definition of the public relations industry: "Public relations is a strategic communication process that builds mutually beneficial relationships between organizations and their publics" (PRSA, n.d.).

The definition emphasizes the goal of public relations – *relationships*. More than that, it is the relationship that both parties find beneficial. Customers find it beneficial to buy a product or service, and the organization finds it beneficial to sell the product or service. Employees find it beneficial to work at the organization, and the organization derives benefits from these employees. Students find it beneficial to enroll at a college, and the college benefits from these students. Many people around the world enjoy using iPhones (see Figure 2.2) – nobody makes them buy iPhones over other phone brands. In fact, iPhones are so popular that Apple can charge a premium price and sell iPhones for more money in comparison with their competitors. Both parties – Apple and its customers – enjoy this relationship: customers get a premium product; Apple gets a premium price. And, of course, this relationship gets reflected in the reputation – Apple has a reputation of a provider of premium phones, and Apple customers have a reputation of people who are willing to pay a premium price.

How does public relations build these *mutually beneficial relationships*? The answer to this question is dependent on a particular public. There is no one universal approach

Figure 2.2   iPhone Is a Popular Consumer Product. *Source:* ET-ARTWORKS/Getty Images.

to relationship building. Every public may want different things and often these demands may be contradictory to each other. Customers may want the organization to build more products and sell them at a cheaper price; on the other hand, employees of the same organization may want to work less and be paid more. But in order to pay them more, organizations may have to charge customers more for the final product – employees and customers may have opposite demands. And at the very same time, investors may want to charge customers more and pay employees less in order to secure more profits that can be used to pay out dividends, while the organization's top management may also want more profits but instead of paying them out as dividends, they may want to reinvest them in research in order to develop even better products in the future and grow the organization's market position. As a result, every organization has a complex knot of competing interests of different publics aimed at it.

Relationship Management

Public relation's job, as a result, is to be on the forefront of *relationship management*. Public relations professionals serve as *counselors* to the organization's leadership, helping them identify various publics and prioritize them. Based on prioritization, the organization decides how much to invest in relationship management with each of these publics and how to engage with them. Of course, this is a never-ending process, since public's importance is constantly changing, relationships are constantly evolving, and what seemed like a public with no connection to the organization may suddenly become of vital importance. Was it possible for Malaysian Airlines' CEO to imagine that military combatants in Ukraine must be an important public for an organization? It is unlikely that prior to July 17, 2014, Malaysian Airlines' management considered this public in any of its planning. Yet, on July 17, 2014, after a Malaysian Airlines passenger jet was mistakenly shot down over Ukraine, the combatants in Ukraine became one of the most important publics for the organization.

In an ideal world, public relations counselors at Malaysian Airlines would have predicted the possibility of such an outcome and acted to change the routes of its plane, saving 298 people. There is a saying in public relations that the best crisis is the one that never happened. But it is difficult, if not impossible, to predict everything. Nevertheless, analyzing past and current publics as well as trying to predict future publics and their potential changing relationships is an important part of the public relations professional's responsibilities.

In fact, it is quite common to modify the definition of public relations provided at the beginning of this chapter by adding a qualifier about the publics. Then, the definition would look something like this: Public relations is a strategic communication process that builds mutually beneficial relationships between an organization and its publics on which its success or failure depends. Such a modified definition highlights an important aspect of reputation management: environmental scanning. Environmental scanning conducts constant monitoring of the environment in which the company operates, and identifies key publics that are affecting or can potentially affect the organization. The process concludes with developing strategies on how to respond to these challenges and opportunities that the constantly changing publics and environment present.

Communication and Action

Another common point of debate when discussing the definition of public relations is the word communication as in the *communication process*. Communication is a foundation of many relationships – we communicate in order to establish and support all kinds of relationships. You can think of your own personal relationships, for example. Some of the most important relationships we have is with our family – as a result, we usually communicate the most with our family. Depending on your stage in life, your parents, your siblings, your significant other, or your children are constantly in your recent contacts on your phone, in your messaging apps, emails, social media, plus, you talk with them in person when you get a chance as well. You tell them how much they mean to you, and they likely remind you of their love. All these communications are integral parts of your relationship. You may also have professional relationships with students, colleagues, professors, and you also use communication to facilitate these relationships.

The same is true for organizations. Organizations must communicate with their employees – it may be something as trivial as the update on food service in the building, or it can be something as drastic as layoff announcements. In either way, failure to properly communicate can lead to an unhappy workforce or even a significant disaster, while honest, sincere, and appropriate communication can help enhance mutually beneficial relationships.

While communication is an essential part of any relationship – personal or professional – no relationship can survive if communication is all there is to it. In fact, any relationship needs the actual substance in addition to the communications. Communications about going to a dinner together need the actual action of going to this dinner, same way as communications about salary increase need the actual salary increase. Relationships are based on what we do to a larger extent than on what we say. Actions speak louder the words!

The reason we have strong relationships with our significant others is mainly because of what they do for us, not just what they say. Our parents spend countless hours and money to raise us and provide for us, feeding us, clothing us, driving us where we need to go, and so on. If all they do is talk and do nothing for us, we probably would not have a very good relationship; in fact, as little children, we may not even survive.

The same is true for corporations. People love driving Tesla cars, not because of what Tesla news releases communicate but because of the products they make (see Figure 2.3). People pay premium for iPhones not because Apple says how great these phones are but because Apple makes them simple to use, reliable, powerful, and with lots of useful applications. The substance is usually more important than communications.

Thus, many scholars and professionals suggest that if public relations is truly a function of managing relationship, the word communication in its definition should be replaced with the word *management*. Then, the definition of public relations would look like this: Public relations is a strategic *management* process that builds mutually beneficial relationships between an organization and its publics on which its success or failure depends.

The word management implies the management of all aspects of the relationship – *substantive* and *communicative* components of it. If customers are not happy with the

Figure 2.3   Tesla Model S. *Source:* Hadrian / Shutterstock.com.

new Tesla self-driving software, a good public relations response would involve both communications about it (acknowledging the issue, informing all the relevant parties, discussing proposed resolutions) as well as fixing the issue (delivering the public's feedback to the engineers and top managers at Tesla, participating in the troubleshooting and addressing the problems found, and developing the actual improvements to the product as part of the team). The news releases cannot fix bad software, thus the software must be fixed and then this information should be communicated.

Devil's Advocate

Public relations as a management function becomes an *intermediary* between the public and the organization. A public relations manager often plays the role of *devil's advocate*, representing the interests of the public involved within the organization but representing the interests of the company when dealing with the public. For example, if a Tesla self-driving software update is getting a lot of criticism, the public relations manager will collect all the feedback and analyze it. Then, they would present their insight to Tesla's management team and engineers, and facilitate proper analysis and evaluation of such feedback. The engineers may identify the errors and then the top management team would develop a solution to the problem. But let us say engineers find out that the software works just as it was designed, and it is the drivers that do not use it correctly. Then, it becomes the job of the public relations manager to focus on the communication aspect and ensure proper communications and issuance of relevant training information to help the public use the software properly.

Two-Way Symmetrical

Another popular definition of public relations also adds *two-way symmetrical* process to the text. Two-way symmetrical process implies that both parties involved in the relationship have a say about this relationship. Imagine trying to troubleshoot a problem with an internet connection. When you call a cable company, it rarely feels like you are in a two-way symmetrical conversation. In fact, it does not matter what you say, once you get to an actual human after waiting on the line for hours, the response will most likely be following a template that the customer service agent must use – they will make you restart the computer, check the password, reset the router. It would not matter what you say at all or if you did all these steps already, you will not have any power in this relationship. The relationship is not going to be symmetrical in any way.

A two-way symmetrical relationship does not mean that both the customer (or any other public) and the organization always have equal power. This would be impossible. As we discussed, any organization has many different publics and the balance of power is constantly moving. Instead, two-way symmetrical means that both parties in the relationship derive benefits from the relationship and both have an influence on this relationship. A customer may decide to buy a new model of a phone or not to buy it and they may freely communicate their satisfaction or lack of satisfaction with such phones. A lot of customers choosing not to buy a product and even worse communicating their unhappiness with the product, can send a very powerful message to the organization selling such product and force it to improve the product based on the customers' feedback. Thus, the modified definition of public relations would look like this: Public relations is a strategic *two-way symmetrical management* process that builds mutually beneficial relationships between an organization and its publics on which its success or failure depends.

Maintaining the Relationships

Another important omission of this public relations definition is its focus on building new relationships rather than on *maintaining* the existing ones. In fact, it is possible to argue that maintaining existing relationships should be more important than building new ones. For example, imagine an iPhone user who used iPhones for many years, upgrading to new model after new model of the device. When Apple releases a new iPhone, this dedicated user is more likely to buy another iPhone than a person who used Samsung phones for years and got used to the Android environment. But this is true only if the iPhone user is happy with the product and loyal to the brand. In fact, investing in developing relationships with existing customers and building brand loyalty is likely to generate more return on investments than trying to switch customers from competitors' products.

Nonprofit organizations knew about this for years. A person who donates even a dollar or volunteers even for a few hours with an organization indicates that they support the cause of the organization and are willing to donate their time or money to it. Such a person immediately becomes the prime focus of this nonprofit organization. So, if you ever donate to a nonprofit, the number of requests for new donations from such nonprofit are likely to increase and not decrease because your prior actions indicate that you are a valuable prospect. It would make sense for animal shelters to focus on people who donate for animal causes and volunteer with animals rather than to focus on people whose priority may be on something else like poverty or domestic violence. Animal shelters may still target those people, but it is more likely to generate the most return on investment from the animal lovers.

The largest nonprofits are able to raise millions and even billions of dollars from private donors because they are efficient not just at identifying new prospective donors but because they can maintain their relationships with existing donors. By cultivating those relationships and showing appreciation for even the smallest donations, they encourage their donors to increase their support. In the United States, just the largest 100 charities received almost $60 billion combined – with the largest one, Feeding America, raising $4.06 billion in donations (see Table 2.1)! And there are more than 1 million nonprofits in the United States (Barrett, 2022).

Compare it, on the other hand, with what businesses are doing sometimes when they focus on building new relationships and completely forget about maintaining the existing ones. T-Mobile, for example, tends to announce a new deal every month for its new customers, giving them free phones, discounted subscription rates, or additional features, but not offering any of these perks to its existing customers. In the case of cellular providers, they are counting on big costs of switching services – it requires some effort to cancel a line at T-Mobile and get a new line at AT&T – thus, they think they do not have to work hard on the existing relationships. However, they still force cost-sensitive consumers to constantly open new lines and close new lines with the same carrier, and sometimes actually switch carriers if the deals are sufficiently lucrative. All of this creates significant hidden costs for the companies and also hurts the loyalty and relationships between the business and the customers.

At the same time, businesses where switching costs are low learned their lesson and invested significant resources in maintaining existing relationships in addition to building new ones. Airline companies constantly show appreciation to their loyal frequent fliers with early boarding, upgrades, and special deals. When a person books a flight, they can choose absolutely any airline without much effort. However, if a person has a certain status in a frequent flier program of Delta Airlines, they are more likely to deliberately seek out a Delta flight first before considering other airlines. If their status with the airline gives them additional bonuses – like free bags or priority boarding or even business class upgrade – they would be even more likely to focus on their flight options from Delta Airlines only.

It is also quite easy for consumers to buy cars of different brands – there is really not much in terms of switching costs – they ride on the same road, park in the same garage, and use the same gas stations. So, car companies maintain fan clubs and organize special events for their loyal customers. Mazda, for example, had its famous Zoom-Zoom Live Tour where thousands had a chance to race Mazda cars, while Ferrari owner's clubs around the world organize more exclusive social events, publish a quarterly magazine, and even arrange Ferrari factory tours for the members.

A person who already owns a Ferrari and enjoys participating in Ferrari owner's club events is more likely to buy another Ferrari than an owner of a Lamborghini or McLaren (see Figure 2.4). Through these relationship-building activities, Ferrari becomes part of a

Table 2.1 30 Largest Charitable Organizations in the United States.

Rank	Name	Category	Donations
1	Feeding America	Domestic Needs	$4.06 billion
2	United Way Worldwide	Domestic Needs	$2.77 billion
3	St. Jude Children's Research Hospital	Medical	$2.42 billion
4	Salvation Army	Domestic Needs	$2.34 billion
5	Direct Relief	International Needs	$2.21 billion
6	Good 360	International Needs	$1.69 billion
7	Goodwill Industries International	Domestic Needs	$1.44 billion
8	YMCA of the USA	Youth	$1.41 billion
9	Habitat for Humanity International	International Needs	$1.27 billion
10	Americares	International Needs	$1.22 billion
11	Boys & Girls Clubs of America	Youth	$1.18 billion
12	Compassion International	International Needs	$1.14 billion
13	Catholic Charities USA	Domestic Needs	$1.04 billion
14	Samaritan's Purse	Domestic Needs	$953 million
15	Nature Conservancy	Environment/Animal	$884 million
16	World Vision	International Needs	$882 million
17	Food for the Poor	International Needs	$837 million
18	American National Red Cross	Domestic Needs	$835 million
19	MAP International	International Needs	$819 million
20	Step Up for Students	Education	$819 million
21	Mayo Clinic	Medical	$783 million
22	American Cancer Society	Health	$683 million
23	Task Force for Global Health	International Needs	$673 million
24	Mount Sinai Health Systems	Medical	$660 million
25	Lutheran Services in America	Domestic Needs	$626 million
26	Doctors Without Borders USA	International Needs	$625 million
27	Cru	Religious	$598 million
28	Memorial Sloan Kettering Cancer Center	Medical	$585 million
29	Feed the Children	Domestic Needs	$583 million
30	Planned Parenthood Federation of America	Domestic Needs	$579 million

Source: Forbes, Americas Top 100 Charities, December 13, 2022. https://www.forbes.com/lists/top-charities/?sh=6604a6805f50

person's life – it goes beyond brand loyalty to brand integration into the customer's own identity. Even more, these events build relationships not just between the brand and the customers, but also between the customers. Switching to a different brand will be not just betraying the brand but also betraying all your friends that you acquired through these events.

Figure 2.4 Ferrari on a Race Track during Imola Classic Event. *Source:* Mau47 / Shutterstock.

Definitions

Thus, the definition of public relations, once again, needs to be modified: Public relations is a strategic *two-way symmetrical management* process that builds *and maintains* mutually beneficial relationships between an organization and its publics on which its success or failure depends. This is similar to one of the earliest and most cited definitions of public relations: "Public relations is the management function that establishes and maintains mutually beneficial relationships between an organization and the publics on which its success or failure depends" (Broom and Sha, 2013, p. 5).

Of course, by now with all these additions, the definition becomes quite complex and difficult to remember. So, instead, we can offer a simplified definition: *Public relations is managing relationships.* We must manage new and existing relationships; we must be strategic about it; the relationship must be beneficial to all involved, otherwise there would be no relationship; and we need to know the people on the other end of the relationship – so, the public's research is still very much involved. All these relationships that public relations professionals manage serve as the foundation for the organizational reputation. In the end, this makes *public relations a strategic function of organizational reputation management.*

Reputation of Public Relations

Unfortunately, over many years of its existence public relations professionals did not focus enough on the profession's own reputation. As a result, many people do not know what public relations is, or think about public relations as a supporting tactical function, or even have quite a derogatory perception of public relations. Some equate public relations with writing news releases and booking media time for the corporate executives. Indeed, public relations professionals may perform these tasks, but equating public relations with media relations is the same as equating the work of physicians with writing prescriptions. Medical professionals do write prescriptions, but they do more than that – they diagnose the issue, analyze the data, and select proper treatment based on their experience – the prescription at the end is based on all these complex tasks that require very specialized and deep knowledge of medicine. Same as public relations professionals may send out a news release based on the research they conducted to identify the issue the organization faces, the publics that are involved in that issue, and analyze that the best way to address that public about that issue would be through the mass media. This also requires specialized knowledge and experience.

Public relations professionals do not get everything right every single time – same as medical professionals, they make mistakes. They may invest lots of organizational efforts and money into organizing a special event like an employees' holiday dinner just to learn that employees hate this idea and there would be no strategic benefit from all these investments. Same as medical professionals treating the wrong issue in a patient, they would learn from that experience and conduct more research to find out what would be a better solution to the problem.

Thus, when we use public relations in its strategic and managerial form, it becomes the main component of reputation management that can provide a competitive advantage to the organization. There is no reputation in a vacuum, outside of the relationship – relationship provides the context for anything else that happens between an organization and the publics. The question then becomes how do we measure and, subsequently, manage the reputation? How can we estimate what car brand, for example, has a better reputation – Ferrari, Lamborghini, McLaren, or maybe Porsche – and what can they do to make their reputations better? Thus, the next chapters will discuss the approaches to managing and measuring reputations.

Chapter Summary

Public relations is managing relationships. Organizations have a lot of publics, such as customers, investors, and employees, and it is essential to build and maintain relationships with all of these publics in order for the organization to survive and prosper. For any relationship to be successful it must be mutually beneficial, with everyone involved receiving a benefit from being in a relationship. It also must be two-way symmetrical, with everyone involved having a say about the relationship. These relationships serve as the foundation for the organizational reputation. This makes public relations a strategic function of reputation management.

Five Key Terms to Remember

Public Relations
Publics

Relationship Management
Two-Way Symmetrical
Mutually Beneficial

Discussion Questions and Activities

1 Discuss the definition of public relations as a relationship management function and its key components. What other components would you add to the definition that the chapter did not touch upon?

2 The concept of relationships came to the business literature from the interpersonal literature. Do you think it is appropriate to compare relationships between people with relationships between people and organizations and even with relationships between organizations? Should another term be used for this other than relationships? Why or why not?

3 Think about any organization that you are a common customer of – the car wash you use a lot, the coffee shop you frequent, the gym you are a member of, or your favorite fast food chain. What do they do to maintain their relationship with you? Are they doing a good job or not from your perspective? What other things do you wish they would be doing?

References

Barrett, W. P. (2022, December 13). America's top 100 charities. *Forbes*. https://www.forbes.com/lists/top-charities/?sh=6604a6805f50

Broom, G. M., & Sha, B. L. (2013). *Cutlip and Center's effective public relations*, (11th ed.). Pearson Prentice Hall.

Center, A. H., Jackson, P., Smith, S., & Stansberry, F. H. (2008). *Public relations practices: Managerial case studies and problems*, (7th ed.). Pearson Prentice Hall.

Ferrell, O. C., & Hartline, M. D. (2005). *Marketing strategy*, (3rd ed.). Thomson.

Kelleher, T. (2018). *Public relations*. Oxford University Press. PRSA (n.d.) About public relations. https://www.prsa.org/about/all-about-pr

3

Managing Reputation: The Never-Ending Process in F.O.C.U.S.

LEARNING OBJECTIVES

1. *After reading this chapter, students will be able to write goals and objectives.*
2. *After reading this chapter, students will be able to develop strategies and tactics.*
3. *After reading this chapter, students will be able to apply the public relations process.*

As we discussed in Chapter 1, reputation is one of the most valuable assets for any organization no matter what country they are in or what type of organization they are. All the equipment, innovation, or human capital may mean nothing without a good reputation. Thus, organizations invest significant financial and non-financial resources in managing their reputations. In this chapter, we will discuss how the reputations are built and maintained.

RPIE

Public Relations Society of America (PRSA) has long proposed a process for developing and conducting public relations campaigns: RPIE. RPIE stands for Research, Planning, Implementation, and Evaluation (PRSA, 2021). The roots of the RPIE process can be traced back to one of the founders of public relations, Edward Bernays (1928). Over the years the process went through many modifications and many different acronyms, but the core principle remained: prior to jumping to any action it is important to conduct research in order to understand what the actual issue is; then, based on the research conducted, it is essential to develop a plan to identify the most effective and efficient course of action; after that, the campaign can actually be launched; and, finally, after the campaign's conclusions the results of all those efforts must be measured and documented. PRSA's Study Guide (2021) for its accreditation exam explains the importance of the process: "Start at the beginning. Don't rush to solutions or jump into tactics before you have done adequate research to analyze the situation, define the business problem, determine key publics and set measurable objectives. By beginning with research, you reduce uncertainty in later decision-making" (p. 23).

Organizational Reputation Management: A Strategic Public Relations Perspective, First Edition. Alexander V. Laskin.
© 2024 John Wiley & Sons, Inc. Published 2024 by John Wiley & Sons, Inc.

The same is true for reputation building and maintaining. Even at a time of crisis when fast action is warranted, it is important to properly understand the issue before jumping into action. As a result, we propose a process of reputation management similar to PRSA's RPIE process and we call it F.O.C.U.S (see Figure 3.1).

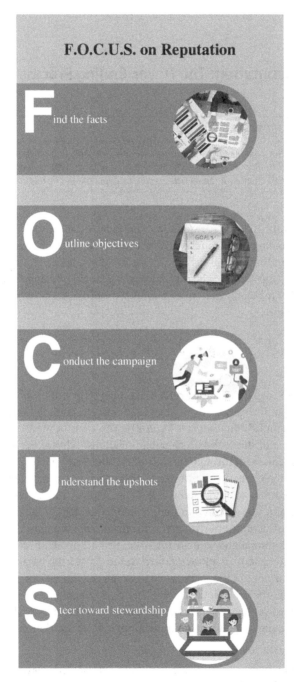

Figure 3.1 F.O.C.U.S. on Reputation: Organizational Reputation Management Process.
Source: Rawpixel.com/Adobe Stock, SDI Productions/iStock/Getty Images, vladwel/Adobe Stock, Stockgiu/Adobe Stock.

F.O.C.U.S. on Reputation

The five-step process of reputation management can be summed up through an acronym: F.O.C.U.S. In this acronym, *F* stands for *Facts*, *O* stands for *Objectives*, *C* stands for *Campaign*, *U* stands for *Understanding*, and *S* stands for *Stewardship*. This is similar to PRSA's RPIE process but adds an important fifth step, *Stewardship* – essential for successful reputations.

Step 1. Finding the Facts

The first step of the process of building and maintaining reputation is finding the facts. Any campaign should start with research. Organizations must understand what the problem is in order to develop an effective plan for solving that problem. If customers are not buying a new phone a company is trying to sell because it is just too expensive, the most effective way to address it is with a discount, coupon, trade-in program, or another tactic designed to lower the price the consumers have to pay. If, on the other hand, the customers are not buying the phone because it is perceived as an uncool product, discounts may not help – instead, a right celebrity endorsement may help change customers' minds. Whatever the reason, without knowing the problem, the organization cannot properly address it and cannot design the most effective campaign.

Another key fact-finding mission is establishing where an organization stands now. This is called a *baseline measure*, or, sometimes, the *before measure*. The baseline measure helps establish the starting point of any effort aimed at improving the organizational reputation. Knowing the starting point helps better plan for what needs to be done. If an organization decides to launch a national TV advertising campaign to sell its product, it is important to have the before measure – how much sales the company's product generates prior to the ads being shown, and the after measure – how much sales the company's product generates after the ads. This helps the organization to estimate the effect of the ads on sales and calculate the return on investment, ROI, of the ad campaign: how much did the ad campaign cost and what was the increase in sales the ads generated. Again, without recording the baseline measure, it would be impossible to know the ROI of the campaign.

In addition to helping an organization understand the problem or issue it deals with and establishing the baseline measure, research allows an organization to understand its place in the competitive environment. Sometimes referred to as *environmental scanning* it is a process of monitoring and analyzing the trends, threats, and opportunities that can affect the reputation of the organization or the way the organization can manage its reputation. For example, if an organization learns during environmental scanning that many of its current or potential customers are joining TikTok, it would be logical for this organization to consider developing its own presence on the app itself. As the saying goes, fish where the fish are – or, in other words, to reach your customers you need to go where they are present, in this case, on TikTok.

SWOT

Many techniques exist to help organizations with research. For example, one of the most popular approaches is called *SWOT – Strengths, Weaknesses, Opportunities*, and *Threats* (see Figure 3.2). The roots of SWOT analysis date back to the 1950s and since then

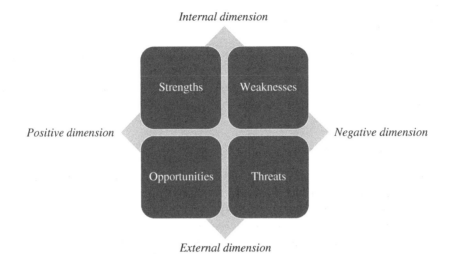

Figure 3.2 SWOT Analysis.

it has become one of the leading analytical approaches in a variety of fields from management to psychology (Puyt et al., 2020).

When conducting SWOT, one analyzes the organization's internal and external dimensions. Two of the four categories in SWOT – Strengths and Weaknesses – measure internal dimension of the organization. *Strengths* represent what the organization does well and what it can rely on as part of its reputation-building activities. For example, the organization may have developed an amazing technology for charging electric vehicles (EVs) that allows its charging stations to provide full charge to cars in less time than any of its competitors.

Weaknesses, on the other hand, represent potential pressure points within the organization. For example, this same organization may know that while its technology is very fast at charging, it also costs significantly more to install and maintain – this puts the organization at a disadvantage versus its competitors, other electric car charging networks, like Electrify America, EVgo, or Charge Point.

Strengths, however, do not automatically create a great reputation for an organization, and Weaknesses do not automatically prevent an organization from having a great reputation. Instead, both Strengths and Weaknesses serve as starting points in developing a better understanding of the organization that later can help in planning successful reputation management activities and managing relationships with the organization's publics.

Opportunities and *Threats* represent external dimensions for the analysis of the organization. If we continue with the same example of a fictitious charging network, an exponential growth in electric car sales represents an excellent opportunity for the EV charging networks because more electric cars will require more charging stations. Consequently, any development that leads to more EVs on the roads would also be opportunities for this organization – for example, federal tax credits on EV sales, increases in gas prices, or even advertising campaigns by EV manufacturers. All of these are *Opportunities* that the charging network can capitalize on to increase its business and build its reputation.

Threats are the events that can jeopardize the growth or even existence of the organization. For example, removal of the federal tax credit on EV sales, decrease in gas prices, or lack of advertising of electric cars may all be threats for the EV charging network. In other words, Threats and Opportunities are often two sides of the same coin.

External and internal dimensions are often connected – this makes SWOT even more valuable as it helps the leaders of the organization see how the internal changes inside the organization may be perceived outside the organization. In other words, it may help organizations understand and manage relations between identity, image, and reputation as we discussed in Chapter 1. For example, a popular influencer posting their praise about how fast they were able to charge their EV at the organization-owned charging station is a great opportunity for further reputation-building activities. This opportunity is directly based on the organization's strength of pioneering a new technology that enables such fast charging speeds. On the flip side, an influencer posting about how expensive it was to charge their EV at one of the network's charging stations presents a threat to the organization's reputation and this threat exposes an organization's weakness about their technology: high cost of charging.

Porter's Five Forces

Another popular tool to use during the initial research step focused on finding the facts about the organization is *Porter's Five Forces* (see Figure 3.3). This analytical technique developed by the Harvard University's Professor Michael E. Porter (1980) focuses on the organization's competitive environment and helps understand where

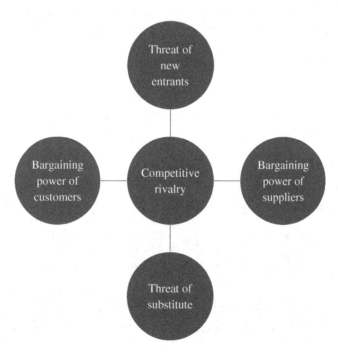

Figure 3.3 Porter's Five Forces.

the organization must concentrate its efforts in order to remain successful and maintain its reputation. The five forces that affect the organization are: (1) threat of new entrants, (2) intensity of rivalry among existing firms, (3) threat of substitute products or services, (4) bargaining power of buyers, and (5) bargaining power of suppliers.

Threat of New Entrants analyzes how easy or hard it is for new competitors to appear in the particular industry. For example, if you are running a restaurant, the threat that another restaurant may open next door is pretty high. It does not take much to open a restaurant. For example, in the small town of Cheshire, CT, a 1950s restaurant Rose Dairy was among the local favorites for its famous Butch Burger. It was standing all by itself when it opened over 70 years ago and as a result it did not have to compete for customers with other establishments. Over the years, however, right on the side of the Rose Dairy, a building was added that today houses two more restaurants – C.J. Sparrow and Anthony's Pizzeria & Deli. Anthony's Pizza is the most recently opened of these three – it opened just a couple of years ago in place of another restaurant that had gone out of business, Sweetpea. And within just yards to the right and to the left, potential customers would find two chain restaurants as well: McDonald's and Starbucks (see Figure 3.4). All that not even counting several restaurants directly across the street from the Rose Dairy where a large shopping plaza developed over the years with such restaurants as Bagelicious, Jersey Mikes, Wayback Burgers, and Sahana. The ease of opening a restaurant places the restaurant industry at a very high risk from new entrants. On the other hand, if the organization runs a nuclear power plant it probably does not have to worry much about another nuclear power plant suddenly appearing next door. Nuclear energy is a highly regulated and highly complex industry making it extremely difficult to open a new nuclear plant. As a result, the threat of new entrants in the nuclear energy sector is low.

Intensity of Rivalry among Existing Firms speaks to the level of competition in the industry. For example, if you are a restaurant, competition is typically high. It is easy for customers to switch their plans from one restaurant to another if they see an advertisement, a commercial, or even hear a word-of-mouth endorsement. For nuclear

Figure 3.4   Restaurant Rose Dairy in Cheshire, CT.

power plants, on the other hand, much of the sales are based on long-term contracts and tied to the electrical distribution network, decreasing the level of competition in the industry. That's why if you open a local newspaper you are likely to find many ads of local restaurants but are unlikely to find ads from local power plants.

Threat of Substitute Products or Services refers to the ability of customers to replace what the organization offers with a different product or service. If we go back to the Rose Dairy restaurant, we might think that their product, food, cannot really be replaced. On the other hand, its service can easily be replaced as people can buy food at the grocery store and cook it themselves at home. Thus, eating at home is a substitute product for going to the restaurant. In the case of a nuclear power plant, solar panels can serve as a substitute product that would replace the need for buying energy from the power plant. Of course, it is significantly easier to substitute going to a restaurant with a home-cooked meal in comparison with substituting getting power from the grid with your own solar panels. On the grid, however, nuclear energy can be substituted with energy produced in a lot of other ways – natural gas plants, coal plants, oil plants, hydro power plants, tidal power plants, solar power plants, wind power plants, geothermal power plants, and so on. This makes a threat of substitution quite high for nuclear power. The last nuclear power plant in California, Diablo Canyon Power Plant, is on the verge of closing as the state incentivized renewable energy to the point of solar energy becoming cheaper than the price of nuclear energy production. The solar production, in other words, substituted the nuclear production (Mulkern, 2022).

It is important to note, however, that substitutions are not the same as the original products. This is significant to consider when analyzing the substitutions as it may help an organization develop communication response strategies. For example, while it may be cheaper to eat at home versus eating at a restaurant, eating at home involves going to a grocery store, cooking, serving, and then cleaning. All of these activities take time that could be spent doing something else and also add costs that are rarely included in the calculations: transportation costs to and from the store, water costs to wash the dishes, electricity costs to cook the meal, and so on. The same is true for nuclear energy – one of the most stable ways to produce electricity. However, replaced with solar energy that peaks during the middle of the day, the grid may suffer from lack of supply at night leading to outages, and may experience oversupply around noon when the demand is not that high but the production is at all-time highs.

Finally, the last two measures in Porter's Five Forces are the *Bargaining Power of Suppliers* and the *Bargaining Power of Buyers*. These indicators talk about the power that consumers and suppliers may have over the organization. For example, in the restaurant business the power of consumers is very high – it is very easy for a consumer to choose to eat lunch today at McDonald's, tomorrow at Burger King, and the third day at Wendy's. There are no extra costs associated with switching from one restaurant to another. On the other hand, for cable companies the power of consumers is not that great. If you are a Comcast subscriber, you cannot suddenly decide that today for lunch you will use the internet connection from Cox and tomorrow from Frontier. It may take days if not months to switch from Comcast to Cox, if another cable provider is even available in your area. There are quite a few places in the world where the only alternative to the one cable company in town would be a satellite provider.

The power of suppliers is a similar concept – the only difference is it focuses on what the organization needs to produce its products or provide its service. During COVID many organizations experienced a shortage of supplies. Perhaps the most debilitating shortages involved semiconductors and processors. Some car companies even had to limit their production as they could not get semiconductors for their cars. For example, *CBS News* reported in 2022 that Tesla had to temporarily abandon release of new models because of the chip shortage (CBS/AP, 2022). Furthermore, for the car companies and other companies releasing highly technological products, it may be quite a lengthy process to switch from one chip manufacturer to another as the overall design of their products may be affected if they are forced to use chips with different characteristics. On the other hand, in the restaurant business, it may be significantly easier to switch from one supplier of potatoes or tomatoes to another – thus, the power of suppliers in the restaurant is less important than in the electronics industry.

In addition to the SWOT analysis and Porter's Five Forces, there are many other techniques to help understand the position of an organization in its environment in order to better assess its current reputation and identify ways to improve and enhance the reputation going forward. The specific analytical technique used may depend on the organization, industry, or an issue at hand. Nevertheless, SWOT and Porter's are very popular starting points in almost any situation. Whatever technique is used, however, the research conducted becomes the foundation for any further effort for building and maintaining reputation. This foundation allows for the organization to establish goals and objectives for any future public relations activities.

Step 2. Outlining the Objectives

The second step in any public relations, strategic communication, or reputation building activities is developing goals and objectives. *Goal* is what you are aiming for, what you want to achieve. The importance of having a specific goal is expressed in almost any language and almost any culture: from the Chinese saying that if you aim at nothing, you hit nothing to the Russian saying that if you chase after two hares, you'll end up catching none. In English language, the same sentiment is usually expressed by the modified quote attributed to Lewis Carroll and Yogi Berra – you won't be able to reach your destination if you don't know where you are going.

Thus any campaign aimed at improving reputation must have a clear goal in mind. Perhaps an organization during its research learns that consumers have a significant power for the organization's existence and success, yet the relationships with consumers are quite bad and are in dire need of improvement. Then, the organization may decide that their next goal would be to improve their consumer relationships and may propose a specific campaign targeted at consumers.

The goal, however, is a very broad concept – it requires additional clarification and interpretation. If we want to improve the company's relations with consumers, then by how much? By what date? With what budget? What exactly needs to be done? What would the successful end result look like? All these questions need to be answered in the planning stages of the campaign. This is when organizations would develop their Objectives.

Objectives may be developed for a specific campaign that an organization wants to implement in order to, for example, improve its consumer relations. Or objectives may be developed for the next budget year or five years and may also focus on consumers, investors, employees, any other public, or even several publics. A 1981 article,

"There's a S.M.A.R.T. way to write management's goals and objectives," proposed that good objectives must be *S.M.A.R.T. – Specific, Measurable, Attainable, Relevant,* and *Timely* (Doran 1981).

Specific focuses on clearly outlining what it is the organization tries to accomplish. It may be beneficial to provide a clear vision of the end result – how exactly it would look like for the organization after the campaign is over.

Measurable focuses on clear ways to quantify the end result of the campaign. It is not enough to say we want to improve reputation – instead, quantify it by how much the reputation will improve and how it could be measured.

Attainable (originally called assignable) focuses on the organization's ability to achieve the stated objective with its current resources. Is it possible to try to reach the certain target considering the organization's budget, starting position, competitive environment, and so on?

Relevant (originally called realistic) focuses on the impact of the proposed objective on the organization. Will it make any difference at all? Is it worth it to try to achieve this target or will reaching it make no difference at all and then there is no point in trying at all?

Timely (originally called time-related) focuses on the time dimension of the objective. A good objective always specifies the time frame in which it is going to be implemented. If a campaign is infinite, an organization would not know when it starts and when it ends, and when it is time to evaluate its success or failure and thus it can never succeed or fail.

For example, if an organization states that it wants to make itself stand out as the best place to work for its employees, it is very vague and unclear of what exactly the organization plans on doing. Instead, a S.M.A.R.T. objective related to improving relationships with employees may sound like this:

> By the end of this fiscal year, the employees' approval of the new health insurance benefit will increase from 30% to 60% as measured by the annual employee satisfaction survey.

Let us look at this objective closely. First, the objective must be *specific*. We can clearly see what this objective is about. It is about the employees' approval of the new health insurance benefit. When organizations change their policies related to employees' benefits, it is quite common to have to invest efforts in employee education in order to clarify and explain what these changes may mean. This is what this objective focuses on – affecting the employees' acceptance of the new policies. The objective is also *measurable*. We can see a very direct target the objective is setting: 60% approval. Is this number *attainable*? While it is difficult to judge how attainable this objective is in this hypothetical example, the objective specifies the starting point, or, in other words, the current level of support that stands at 30%. In other words, it seems like already today 30% of employees are in support of the new benefit plan. This suggests that it may be an attainable objective to gain another 30% of supporters over the current year. In addition, the objective very clearly states how the end result will be evaluated – it is based on a question or several questions about the employees' approval of the health insurance benefit in the annual employee satisfaction survey – this speaks once again to the objective being measurable as well as attainable since at least the measurement process (the survey) had been already done earlier. The objective also suggests that this would be quite a *relevant* outcome for the organization. If the objective's target is achieved the number of employees approving of the new policy will go from minority (30%) to majority (60%) – while again in a hypothetical scenario it is difficult to properly estimate the relevance of this result, it seems like any organization would like most of the employees to support its policies. Finally, the objective has a clear *time frame* for its implementation – current fiscal year – thus, it is known when the completion of the work is expected and when it would be appropriate to evaluate the results.

Another important consideration that specifically applies to the reputation management objectives is the need to clearly state what public the objective is aimed at. In public relations literature, it is known as the requirement for objectives to be *public specific*. Indeed, as we discussed earlier in this book, different organizational publics may often have different, even competing or directly opposite, demands to the organization. The objective we looked at above focused on employees. And in this example, employees may have a desire for better health insurance even if it is more costly for the organization. Investors, on the other hand, may want to cut costs on the health insurance benefit and downgrade the employees' coverage. Customers may be indifferent about the employees' health insurance. And, of course, with different demands come different communication approaches. Thus, objectives must be crafted with a specific public in mind. That is why in our example of the objective we specifically stated that this objective is aimed at the organization's employees. This would make objectives related to reputation management not just *S.M.A.R.T.* but *P.S.M.A.R.T.* with the first P indicating the specific *Public* it is focused on.

Step 3. Conducting the Campaign

Once the goals and objectives of the reputation management program or campaign are in place, it is time to develop strategies and tactics. *Strategies* and *tactics* are specific ways to achieve the stated objectives. Of course, strategies and tactics are developed prior to the actual start of the campaign, but they are what the campaign actually is – they are the content of the campaign and, as a result, we discuss them in the Conducting the Campaign step of the F.O.C.U.S. model. In public relations literature, this step is also known as the implementation step, when the strategies and tactics are implemented.

The concept of strategies and tactics and the separation between the two goes back to early military training. People engaged in wars since the very early days of their existence, and victory or defeat always had very severe consequences – thus, lots of efforts were invested in making sure they would be successful. Thus, it was always important to plan for warfare and analyze what could and should be done. These plans consisted of strategies and tactics.

One of the earliest known books on warfare, *The Art of War* by Sun Tzu explains, "All men can see these tactics whereby I conquer, but what none can see is the strategy out of which victory is evolved" (2010, p. 19). In other words, *strategy* is a conceptual idea on how to reach our objective; it is not directly observable but it guides all our actions and our tactics. For example, a military objective may include occupying a particular town. In this case, the strategy may be an unexpected attack when the enemy cannot see the advancing troops.

Tactics, then, would be the specific tasks needed to implement this strategy. For example, in this military example it may be decided that the best time to attack unexpectedly, as the strategy calls for, would be at 3 a.m. when it is still dark, the enemy is asleep, and even the guards are falling asleep in this early morning hour. To ensure quiet approach, another tactic implemented may be to use only infantry with light weapons instead of horses and carriages. Another tactic may be to avoid major roads and instead travel through the forest.

Altogether the strategy gives you a general direction in which you should act, while the tactics include the specific list of activities to be implemented. Strategy is like an idea that lives in your mind, while tactics realize the strategy and implement it in real life. Famous chess player Max Euwe used to say that *strategy requires thought, tactics require observation* – in other words, it is possible to see what tactics are being used, but one would have to think hard in order to figure out what strategy all these tactics combined together try to implement.

Both strategies and tactics, however, are aimed at achieving a particular objective. These concepts are widely applicable in a lot of fields – business, psychology, medicine, and, of course, public relations and reputation management. For example, we can go back to our previous example when we stated the goal to improve the organization's relationship with its employees and the objective was: *By the end of this fiscal year, the employees' approval of the new health insurance benefit will increase from 30% to 60% as measured by the annual employee satisfaction survey.* How can we achieve this objective? Well, one strategy we can focus on would be educating employees about the details of the new health insurance benefit. If we believe that the problem with employees' disapproval of the new plan is the lack of knowledge about it, the strategy focused on education would make sense to combat such lack of knowledge.

If this is our strategy, then the tactics would be the specific educational activities we can undertake. For example, we can build a special page on the website dedicated to showing the comparison between the new health insurance and the old one. Another tactic may be direct mail where we would mail employees and their dependents information packages about the new health insurance. Yet another tactic may be holding open hours with HR where any employee can stop by and ask any questions about how the changes affect them personally. And so on and so forth.

Overall, we can think of a variety of different tactics to implement our strategy in order to achieve our objectives. Yet, our imagination is not the only limiting factor. Other factors that should be considered are time and budget. As we discussed before, every objective has a time component. So, if we need to achieve this objective in one month, it means we can have only a month's worth of tactics to implement. If we have a year, we have a year-long time frame to work with. Time is a very important consideration – it also limits what external events we can participate in. If we think it'd be great for our organization to develop a commercial for the Olympic Games, but our objective's time limit expires before the next Olympic Games are even set to begin, we would have to abandon that tactic as it would not help us with our specific objective by falling outside of its time frame.

The same is true for the budget. The budget can limit what we can realistically do – if the commercial during the Olympic Games would cost us half a million dollars and our whole budget is only half of that, it would mean that we cannot implement that tactic. Time and budget's limiting nature is not always a bad thing – it helps reputation management professionals develop focus on what's attainable and realistic – two key components of any objectives – and, ultimately, help the organization achieve its goals.

In public relations and strategic communication campaigns, a variety of different tactics can be used to help organizations build, maintain, protect, or improve their reputations. One of the most developed classifications of these tactics is called *PESO*. In the PESO classification, P stands for *Paid* tactics, E stands for *Earned* tactics, S stands for *Shared* tactics, and O stands for *Owned* tactics.

Paid tactics usually include placing advertising in print and on social media, displaying commercials on TV and streaming platforms, and similar activities. The organization pays for the opportunity to communicate to its publics by buying a commercial on TV, an ad on Facebook, or billboard along the road. Paid media can also be called interrupting media – it usually interrupts whatever we are doing – like a commercial that suddenly appears during a YouTube video we are watching and we cannot wait for the Skip button to appear. Since it tends to interrupt our activities, people usually do not actively consume the paid content. During commercials on TV, people tend to shift their attention to something else – conversations with others in the room, checking their phones, or going to the kitchen for a snack.

Earned tactics include various publicity efforts. For earned media, the organization persuades various intermediaries, for example, journalists, that whatever the organization wants to communicate is newsworthy and, as a result, the news media report these stories as part of the news segment. For example, when Apple unveils its new iPhone model, it typically makes the news coverage online, on TV, and in print publications without having Apple pay these news organizations to run those stories. In other words, the organization earns the coverage instead of having to pay for it. Earned media is the actual content that people consume – thus, people pay attention to this content and are active users of it.

Shared tactics are sometimes called social tactics or social media tactics. The organization may have a Facebook page where its customers share stories about their experience of using the products the organization sells. The organization may also use their social media presence to communicate directly to their publics, collect feedback from them, organize contests and promotions, and even crowdsource marketing, design, and fundraising activities. Overall, shared tactics involve collaboration between the organization and its various publics.

Finally, *owned* tactics involve various activities on media platforms that an organization owns. These may include the organization's own website, the organization's newsletter, and even the façade of the organization's corporate headquarters.

Different tactics within the PESO model give the organization using them varying levels of control, expense, trustworthiness, and so on. For example, if the organization claims on its own website that their pizza is the best pizza ever, consumers may be skeptical; on the other hand, if independent experts in the leading publication about pizza claim that the organization's pizza is the best pizza ever, consumers are more likely to believe these claims. But then again if the organization simply pays for an ad with the claim that their pizza is the best one ever, it would not carry as much weight as the independent experts' testimony.

If the organization needs to say something important about, for example, a crisis it is involved in, owned media may be the best way to go as the organization can craft the wording, message design, and placement exactly how it wants it to be. With the earned media, the organization may win credibility, but they would lose any control over how the organization's message would be presented, including if it would be presented at all.

In a typical campaign aimed at building or improving reputation, organizations tend to use a mix of tactics from the PESO model. In this case, it becomes important to properly monitor these tactics and arrange them in logical order so that they could benefit from and not interfere with each other. For example, a commercial shown during a Super Bowl may direct consumers toward a social media page where consumers can participate in a contest. Later, their contest entries may be used for direct mail to send consumers coupons or other materials.

In order to track the implementation of all the tactics, it is common to use a specialized tool known as the *Gantt chart*. The chart, named after Henry Gantt, an American engineering and management consultant, was actually invented by one of the early pioneers of management science from the Russian Empire, Karol Adamiecki (Marsh, 1974). Henry Gantt, however, widely popularized the use of the chart as a project management tool and applied the chart in various contexts. The Gantt chart allows managers to see when a particular tactic starts and when it should end, who is responsible for each tactic at every stage of its progression, and, most importantly, how this tactic relates to all other tactics. It allows managers to plan the workload of the employees and plan future work responsibilities, but also to ensure that all tactics complement each other and can build on each other in order to implement the overall organizational strategy. For example, here is the Gantt chart of the agency showing simultaneous work for three different clients over multiple weeks with tasks completed marked in black (see Figure 3.5).

Step 4. Understanding the Upshots

Once all the tactics are completed, it is time to measure the results – was the organization able to achieve its objectives or not? This can be done at the end of the campaign (called campaign evaluation), or at the end of the year (called annual evaluation). Some organizations set quarterly or even monthly objectives – then, it is important to conduct quarterly evaluations and monthly evaluations. The public relations RPIE process includes evaluation as its final fourth step.

This is the step where one could learn if all the efforts invested in the strategic campaign are paying off or not. For the public relations, reputation management, and marketing agencies this is an extremely important step because they get to show their clients how much value they were able to contribute and that the expensive fees the agencies charge for their services were actually worth the investment. Internal departments have to prove their value as well – CEO, CFO, CCO, and other C-suite managers constantly reevaluate their budget allocations on an as-needed and periodic basis. If the marketing department's evaluation of its recent campaign can show how beneficial that campaign was, during the next budget cycle more money could be shifted to this marketing department from, for example, the public relations department. If the public relations department, however, can show during its evaluation that its work far

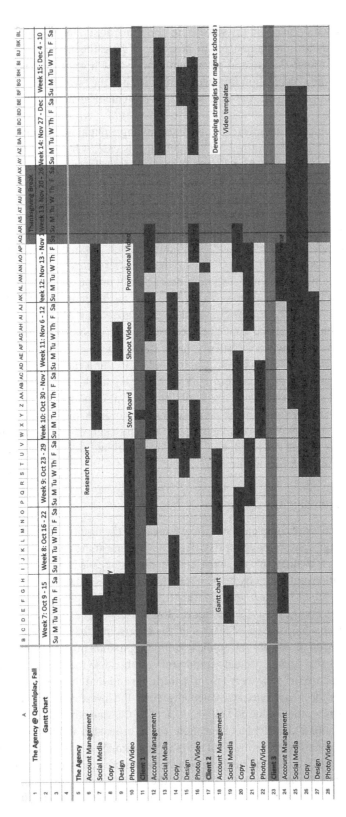

Figure 3.5 Example of a Gantt Chart Used by The Agency @Quinnipiac.

outperforms investments in marketing, then the money could be shifted the opposite way: to public relations and away from marketing.

As a result, it is more and more common to hear the term *ROI – Return on Investment* – when evaluation of communication activities is involved. ROI, originally an investment term, compares financial investments into an activity with the return this activity produces. For example, if investing one dollar into Activity A brings a profit of $100, while investing one dollar into Activity B brings a profit of only $10, then it can be stated that ROI of Activity A is higher than ROI of Activity B and thus investments should be made into Activity A, as they would bring more profit.

Today, however, ROI moved from its narrow original application in financial analysis and is often used outside of the investment context, as the term became part of the popular discourse. People talk about ROI of education, ROI of exercises, and, of course, ROI of reputation – just to name a few examples. In the field of strategic communication there was even an attempt to adapt ROI specifically to communication changing its name from ROI to *ROC – Return on Communications* (Laskin, 2016).

The reason for popularity of ROI-type measures in corporate reputation is often attributed to the need to show the value of various activities in the environment of limited resources. For example, if an organization has only certain amount of dollars in its marketing/communication budget, it needs to decide where this money can produce the most return – will it be a TV advertising campaign, a sponsorship deal, a newsletter for employees, or something else entirely? Thus, people advocating for investments in specific reputation-enhancing activities need to show the value that such activities can bring to the organizational bottom-line.

It is, however, quite challenging to equate reputation with dollar amounts in order to calculate the return. In fact, various strategic campaigns may be targeted at different goals – a campaign to decrease employee turnover may be challenging to compare with a campaign to generate sales for a new product or a campaign to place corporate shares on the stock market. When managing relationships with a variety of publics, it becomes difficult to draw comparisons. In fact, one can argue that such comparisons are pointless and thus, ROI, designed to compare what investment activity would generate the most return, cannot be applied at all to the reputation management. One simply cannot completely abandon relations with its employees even if calculations would show that investments in improving customer relations generate more dollars. In order to survive and be successful, any organization needs to maintain relationships with employees, customers, investors, suppliers, and a host of other publics simultaneously. On the other hand, one cannot manage what one cannot measure – thus, it is still essential to engage in measurement and evaluation on a consistent basis. Due to the high importance of measurement and evaluation, we would discuss the specific approaches to measuring and evaluating reputation in a standalone chapter, Chapter 4, Measuring Reputation.

Step 5. Steering toward Stewardship

The fifth and final step in the F.O.C.U.S. model of reputation management is *Stewardship*. Stewardship talks about the need for the organization not to forget about its publics even when the organization does not really need anything from them. Stewardship focuses on maintaining relationships rather than looking to create the new ones, and on reinforcing the existing attitudes and behaviors rather than trying to create the new ones. This is extremely important – as Kathleen Kelly, who is responsible for developing the concept of stewardship in public relations, explains: "It is easier to keep a friend than to make a new friend" (Kelly, 2001, p. 279).

Yet, organizations often forget about their existing relationships. Think about many cell phone providers who always have deals for new customers but rarely offer free phones or other limited-time deals to their existing customers. Same is often true for cable companies that try to lure in new customers with deep discounts and promotions but rarely offer those to their existing customers. The situation often applies to other publics as well – new employees may get sign-up bonuses that existing employees are not eligible for; new students may get free T-shirts and other university souvenirs in the mail for paying their deposit but the returning students rarely get such perks, and so on. Even the official professional definition of public relations states that the activities must be focused on building relationship but does not mention maintaining the existing ones (PRSA, n.d.). Stewardship, however, argues that we should not forget about our existing customers, employees, students, and so on and invest efforts into maintaining relationships with them.

The roots of the concept of stewardship go back to the discipline of fundraising. Fundraising professionals noticed that past donors of the organization are more likely to donate to their organizations again in the future in comparison with new donors who never contributed to the organization or this particular cause before. Indeed, if somebody previously donated to, for example, Greenpeace, they showed that they do have the means and inclination to engage in philanthropy, they care about environmental causes, and they do think that Greenpeace is a respected organization that actually contributes positively to the environmental causes. In other words, if Greenpeace reaches out to these donors again, their job is already halfway done – they do not have to persuade them how important the environment is or educate them about Greenpeace. This makes prior donors a very important public for fundraisers and suggests the need for maintaining relationships with them: "Because the best prospects for new gifts are past donors, programs that provide careful stewardship and provide donors with timely information on the impact of their gifts can pay significant dividends in continued support" (Worth, 1993, p. 13).

Today there is little doubt that stewardship is important not just in fundraising but can be applicable to any organization and any organization's publics. When Apple releases its new iPhone, it is more likely to sell these new phones to people who are already users of previous models of iPhones. They already know the brand, they use it, and they are likely to be integrated into the infrastructure – maybe using iCloud storage, Apple Music, having all their conversations on iMessages, and so on. Same way as with fundraising, your previous donors and your previous customers are likely to be your future donors and your future customers. It does not mean that Apple cannot sell iPhone to users of Samsung phones or Google phones, but targeting them is likely to be more difficult and the efforts invested in making the sale will be more expensive. The same is true for political communications – people who voted for Democrats before are more likely to vote for Democrats again; and people who voted for Republicans are more likely to vote for Republicans in the future as well. It will take less effort to reinforce and maintain their beliefs rather than to persuade somebody to change their opinions completely.

As a result, stewardship is vital for successful reputation management. Organizations must nurture the relationships with publics that already support the organization – long-term employees, loyal customers, large investors, and so on. Those who already have a positive relationship with the organization can be great contributors to the positive and enduring reputation. It is easier to maintain a good reputation than to build one from scratch. So, how can organizations ensure they conduct their stewardship activities properly and maintain their reputations?

Kelly (2001) proposed four pillars of a good stewardship program – the four *Rs of Stewardship*: *Reporting, Responsibility, Reciprocity*, and *Relationship Nurturing*.

Reporting

Reporting speaks to being open and transparent with your publics. For example, if a university has a large fundraising campaign, it should later inform the donors how much money was raised and what exactly the money was spent on. For governments, it is also customary to expect a report of what was accomplished and what was not – mayors, governors, and presidents usually report to voters what they were able to achieve during their term in office (see Table 3.1). For many corporations, the idea of

Table 3.1 The White House Statement. FACT SHEET: 100 Days In, Biden-Harris Administration Makes History with Presidential Appointees.

Today, the White House Office of Presidential Personnel is releasing new data about the historic number and diversity of presidential appointees hired by Day 100 of the Biden-Harris Administration.

The Biden-Harris Administration put in place its Statutory Cabinet faster than any other Administration since President Reagan. President Biden has also announced his intent to nominate 233 individuals to serve in Senate-confirmed leadership roles across the Executive Branch – more nominees than any past administration has announced by the 100-day mark. Many of these Administration leaders have broken new ground. Lloyd Austin is the first Black Secretary of Defense. Janet Yellen is the first woman to be Secretary of the Treasury. Alejandro Mayorkas is the first Latino and immigrant to serve as Secretary of Homeland Security. Xavier Becerra is the first Latino to serve as Secretary of Health and Human Services. Deb Haaland, the Secretary of the Interior, is the first Native American to ever serve as a Cabinet Secretary. Pete Buttigieg is the first openly LGBTQ person to serve in the Cabinet. Cecilia Rouse is the first woman of color to chair the Council of Economic Advisors and Katherine Tai is the first woman of color to serve as U.S. Trade Representative. Avril Haines is the first woman to lead the U.S. intelligence community. Rachel Levine is the first openly transgender person to be confirmed by the Senate. If confirmed, Robert Santos will be the first person of color to be Director of the United States Census Bureau and Stacey Dixon will be the highest-ranking Black woman in the intelligence community.

Even as the Senate continues to confirm the President's highly qualified nominees, the White House Office of Presidential Personnel has hired nearly 1,500 presidential appointees to serve in key agency positions that do not require Senate confirmation – double the number of appointees hired by any prior administration by the 100-day mark. And, consistent with President Biden's commitment to leveraging the talent, creativity, and expertise of the American people to build an Administration that looks like America, more than half of all Biden appointees are women, and half identify as non-white – numbers that set a new bar for future Administrations.

(Continued)

Table 3.1 (Continued)

Of the approximately 1,500 agency appointees hired by President Biden so far:

58% are women
18% identify as Black or African American
15% identify as Latino or Hispanic
15% identify as Asian American or Pacific Islander
3% identify as Middle Eastern or North African
2% identify as American Indian or Alaska Native
14% identify as LGBTQ+
4% are veterans
3% identify as disabled or having a disability
15% were the first in their families to go to college
32% are naturalized citizens or the children of immigrants

President Biden's commitment to representation from communities that haven't always been at the table can be seen across the federal government. At the U.S. Department of Labor – the agency on the frontlines of the crisis facing women in the workforce across the country – nearly 70% of all appointees are women. At the U.S. Department of Homeland Security, nearly 40% of all appointees are first-generation. At the U.S. Department of Education, one in four of all appointees are the first in their family to graduate from college and one in three are former educators. And at the U.S Department of Interior, one in five of all appointees are American Indian or Alaska Natives.

Source: The White House. https://www.whitehouse.gov/briefing-room/statements-releases/2021/04/29/fact-sheet-100-days-in-biden-harris-administration-makes-history-with-presidential-appointees

reporting is not just an expectation but a legal requirement – public companies are mandated by disclosure regulations to submit both periodic and current reports to inform all interested publics about what's going on within the company.

Responsibility

The second R, *Responsibility*, simply means that organizations are expected to keep their word and not lie. If we use the same hypothetical example of a university that engaged in fundraising activities to, for example, build a new library on campus, the donor would expect that the money would be actually used to build a new library on campus. This university would violate the tenant of responsibility if, instead, it used the money to build a new football stadium or luxury dorms. Governments, non-profits, and corporations are all intertwined in society and we have expectations on how they should behave. We build these expectations in part on what they say, and if their actions fail to reflect their promises, our expectations would be violated. This will no doubt hurt our relationship with these organizations and, as a result, their reputation.

When it became known that Volkswagen's promises of clean diesel were a lie and the company cheated on their engine emission tests, VW's reputation was negatively affected. This required extraordinary measures to even keep existing customers let alone attract new ones – in fact, more than 340,000 owners of VW cars demanded the company buy those cars back from them, and the company had to agree to a $14.8 billion settlement. It is still not completely clear if all these efforts were enough to save the company from "its own toxic vapors" (Atiyeh, 2019). Responsibility also has parallels to a well-known concept of Corporate Social Responsibility (CSR). However, as we already discussed, the concept of responsibility should apply not just to corporations but to all kinds of organizations. Responsibility "demands that organizations act in a socially responsible manner to publics that have supported the organization and its goals in the past. The concept of social responsibility simply means that organizations act as good citizens" (Kelly, 2001, p. 285).

Reciprocity

The third R is *Reciprocity*. The idea of reciprocity is one of the central concepts of humanity – it is rooted in the expectation of a balance in the universe. If a person helps another person, that other person typically feels an obligation, a debt, to do something back for the first person in order to restore the balance. The same is true in fundraising – a non-profit organization may send you free address labels with a request for a donation in order to create a need for reciprocity and to encourage you to donate again. Or a university may promise its donors that for every donation of $100, donors will receive a free T-shirt – this, again, brings balance to the donation and makes the donor feel appreciated. Reciprocity can be found in the context of governments and politics with *I Voted* stickers or even tax deductions for charitable contributions; and in the corporate world, where, for example, buyers of Samsung Galaxy phones receive for free an exclusive Galaxy skin they could use in the virtual world of *Fortnite*.

Relationship Nurturing

Finally, *Relationship Nurturing* strategy of stewardship focuses on maintaining connections with the organization's current supporters. It may be as simple as having a monthly newsletter for donors of a local non-profit organization. Such a newsletter keeps the organization's supporters informed about what is happening, reminds them about the organization in general and about the bond they have with the organization, and perhaps even suggests the needs of the organization that a future or even current fundraising campaign may help address. Such a newsletter may also add elements of reciprocity, responsibility, and reporting, if done well. Of course, relationship-nurturing is important for all types of organizations. Buyers of Ferrari cars, for example, buy more than a car, they also become part of the Ferrari Club with access to exclusive track events, where the car company has a chance to emphasize their unique car characteristics, provide racing training, and of course reinforce the relationships between the Ferrari and its customers. In North America alone, Ferrari Club of America has about 900 events a year – this is a strong commitment to relationship nurturing with its customers.

Chapter Summary

Managing organizational reputation is a strategic process that can be represented through an acronym, F.O.C.U.S. In this process, F stands for finding the facts when the organization conducts research to better understand what the issues are. O stands for outlining the objectives when the organization develops plans of activities based on their research and organizes those plans into goals and P.S.M.A.R.T. objectives. C stands for conducting the campaign when the organization works on achieving their objectives through strategies and tactics. U stands for understanding the upshots when the organization evaluates the results of all their efforts and determines if their investments produced any returns. The final letter, S, stands for steering toward stewardship, where the organization works non-stop at maintaining the relationships with all their publics through reporting, reciprocity, responsibility, and relationship nurturing strategies.

Five Key Terms to Remember

FOCUS
Goal
Objective
Strategy
Tactic

Discussion Questions and Activities

1 Discuss the concept of the reputation management process F.O.C.U.S. Can you propose your own acronym for this process?
2 Discuss the differences between goals and objectives and strategies and tactics. Provide examples of your personal goals and objectives for this year. What strategies and tactics are you planning for this year to help you reach your goals and objectives?
3 Explain what makes objectives P.S.M.A.R.T. Write a reputational objective for any organization.
4 Choose any organization – it may be a university you attend, a store you shop at, or a restaurant you like to dine in. Conduct a SWOT analysis of this organization.
5 Choose any large organization – for example, a corporation from the Fortune 500 list or a non-profit from *Forbes'* largest charities list. Monitor a conversation about this organization for seven days (for example, using Google Alerts). Prepare a report as if you were writing for the CEO of that organization with the summary of your monitoring and conclude with your recommendations for the organization.

References

Atiyeh, C. (2019, December 4). Everything you need to know about the VW diesel-emmissions scandal. *Car and Driver.* https://www.caranddriver.com/news/a15339250/everything-you-need-to-know-about-the-vw-diesel-emissions-scandal

Bernays, E. (1928/2005). *Propaganda*. Brooklyn, NY: Ig Publishing.

CBS/AP (2022, January 27). Tesla won't roll out new models in 2022 because of chip shortages. https://www.cbsnews.com/news/chip-shortage-delays-tesla-cybertruck-new-models-2022

Doran, G. T. (1981). There's a SMART way to write management's goals and objectives. *Management Review, 70*(11), 35–36.

Kelly, K. S. (2001). Stewardship: The fifth step in the public relations process. In R. L. Heath, Ed., *Handbook of Public Relations* (pp. 279–289). Thousand Oaks, CA: Sage.

Laskin, A. V. (2016). Levels of evaluation: An agency's perspective on measurement and evaluation. *The Public Relations Journal, 10*(2), 1–31.

Marsh, E. R. (1974). The harmonogram of Karol Adamiecki. *Academy of Management Proceedings.* https://doi.org/10.5465/ambpp.1974.17530521

Mulkern, A.C. (2022, July 19). Calif.'s last nuclear plant faces closure. Can it survive? Energy Wire. https://www.eenews.net/articles/calif-s-last-nuclear-plant-faces-closure-can-it-survive/

Porter, M. E. (1980). *Competitive strategy: Techniques for analyzing industries and competitors.* New York: Free Press.

PRSA (2021). *Study guide for the examination for accreditation in public relations.* New York: Universal Accreditation Board.

PRSA (n.d.). *Learn about public relations: What is public relations?* https://www.prsa.org/prssa/about-prssa/learn-about-pr

Puyt, R., Birger Lie, F., De Graaf, F. J., & Wilderom, C. P. M. (2020). Origins of SWOT analysis. *AOM Proceedings.* https://doi.org/10.5465/AMBPP.2020.132

Tzu, S. (2010). *The art of war.* New York: Cosimo Classics.

Worth, M. J. (1993). *Educational fund raising: Principles and practice.* Phoenix, AZ: American Council on Education.

4

Measuring Reputation: You Cannot Manage What You Cannot Measure

---

LEARNING OBJECTIVES

1. *After reading this chapter, students will be able to explain various levels of evaluation and the connections between them.*
2. *After reading this chapter, students will be able to compare and contrast various approaches to measuring and ranking organizational reputations.*
3. *After reading this chapter, students will be able to apply the Relational Reputation Ranking (RRR) approach to analyzing reputations of various organizations.*

As we discussed in Chapter 1, reputation is one of the most valuable assets of an organization. All the equipment, innovation, or human capital may mean nothing without good reputation. Thus, organizations find it important to measure their reputational assets. As Peter Ducker's famous saying goes, "you cannot manage what you cannot measure." And organizations take managing their reputations seriously. That's why there are several competing approaches to measuring reputations with many rankings, agencies, and consultants offering a variety of reputation measuring services.

In fact, many popular publications and associations in different parts of the world at some point developed their proprietary rankings of reputations. The list includes *Fortune*'s America's most admired companies, *Fortune*'s global most admired companies, *Financial Times*' world's most respected companies, *Industry Week*'s best managed companies, *Far Eastern Economic Review*'s Asia's leading companies, *Management Today*'s Britain's most admired companies, Asian Business's Asia's most admired companies, and *Manager Magazine*'s ranking of German manufacturing, and many more. However, despite their promises to measure reputations, many observers noted that they in fact measure primarily financial performance of the organizations instead of reputation (Brown and Perry, 1994; Laskin, 2013). Fryxell and Wang (1994) summarized their research, "We conclude that the dominant factor underlying the database appears to be predominately financial in its construct domain" (p. 11). Let us look at the methodology of one of such rankings, *Fortune*'s Most Admired Companies.

Organizational Reputation Management: A Strategic Public Relations Perspective, First Edition. Alexander V. Laskin.
© 2024 John Wiley & Sons, Inc. Published 2024 by John Wiley & Sons, Inc.

Fortune's Most Admired Companies

Fortune's ranking of corporate reputation is one of the oldest and well-respected approaches, dating back to 1984 when the first list of America's Most Admired Companies was released. It is important to note whose opinions *Fortune* measures in order to gauge reputations: *Fortune*'s ranking primarily evaluates the corporate reputations among the business publics. In its methodology, *Fortune* explains that in order to arrive at the final ranking of the most admired companies they, in partnership with Korn Ferry, surveyed "executives, directors, and analysts to rate enterprises in their own industry" (*Fortune*, 2021). Indeed, it makes sense to ask the experts on the subject to rank the companies. Plus, who could be more knowledgeable about all the intricacies of what is happening with a corporation than a financial analyst specializing in the industry the company operates. On the other hand, it is doubtful that what financial analysts admire is the same as what consumers appreciate about the organization or what the local community residents would find important. Thus, one may question whether the measures generated by the industry insiders are transferable to other publics.

In addition to a rather unique choice of publics to rank the corporations, many of the criteria *Fortune* uses in its ranking are also financially oriented. *Fortune* uses such criteria as, for example, financial performance of corporations, wise use of corporate assets, and long-term investment value – all financially oriented measures. At the same time, there are other criteria as well, for example, products and services, innovativeness, or societal responsibility. However, because of such a strong focus on business performance in its list of criteria and among the people conducting the ranking, several scholars noted that *Fortune*'s approach instead of admiration or reputation primarily measures financial success (Fryxell & Wang, 1994; Laskin, 2013).

With its focus on financial success and evaluation based on the industry insiders, it is no surprise that the leaders of *Fortune*'s list of most reputable companies are actually the most profitable corporations. In fact, the front-runner of the 2021 *Fortune*'s World Most Admired Companies was Apple, Inc., a company that demonstrated outstanding financial success in 2021. Apple was followed by Amazon, Microsoft, Walt Disney, and, in fifth place, Starbucks. Finishing up the top ten were Berkshire Hathaway, Alphabet, JPMorgan Chase, Netflix, and Costco Wholesale.

The creators responsible for developing the calculations of annual rankings for *Fortune*'s list of most reputable companies recognize the strong influence of financial performance on the overall results in their rankings and conclude that financial performance is responsible for almost 50% of the index's overall score (Reese and Sookedo, 1993). Combined with the fact that people who actually get to rank reputations are Wall Street financial analysts, CEOs of corporations, and other executive and business leaders, overall, *Fortune*'s list, unfortunately, fails to demonstrate a comprehensive approach to measuring various aspects of reputation.

RepTrak

A more comprehensive approach to measuring reputations was developed by the RepTrak company (formerly known as the Reputation Institute). For years, RepTrak analyzed reputations of corporations from around the world in order to find the most reputable firms overall as well as most reputable firms in various industries such as retail or banking. For example, the most reputable company in 2021 was Lego, followed by Rolex and Ferrari. Top 10 also included Bosch, Harley-Davidson, Canon, Adidas, Disney, Microsoft, and Sony. In order to measure corporate reputation (RepTrak, 2021c), RepTrak's methodology analyzes seven drivers of the corporate reputation. The measures of reputation drivers focus on answering the following question: "What do your customers think about your company?" (RepTrak, 2021a).

The first driver of the reputation is the company's *products and services*. This measure focuses on the perceptions of quality, value, and reliability of what the company is offering to its consumers. For many retail firms, this may be their most important driver of the overall reputation, as their consumers know them first and foremost through their products and services. *Innovation* is the next driver of the reputation. It is also concerned with products and services but evaluates how advanced and modern those are perceived. In the past, innovativeness was considered a part of the products and services category, but more recently RepTrak designated it as a standalone measure. In fact, one could argue that innovativeness of a company can go beyond just its products and services – the company can innovate in how it markets itself or how it manages its employees or how it raises its funding. There are many venues for innovation outside of products and services. But even innovation in products and services can raise the reputation of a company as an innovative company overall rather than just a company making innovative products. In fact, the companies want to be viewed as ground-breaking pioneers rather than backward dinosaurs in the eyes of its consumers. Consider the difference in perceptions between Apple with its iPhones and phones made by, for example, Nokia or Motorola.

Another driver of corporate reputation is the *governance*. It is a measure of the company's ethical behavior, transparency, and fairness. Close to governance is another driver, *citizenship*. Citizenship measures the firm's contributions to making the world a better place – "most frequently through environmental and social efforts" (RepTrak, 2021b, p. 3). One way to distinguish governances and citizenship is the end focus of these efforts. Governance has more of an internal focus within the organization: diversity, equity, and inclusion environmental sustainability practices of the firm, corporate transparency, fairness of the supply chain, and similar. Citizenship, on the other hand, may focus on all the same issues but outside of the organization – what does the firm do to promote diversity, equity, and inclusion in society or what does the firm do to improve the sustainability practices in society at large? In fact, in the past the citizenship category was labeled as a social responsibility category.

These seven measures of reputation - Products, Innovation, Governance, Citizenship, Workplace, Leadership, and Performance - are called drivers of reputation, as they form the foundation for the firm's reputation. But these drivers are viewed through the prism of the emotions labeled as *Trust, Feeling, Esteem,* and *Admire.* In the earlier models, emotions used to be one of the drivers of corporate reputation known as *emotional appeal*, but in later modifications of its approach RepTrak pulled emotions out of the list of drivers and made emotional appeal an intervening variable (Fombrun & van Riel, 1997; Fombrun & Foss, 2001). Indeed, many of customer's views on the company's products or performance are filtered through the lens of emotions and thus it is important to account for these emotions whether they are identified as a standalone driver of the reputation of the intervening dimension.

The Harris Poll's Reputation Quotient

Another popular measure of corporate reputation is the *reputation quotient* (RQ). The 2021 Axios Harris Poll 100 (The Harris Poll, 2021), based on the RQ methodology, identified Patagonia as the company with the best reputation. Patagonia was followed by Honda, Moderna, Chick-fil-A, and SpaceX, rounding out the top five. The poll was limited to the United States and it started with asking Americans to name the company with the best reputation and also to name a company with the worst reputation. These companies formed the list of the most visible corporations in America. In the second round, these most visible companies were ranked based on the seven dimensions that are almost identical to the dimensions RepTrak uses: *products & services, growth, vision, trust, culture, ethics, and citizenship.*

Indeed, it is impossible to deny the similarities between the reputation quotient and RepTrak's methodology. Likewise, the *Products & Service* category is the same in both measures. The same is true for the *Citizenship* category. Other categories may have different titles but they describe the same phenomena. For example, the company's workplace culture is measured by the *Culture* category in the RQ approach and it is measured in the *Workplace* category in the RepTrak approach. Perhaps the largest difference between the two is the emotions category – while in the RepTrak, emotions are the intervening variable, in the RQ approach, emotions are listed under the *Trust* category, which is one of the seven main categories.

The similarities between the reputation quotient and the RepTrak may be explained by the fact that both approaches were essentially developed from the same methodology and can be traced back to the Harris-Fombrun Reputation Quotient. Charles Fombrun, who at the time was a professor of management at the Stern School of Business, New York University, partnered with Harris Interactive (which is now The Stagwell Group) in order to develop a comprehensive measure of reputation. Later, Charles Fombrun founded the Reputation Institute that developed the RepTrak methodology, while Harris Interactive continued working on the reputation quotient (Reputation Institute, 2008).

Fortune's list, RepTrak measure, and the reputation quotient were all developed with corporations in mind. The way the data are collected and the type of categories used in calculations point to the primary focus of these measures – the largest corporations. This creates significant weaknesses of these metrics and often makes the measures invalid, if one would try to use these rankings in order to measure reputations of other kinds of organizations. For example, a nonprofit organization should not be measured with the same stick as a publicly traded corporation; the same is true for a local municipality or a presidential candidate. However, over the years, there were several attempts to apply these measures outside of the corporate context. For example, RepTrak's related instrument was modified into *Fombrun-RI Country Reputation Index* (CRI) that Passow, Fehlmann, and Grahlow (2005) applied to measuring the reputation of the principality of Lichtenstein. RepTrak, in addition to the most reputable corporations, also produces the list of most reputable countries, Country RepTrak. Laskin (2014), after reviewing all this prior research on country reputations, including Country RepTrak and CRI, proposed a new approach, *global reputation measurement* (GRM). He applied GRM to measure the reputation of the Russian Federation in the United States of America.

Relational Reputation Ranking: RRR

While reputation quotient and other measures based on RQ primarily focus on the perspectives of corporate consumers, and *Fortune*'s list of most admired companies primarily focus on the perspective of the financial audiences, there is really no multi-stakeholder approach that would focus on different publics and their different relationships with organizations. In addition, prior approaches were developed for corporations and may not be always appropriate for usage with nonprofit organizations, governments, celebrities, or other entities (of course, some modifications were developed earlier such as CRI or GRM to measure reputations of countries, but they did not gain a widespread adoption).

Yet, since relationship is the key component of reputations, with different publics having different relationships with and focusing on different issues related to the organization studied, it is important to develop such an approach focused on a variety of diverse stakeholders. This is exactly what *relational reputation ranking* (RRR) promises to achieve. RRR follows a two-step approach. First, the organization identifies key publics that can affect its success or even simply survival. This publics-first approach requires the organization to carefully review its environment and understand how it operates in its external and internal ecosystems, and prioritize its publics based on the current situation.

For example, for a university, the key relationships for success and survival may be students, students' parents, faculty, local community, and donors. The university's leadership may then prioritize these publics and assign different weights to its relationships with them as displayed in Figure 4.1. For example, students may receive 30% weight, students' parents also 30%, faculty – 20%, local community – 10%, and donors – also 10%. Of course, the specific publics and their weights may differ for different universities – for a state school, state legislature may be more important than students; for research intensive universities, grant-issuing organizations may be more

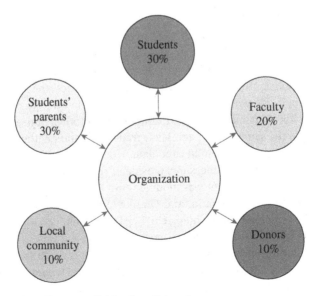

Figure 4.1 Ranking of Important Publics for a University.

important than donors; for universities with popular athletic programs, athletics boosters may be a priority. Plus, the priorities may shift from year to year, making it important to re-identify and re-evaluate the importance of different publics for the organization on a periodic basis.

Whatever the organization being measured, its leadership would need to work carefully to identify the most important publics and prioritize them as the first step of the RRR approach. After that is done, the second step is measuring the image of the organization in the eyes of these publics and the quality of the relationships between the organizations and these publics. The sum of the images and relationships will give us the overall organizational reputation.

The RRR approach can be applied to a variety of organizations, from nonprofits to governments of countries to, of course, corporations. Corporation X may have the following four publics it mostly depends on: customers, employees, suppliers, and investors (see Figure 4.2). Corporations may have prioritized employees at the very beginning of its existence when the company was just an idea and an early-stage startup because it needed to have people with the vision who can turn their vision into a reality. Later, Corporation X may have prioritized investors as the company needed money to actually build their products and put them in front of the customers. Then, they may have shifted their attention to customers to make sure the product is a success supported by a strong demand, with sales growing at an ever-accelerating pace. During the COVID pandemic the most important public may have become the suppliers, as investors were willing to invest, employees were willing to build, customers were willing to buy, but there were no materials or parts available for Corporation X because of supply-chain constraints. Thus, the company's reputation and the relationship with suppliers became the main differentiator between success and failure. Finally, today the company may rank all their four main publics equally, assigning a 25% weight to each of these relationship contributions to the overall reputation of Corporation X.

Figure 4.2 RRR: Relational Reputation Ranking with Four Key Publics: Customers, Employees, Suppliers, and Investors. The Ranking Shows Strong Relationships with Employees and Investors, Average with Suppliers, and Very Poor with Customers.

Different publics would have different, and often competing, demands for the organization. As a result, an action an organization takes may please shareholders but anger consumers and thus RRR scores will change for each individual public, but the overall reputation may actually remain unchanged depending on the specific level of changes and the importance of specific weights assigned to the involved publics. However, such change may also cause the organization to revise the importance of weights assigned to individual publics – after all, if consumers stop buying the organization's products, no amount of love from investors can save the company and vice versa.

As a result, it is important to build and maintain close relationships with a variety of publics that are currently affecting an organization's well-being as well as those that could potentially become important in the future. This is a key function of strategic public relations – maintaining relationships with key publics. Later in this book, we will look at some of the most common publics that many organizations would find important. We will start with employees, moving on to shareholders and investors, then discuss customers, regulators, and, finally, conclude with media and influencers. This is not a comprehensive list, however. Each organization should engage in annual *stakeholder audits* to identify main publics specifically relevant for this organization and re-evaluate its relationships with them.

Measuring Results of Specific Campaign Activities

While relational reputation ranking is a useful tool to measure overall organizational reputation and how it changes over time, sometimes organizations need to evaluate a specific strategic campaign or even a specific activity. For example, if a corporation decides to sponsor a New York City Marathon in an effort to improve its reputation, it may be important for such organization to try to calculate if their sponsorship actually helped their reputation. For example, among 2023 New York City marathon sponsors are TCS, MasterCard, New Balance, United Airlines, and even Michelob Ultra beer – their shareholders may ask if these sponsorship investments are actually producing results for the corporations, if there are any returns on those investments.

One of the popular approaches to measuring the effectiveness of various campaigns and activities in the reputation management field is the *return on investment*. Return on investment, often abbreviated ROI, is originally an investment instrument used to rank the profitability of various investment activities.

ROI compares financial investments into an activity with the return this activity produces. For example, if investing one dollar into Activity A brings a profit of $100, while investing one dollar into Activity B brings a profit of only $10, then it can be stated that ROI of Activity A is higher than ROI of Activity B, and thus investments should be made into Activity A as they would bring more profit.

ROI can be expressed through a simple mathematical formula:

$$ROI = \frac{Profit\ from\ the\ activity - Investment\ in\ the\ activity}{Investment\ in\ the\ activity}$$

ROI formula controls for the size of the initial investment, making it possible to compare investments of different amounts between each other.

The return on investment is a part of calculations known as *DuPont analysis*. The name refers to the DuPont Powder Company where this analysis was first developed, making DuPont Powder the first organization to use return on investments in a standardized fashion as part of its management accounting practices. At DuPont Powder, the return on investment information was used purely for evaluating investments of capital and not for evaluating managers and/or different departments. Return on investment was proposed to be used merely as an investment instrument rather than a management tool.

The original formula took into account a variety of operational measures and is significantly more complex than the simplified formula presented above. In fact, return on investment in the original DuPont analysis is calculated as a turnover ratio multiplied by a profit margin, and the formula includes several other financial indicators such as return on assets, return on equity, return on sales, tax burden ratio, and so on.

Today ROI is often used outside of the investment context, as the term became part of the popular discourse. People talk about ROI of education, ROI of public relations, ROI of physical exercises, ROI of communication (or ROC, as we discussed in the previous chapter) – just to name a few examples. And, of course, people talk about ROI of reputation.

As we discussed in the previous chapter, the reason for reliance on ROI measures in reputation is often attributed to the need to show the value of various activities in the environment of limited resources. For example, if an organization has only a certain amount of dollars in its marketing/communication budget, it needs to decide where this money can produce the most return – will it be a TV advertising campaign, a sponsorship deal, a newsletter for employees, and so on? Thus, people advocating for investments in reputation-enhancing activities need to show the value that such activities can bring to the organizational bottom line.

Fallacies of Measuring ROI of Reputation

To measure *ROI of reputation,* one should calculate all the investments into the reputation-building or reputation-maintenance activities on one side and, on the other side, the value they produced – in other words, the reputation's contribution to the organization's profits. Since ROI is a well-established financial metric, using it for reputation-enhancing activities allows executives to better understand the importance of reputation. It also creates opportunities to compare different activities between each other to discover the best value-generating undertakings and thus invest more resources into those.

However, it turns out that assigning dollar amounts to a reputation is a difficult task. Quite often in this context ROI does not mean the actual return on investment but instead is used synonymously with result, impact, or effectiveness. Indeed, in the reputation and communication realms it may be difficult if not impossible to quantify financial return of a particular investment. For example, if a company avoids lawsuits from upset customers through successful strategic communication activities, how could one reliably calculate how much financial value it really generated? In this case, one can perhaps estimate the potential legal fees saved, but what about cost savings from preventing a potential decline in future sales? Or increased employee turnover costs that were avoided? These estimations seem impossible to produce with any reliable degree of certainty. In addition, there is a lack of empirical evidence that investments in reputation-enhancing activities can be directly connected to any bottom-line measures (Kim and Yang, 2013). Thus, it becomes impossible to estimate any kind of return on investment of such activities.

Another challenge with using ROI as a metric lies in the measures of inputs. Indeed, measuring investments in reputation for ROI calculations is as challenging as measuring the final profit from such activities. How would one measure a cost of allowing telecommunicating, for example, as part of the reputational investments? Yet, it can have a very strong impact on the organization's reputation among its employees and increase employees' loyalty, thus leading to improved productivity, thus making customers happier and increasing retention and sales as well.

Finally, identifying the correlation between an organization's actions and changes in its reputation also proves to be a very difficult task. What is the dollar amount of advertising sales decline (or increase) Google experienced as a result of giving in to demands of the Chinese government about censoring the search results in China? Identifying this relationship may prove impossible as many other variables acting at the same time may have influenced revenues of Google.

As a result, while popular, using ROI in the context of building and maintaining reputations is often misleading. Scholars and professionals caution again using the term ROI when discussing the value of such an intangible concept as reputation and propose that few, if any, communication programs can be measured using ROI. Chartered Institute of Public Relations (2005) concludes that the term ROI in public relations is used so loosely that it becomes misleading.

In addition, using ROI for measuring reputation-enhancing activities can be simply unnecessary. Since ROI is designed to compare the profitability of various investment activities to identify the ones an organization should focus on, it assumes that organizations can choose what is the most profitable at building reputation. But it is not always the case when reputation is involved. For example, organizations cannot abandon communication activities targeted at building good reputations among current and prospective employees, even if ROI calculations show that bigger impact on reputation is achieved through marketing of an organization's products toward the consumers. Reputation is a multi-dimensional concept and organizations cannot abandon one of the dimensions no matter how little profitability it produces.

Management by Objective

A better approach to measuring reputation is to focus on the actual goals and objectives of the communication programs as recommended by the Barcelona Declaration of Research Principles (AMEC, 2010). These Barcelona Principles serve as the first global standard for measurement and evaluation in the public relations industry and propose that before launching any campaign, an organization should develop goals and specific measurable objectives it seeks to achieve in the end (see Table 4.1). Then, at the conclusion of the campaign, the final results can be compared to these goals and objectives to evaluate whether the campaign was successful or not.

Table 4.1 The Evolution of Barcelona Principles from 2010 to 2020.

Barcelona Principles 1.0	Barcelona Principles 2.0	Barcelona Principles 3.0
2010	2015	2020
Importance of goal setting and measurement	Goal setting and measurement are fundamental to communication and public relations	Setting goals is an absolute prerequisite to communications planning, measurement, and evaluation
Measuring the effect on outcomes is preferred to measuring outputs	Measuring communication outcomes is recommended versus only measuring outputs	Measurement and evaluation should identify outputs, outcomes, and potential impact
The effect on business results can and should be measured where possible	The effect on organizational performance can and should be measured where possible	Outcomes and impact should be identified for stakeholders, society, and the organization
Media measurement requires quantity and quality	Measurement and evaluation require both qualitative and quantitative methods	Communication measurement and evaluation should include both qualitative and quantitative analysis
AVEs are not the value of public relations	AVEs are not the value of communications	AVEs are not the value of communication
Social media can and should be measured	Social media can and should be measured consistently with other media channels	Holistic communication measurement and evaluation include all relevant online and offline channels
Transparency and replicability are paramount to sound measurement	Measurement and evaluation should be transparent, consistent, and valid	Communication measurement and evaluation are rooted in integrity and transparency to drive learning and insights

Source: AMEC: International Association for the Measurement and Evaluation of Communication. https://amecorg.com/how-the-barcelona-principles-have-been-updated and https://amecorg.com/barcelona-principles-3-0-translations

In fact, such an approach is quite prevalent in management literature and practice. This approach, called *management by objective* (MBO), focuses on measuring success or failure of activities against a certain goal that was established for such an activity beforehand. Instead of one goal of financial return, as in ROI, these goals can be different for different activities. It thus becomes an important task to select the goal most appropriate for a particular activity, whether it is expressed in monetary terms or in any other metrics. Such measures can be expressed as "enhanced cash flow, improved share price and shareholder value, greater productivity, more sales, better market shares, less employee turnover and high earnings per share" (Webster, 1990, p. 18).

Such a goal-attaining approach was also advocated by several public relations experts (Dozier and Ehling, 1992; Grunig et al., 2002; Hon, 1997). PRSA states that during evaluation the results must be measured against the stated goals and objectives of the activity (UAB, 2021). Indeed, instead of trying to artificially attach communication effects of reputation building to the sales or profits, one should focus on what these activities can actually impact – such as customer perceptions, employee attitudes, opinions of local communities, sensitivities of the regulators, and so on.

For example, one of the recent PRSA Silver Anvil Award-winning campaigns declared its goal as enhancing, promoting, and improving the reputation of the salmon industry in general and Verlasso Salmon Company in particular. Verlasso is a young company that chose to differentiate itself as a sustainable farming company in the industry tarnished with reputational problems. With support from the Linhart public relations agency, Verlasso developed a campaign focused on building reputation among chefs, retailers, distributors, and consumers. Instead of looking for ROI, the company developed five key objectives the campaign needed to reach, from placing national stories and landing speaking engagements to generating sales leads. At the end, the results were evaluated against the specific targets for each of these objectives to see if the targets were met or not. These objectives also pointed to various levels of campaigns results – from media level results such as placing stories in publications to organizational level results such as sales. In fact, the public relations industry for years emphasized the importance of measuring results at various levels – proposing different names of different levels such as inputs, outputs, outcomes, business measures, and so on, and organizing these levels in various matrixes. One of the most comprehensive approaches of this type is *levels of evaluation* (Laskin, 2016).

Levels of Evaluation

The diverse communication metric can, in fact, be organized in a standardized system of measurement and evaluation. This approach, labeled levels of evaluation, allows for variability of specific metrics while still presenting a unified structure of measurement. This approach also allows for taking measures at various stages of progression: from the actual reputation-focused activities to the final bottom-line measures impacting the whole organization.

This standardized hierarchical structure can be applied across contexts and organizations and, as such, promote standardization, serving as standard operating procedure (SOP) for measurement and evaluation. At the same time, the model of levels of evaluation does not limit the variability of activities that can be measured. Instead, levels of evaluation define the hierarchy of levels at which any campaign should be evaluated, while the actual activities at each of these levels can vary across clients and campaigns.

The levels of evaluation approach consists of five hierarchical levels: each of these levels measures the effects of specific campaigns from the start, the actual tactics the organization implements, through the intermediaries, such as media or social media, to the target audiences, for example, changes in awareness, attitude, or intended behavior, to the organizational results, for instance, changes in employee turnover ratio, and, finally, effects of the whole economy. The initial level is labeled *Output*; intermediary level, *Outreach*; target audience level, *Outcome*; business results level, *Outgrowth*; and economy level, *Outperform*. These steps are presented in Figure 4.3: from an initial idea to the actual changes in the organization's competitive environment.

Each of the levels requires measurements taken among different publics/environments: the first level, *Output*, is a measure of the productivity – so, the measure focuses

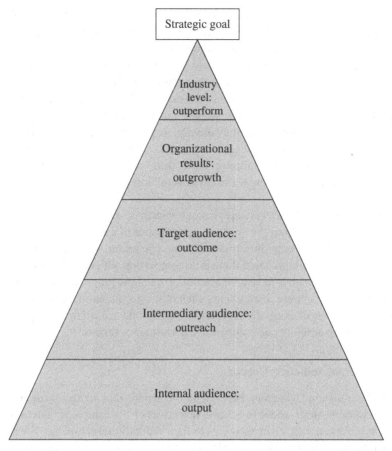

Figure 4.3 Levels of Evaluation: A Multi-Level Approach to Public Relations Evaluation. *Source:* Based on Investor Relations Textbook; https://www.wiley.com/en-us/Investor+Relations+ and+Financial+Communication%3A+Creating+Value+Through+Trust+and+Understanding-p- 9781119780458

on the corporate professionals' efforts or the communication agency hired to conduct the campaign; the second level, *Outreach*, is a measure of how far the message was able to reach in the media, on the internet, or among the opinion-leaders – thus, the intermediary publics are measured; the third level, *Outcome*, measures outcomes among the target audiences and, as a result, the measures focus on the target audiences' awareness, knowledge, attitude, and intended behavior; the fourth level, *Outgrowth*, looks at the overall organizational results – thus, the focus is on achieving the actual campaign's objectives, such as growing sales, or decreasing employee turnover, or raising donations, or getting the votes; and, finally, the fifth level, *Outperform*, puts the results of all the work into the context of the overall economic, social, and political environment in which the company operates, and compares the results with the performance of competitors and similar organizations.

Finally, the model of levels of evaluation always focuses on the organizational goal: it starts with the goal and ends with measuring how the campaign helped to achieve this goal. Although it still cannot prove a definite causal relationship between measures taken at the output level and the campaign's final result, looking at the overall picture of the quantitative and qualitative results for each level of evaluation can help the agency or internal department build this connection between their work and organizational results, and make the fact-supported claim about how the strategic public relations tactics can contribute to the organizational reputation. Furthermore, levels of evaluation can also serve as a campaign development and monitoring tool – for example, having levels of evaluation as part of the campaign's pitch builds the connection between strategic communication activities and organizational goals and objectives from the early planning stages, thus, making the work more proactive, strategic, and relevant to the organization's overall mission (Laskin, 2016; Laskin and Laskin, 2018).

Michaelson and Stacks (2011) note that any system of measurement and evaluation must allow for gauging both the absolute performance of specific programs as well as the comparative performance in contrast with prior years and/or competitive programs. However, without standardization there is no comparison – if every organization, every industry, every campaign is measured according to unique proprietary guidelines, then it is impossible to compare them among each other. So, standardization is important. The model of levels of evaluation allows for such standardization through SOP, and thus enables both absolute and comparative performance measures.

Level 1, Internal Audience: Output

Every communication campaign is based on the actions that an agency or an internal department performs in order to achieve objectives of the campaign. These activities represent the organization's investments in their reputational campaign. For example, an organization may produce news releases, organize special events, update websites, collaborate with social media influencers, and so on. Each of these activities may require significant efforts on the part of the staff and commitment of the resources. Thus, the first step is to measure and demonstrate the actual work involved in all of this – in other words, the output of the production.

The focus of this level is on the work that the organization's staff or the hired agency produces – the output of their efforts. The actual metrics can vary based on the campaign objectives. It is possible, of course, to present clients or supervisors with an actual count of what was produced: for example, 30 news releases were written, or 50 phone calls were conducted, or 150 tweets were posted. Agencies, more often, use the hourly method – presenting the client with the amount of billable hours dedicated to working on the client's account; then, each hour is billed at a predetermined rate.

It is also possible to narrow down the measurement: one news release is not always equal to another one. One can be 400 words while another can go over 1,000 words, thus word count produced on behalf of the client can be measured. Qualitative measures can also be incorporated: for example, some news releases can be about the quarterly results, some about the corporate structure, and some about new research and development. The specific measures should be selected to best reflect the overall goal of the campaign.

No matter what exact measures are used, what is important is that the agency can present to the client what work has been done on its behalf, or the internal department employees can present to the CEO what efforts were invested in supporting the function. This level becomes the foundation that all other levels of evaluation are built upon. Without looking at the actual work produced and investments made it is possible to understand what went right and what went wrong, at the conclusion of the campaign.

Level 2, Intermediary Audience: Outreach

All the investments put into a campaign mean nothing if the outputs of their work do not go anywhere beyond the departments that created them. If press releases remain on the PR staff desks and the social media posts never get seen by the people, the work produces zero effects. The goal of many efforts is communicating a message to the target audiences, so in order to reach these target audiences we usually rely on *intermediaries*: mass media, social media, opinion-leaders, influencers, and so on. Thus, the second level of evaluation focuses on the intermediaries and the channels of communication to measure how far and wide the produced message was able to reach.

For example, when talking about the first level, *Output*, we can note that the agency produced 30 news releases on behalf of the client, but let us say only five of these releases were actually picked up and covered in the news media. Then, when measuring intermediary level, *Outreach*, the agency would report that five news releases were published or broadcast.

Once again, the actual measures may differ as long as they focus on the intermediaries. Instead of the amount of news releases picked up, one can measure the readership of the *Financial Times* or *The Wall Street Journal* where the stories were published. Since *The Wall Street Journal* circulation is about 2.2 million subscribers, thus having a story in *The Wall Street Journal* allows us to say that we reached 2.2 million people. The *Financial Times* reports over 22 million subscribers, thus with the higher circulation numbers, we can report reaching more people with the same message. In addition, different media outlets have different readers – a client may be more interested in *The Wall Street Journal* rather than the *New York Times* because of the demographic profiles of readers of these two publications. Thus, measures of circulations, measures of readership/viewership can and should be incorporated during the measurement and evaluation at the outreach level.

The intermediary measures can also apply to owned media, such as the company's website, or social media, such as Facebook or Twitter – how many people saw the message, read it, commented, and re-tweeted/re-shared; who those people were; how far they spread the message; and whether the message reached the right audiences.

Qualitative measures may and should also be used. For example, the stories that appear in the media can be positive, negative, or neutral; they can briefly mention the client or focus on the client exclusively. Thus, these stories may have different effects on the client's reputation. In other words, these qualitative measures can significantly enhance the relevance and accuracy of the measurements on the intermediary level.

Level 3, Target Audience: Outcome

Having a news release on the topic important to a client prepared and published in an appropriate outlet is not sufficient. In order to call a campaign successful, at minimum, this message should actually produce an effect on the *target audience*. Thus, the target audience level measures the effects of the campaign on stakeholders. Instead of the reach of the intermediaries, the actual target publics must be measured and whether these publics became aware of the message, understood the message, developed an intended attitude toward the message, and, in fact, now plan on acting in response to this message. In other words, what was the outcome of the campaign efforts?

Indeed, placing a message in a business publication or having a financial analyst write a report about a stock does not guarantee that a member of the target audience, an investor, will actually agree with the message or understand the message the way the organization meant it to be understood. In other words, did the campaign generate the intended effect in our target audiences? So, we have to advance from measuring the intermediaries to measuring the actual target audience effects.

Measures of the target audience can be based on *awareness*. If our goal was to increase consumer's knowledge about our new product, we would want to know if the target audience became aware of our new product at the end of the campaign.

But simply knowing about the product is not enough. We also want to measure the *comprehension* – whether the target audience understands what is unique about our new product and how it differs from previous products and from our competitors' products. However, even knowing all this does not guarantee that members of the target audience will like our product. Thus, we can also measure *attitude* – is there a perception that our product is a good choice for the customer? Finally, despite knowing, understanding, and liking the product, one still may not be doing the actual final step of buying the product for a variety of reasons.

Thus, another important measure is the *intent to act*. Indeed, there is little value in making sure the target audience is aware of the product, knows all about it, and likes it, if, at the end of the day, they do not wish to buy it. Thus, measures of the target audience should include awareness, comprehension, attitude, and the intended behavior.

Level 4, Organizational Results: Outgrowth

The organizational results level moves away from measurement of the target audiences and focuses on measuring the actual organization. Here we look at the objectives of our campaign to see if we achieved them. If the focus was on selling our product, instead of measuring intention to purchase among target publics, we would measure the actual sales of our new product. Thus, this level evaluates what actually grew out of the seeds planted by the campaign and, as a result, it is called *outgrowth*.

Once again, the specific metrics can vary based on the goals of the campaign – in the case of increasing share of foreign investors, it can be global diversification of the corporation's overall shareholders' base; in the case of conducting sales, it can be sales numbers for a specific product or time frame; in the case of employee satisfaction, it may be a decrease in employee turnover. It is also important to use both quantitative and qualitative metrics – while quantitate sales numbers are always important, the organization can supplement these measures by looking at sales in different regions and countries of the world, or it can compare direct sales versus sales through distributors and dealers. These nuances may help organizations better understand the effects of the campaign and the effects of the campaign on the organizational reputation.

Level 5, Industry Level: Outperform

The final level of evaluation goes one step above the organization and measures the whole economic, social, and political environment in which the organization operates. For example, for an automaker the sales can go up as a result of the overall economic growth or go down as a result of an economic downturn, no matter whether a specific marketing campaign was successful or unsuccessful. It is possible to record an increase in car sales simply because people have more disposable income and higher consumer confidence, and thus they buy more cars across the board, not just that particular car brand. Thus, this increase in sales will have nothing to do with the campaign efforts but rather with the state of the economy. The sales can also be decreasing across the board in the industry because of the economic downturn or technological changes. If campaign evaluation measures were limited only to organizational level, it would be impossible to identify the influence of the factors outside of the organization's control. Thus, adding the fifth level lets reputation professionals capture this important information.

Looking at the overall economic, social, and political environment as well as the organization's competitors can help identify if the industry is growing or declining as a whole, which competitors are growing and which competitors are declining, and why. As a result, we can see changes in the client's market share. In this situation, a successful campaign can help make the growth larger than the one of the competitors or have the downturn smaller also in comparison with the competitors. As a result, looking at the overall economic environment during evaluation makes the measurement more valid and more reliable.

For example, during a financial crisis, reputations of all banking institutions tend to suffer, but some banks' reputations may decline significantly more than others. For example, a recent study, "the Effects of Financial Crisis on the Organizational Reputation of Banks," notes that some banks suffer larger reputational losses and face harsher criticism even though they may experience similar financial losses as other banks. The study concludes that non-financial reputational factors such as visibility and favorability may have strong differentiating effects during the crisis (Englert, Koch, & Wüstemann, 2020).

As a result, the levels of evaluation model allows public relations and communication professionals responsible for conducting campaigns aimed at improving organizational reputations to build a stronger case for their clients and supervisors in order to show how all investments in organizational reputation campaigns can grow through intermediaries to reach our target audiences to achieve the organizational performance objectives that contribute to the success of the organization in the context of larger social, political, and economic environments.

Chapter Summary

Since reputation is one of the most important assets of any organization, it is important to measure and evaluate any changes in organizational reputation. Over the years different approaches were proposed for reputation measurement, such as *Fortune*'s ranking of reputation, reputation quotient, and RepTrak. However, these measures failed to take into account the diversity of publics the organizations have and the fact that different publics have different demands and expectations for the organizations. As a result, a new approach, relational reputation ranking (RRR), focuses specifically on a variety of different organizational publics and their diverse relationships with the organization. RRR, first, identifies key publics and their effects on the overall reputation; and, second, establishes reputational measures specific for each public. In reputation management, it is also important to measure the return from the specific reputation-building activities and campaigns – such measures must integrate a variety of effects the campaign can produce on a variety of levels from communication outputs to business results as stated in the Barcelona principles. It is also important to build logical connections between all these effects. Such an approach to campaign evaluation is called levels of evaluation as it proposes to measure the results at different levels such as media, target audience, and organizational.

Five Key Terms to Remember

Relational Reputation Ranking (RRR)
RepTrak
Reputation Quotient (RQ)
Barcelona Principles
Levels of Evaluation

Discussion Questions and Activities

1 Discuss strengths and weaknesses of various reputation measurement approaches. What makes them less than comprehensive in measuring the organizational reputations?
2 Apply the relational reputation ranking (RRR) to any organization of your choice such as the university, a local pizza shop, or a nearby convenience store. First, identify the publics that are important for this organization; then estimate the quality of the relationships between the organization and each of these publics.
3 Study the Barcelona principles and their evolution from Barcelona principles 1.0 to 2.0 and to 3.0. Discuss why these changes were made. Propose how you would change the Barcelona principles if you were in charge of drafting Barcelona principles 4.0.
4 Explain how the concept of levels of evaluation can allow public relations professionals to build a strategic connection between the reputation management tactics and the overall organizational results.
5 Identify a recent campaign by a corporation or a nonprofit – it may be a Super Bowl commercial or a direct fundraising email from a local nonprofit. Apply the levels of evaluation to this campaign and propose what specific measures can be taken at each of the levels to measure the effectiveness of this campaign.

References

AMEC: International Association for Measurement and Evaluation of Communication. (2010). *Barcelona declaration of measurement principles.*

Brown, B., & Perry, S. (1994). Removing the financial performance halo from Fortune's "most admired" companies. Academy of Management Journal, 37(5), 1347–1359.

Chartered Institute of Public Relations (CIPR) (2005). *Measurement and evaluation: Moving the debate forward.*

Dozier, D. M., & Ehling, W. P. (1992). Evaluation of public relations program: What the literature tells us about their effects. In J. Grunig, Ed., Excellence in public relations and communications management (pp. 159–184). Hillsdale, NJ: LEA.

Englert, M. R., Koch, C., & Wüstemann, J. (2020). The effects of financial crisis on the organizational reputation of banks: An empirical analysis of newspaper articles. *Business & Society*, 59(8), 1519–1553. https://doi.org/10.1177/0007650318816512

Fombrun, C. F., & Foss, C. B. (2001). The reputation quotient, Part 1: Developing a reputation quotient. *The Gauge: Delahaye Medialink's Newsletter of Worldwide Communications Research,* 14(3), 1–4.

Fombrun, C. J., & van Riel, C. B. M. (1997). Fame and fortune: How successful companies build winning reputations. Upper Saddle River, NJ: Prentice Hall.

Fortune (2021). World's most admired companies. https://fortune.com/worlds-most-admired-companies

Fryxell, G. E., & Wang, J. (1994). The fortune corporate "reputation" index: Reputation for what? *Journal of Management*, 20(1), 1–14.

Grunig, L. A., Grunig, J. E., & Dozier, D. M. (2002). Excellent public relations and effective organizations. Mahwah, NJ: Lawrence Erlbaum Associates.

Hon, L. C. (1997). What have you done for me lately? Exploring effectiveness in public relations. *Journal of Public Relations Research*, 9(1), 1–30.

Kim, Y., & Yang, J. (2013). Corporate reputation and return on investment (ROI): Measuring the bottom-line impact of reputation. In C. E. Carroll, Ed., *The Handbook of Communication and Corporate Reputation* (pp. 574–589). Oxford, UK: Blackwell Publishing Ltd.

Laskin, A. V. (2013). Financial performance and reputation. In C. Carroll, Ed., *The Handbook of Communication and Corporate Reputation* (pp. 376–387). Malden, MA: Wiley.

Laskin, A. V. (2014). Pilot test of the global reputation measurement: What do US students think of the Russian Federation today? *Russian Journal of Communication*, 6(3), 260–274. https://doi.org/10.1080/19409419.2014.960317

Laskin, A. V. (2016). Levels of evaluation: An agency's perspective on measurement and evaluation. *The Public Relations Journal*, 10(2), 1–31.

Laskin, A. V., & Laskin, A. A. (2018). Measurement and evaluation of investor relations and financial communication activities. *The Handbook of Financial Communication and Investor Relations*, 275–281.

Michaelson, D., & Stacks, D. W. (2011). Standardization in public relations measurement and evaluation. *Public Relations Journal*, 5(2), 1–22.

Passow, T., Fehlmann, R., & Grahlow, H. (2005). Country reputation – from measurement to management: the case of Liechtenstein. *Corporate Reputation Review*, 7(4), 309–326.

Reese, J. & Sookdeo, R. (1993). America's most admired corporations: What lies behind a company's good name? Some hard financial realities—including long-term return to shareholders and an abiding record of profitability. CNN Money. https://money.cnn.com/magazines/fortune/fortune_archive/1993/02/08/77483/

RepTrak (2021a). 2021 Global RepTrak 100. https://www.reptrak.com/rankings

RepTrak (2021b). Can't buy me love: The receipts on retail 2021. https://ri.reptrak.com/hubfs/_2021%20RETAIL%20(Cant%20buy%20me%20love)/Retail%20report_X.pdf

RepTrak (2021c). RepTrak platform. https://www.reptrak.com/reptrak-platform/what-is-reptrak

Reputation Institute. (2008). About RI. Retrieved January 1, 2009, from the Reputation Institute website: http://www.reputationinstitute.com/about/index

The Harris Poll (2021, May). 2021 Axios Harris Poll 100. https://theharrispoll.com/wp-content/uploads/2021/05/Axios-Harris-Poll-100-2021-Report.pdf

Universal Accreditation Board (2021). Study guide for the examination for accreditation in public relations (6th ed.). https://accreditation.prsa.org/MyAPR/Content/Apply/APR/APR.aspx

Webster, J. L. (1990). Strategy implementation: some interactive effects of strategy and structure on bank performance. Arizona State University.

5

Maintaining Reputation through Crises and around the World: Legal, Ethical, Professional, and Socially Responsible Perspectives

---

LEARNING OBJECTIVES

1. *After reading this chapter, students will be able to define crisis and explain best practices of crisis management.*
2. *After reading this chapter, students will be able to discuss international issues in reputation management.*
3. *After reading this chapter, students will be able to recognize and analyze legal, ethical, professional, and societal influences on organizations.*

It is important for organizations to be proactive in managing their reputations. Organizations should measure their reputations on a periodic basis and invest in building and maintaining relationships with key publics based on the results of those measurements. Sometimes, however, an unexpected event can happen that would force the organization to act reactively in order to protect its reputation. Such unexpected events are often referred to as organizational crises.

Crisis

A crisis is the most stressful and difficult time for any organization. A crisis is an unexpected, nonroutine event that creates high levels of uncertainty and threatens the existence of an organization or its ability to carry out its mission (Ulmer et al., 2007). This definition focuses on key characteristics of a crisis.

First of all, a crisis must be *unexpected*. It comes as a surprise. As a result, a snowstorm during the winter in Vermont can hardly be called a crisis. It should be expected, and many in Vermont are preparing and planning for it. A snowstorm in Texas, on the other hand, may become a crisis right away if people did not expect it and did not prepare for it. Indeed, if it never snows in Texas, why would anyone even consider

Organizational Reputation Management: A Strategic Public Relations Perspective,
First Edition. Alexander V. Laskin.
© 2024 John Wiley & Sons, Inc. Published 2024 by John Wiley & Sons, Inc.

preparing for a snowstorm there? Thus, crises must be out of the ordinary and violate normal expectations in order to be considered crises.

Another key characteristic of a crisis is its *importance* – the event should be a significant enough threat to the organization or its publics to be called a crisis. Any consumer electronic company can produce and sell defective products from time to time – that's why they offer warranty protections. Normally, a customer would return the defective product and it will be fixed or exchanged for a proper working one. Sometimes, companies may even have a whole line of products with a subpar quality or lacking key features – phones with slow processors, cars with poor ergonomics, or laptops without enough storage. These occurrences are rarely raised to the level of a crisis, however. On the other hand, when new Samsung phone batteries started catching fire, including on planes during flights, forcing the Federal Aviation Administration (FAA) to ban those phones from flights in the United States, this became a crisis (see Figure 5.1). Other countries followed suit, and social media and then traditional media were filled with images of Samsung phones catching fire. At one point it was not even clear if Samsung would ever recover as a phone manufacturer or if it was the end for the Samsung line of Galaxy phones.

The third key characteristic of a crisis is its *urgency*, or a *short response time*. The company must deal with whatever issue the crisis brings up fast – there is no chance to take a pause and postpone the decision about what needs to be done. It may not even be possible to consider all response options or involve all relevant parties as the urgency of the crisis may demand immediate action; inaction is often the worst possible option. If there is a fire, or flood, or snowstorm, action must be taken as soon as possible to save lives. When it comes to reputational crises, the stakes may not always be that high, but if there is a rumor that can hurt the financial solvency of an organization,

Figure 5.1 Samsung Galaxy Note 7 Phone. *Source:* Leszek Kobusinski / Shutterstock.

delay may harm employees, suppliers, customers, and local communities as well. Thus, fast and decisive action would still be required.

Finally, crises produce *uncertainty*. An event that is urgent, significant, and unexpected, but with a clear path of action, hardly qualifies as a crisis. It is more of an important operational event. If, on the other hand, it is unclear what to do next or how the event even occurred, this is a classic crisis scenario. Coombs (2012) suggests that because of this uncertainty component, a crisis is perception-based. The events that rise to the level of a crisis are the events that we perceive as a crisis: no perception of a crisis would mean no crisis.

When we are uncertain on how to act, when we do not know what to do in a situation, we tend to view the situation we are in as a crisis. For example, for an average person, getting into a fist fight is typically a crisis situation because we do not know what to do and how to properly act in a fight, but for a professional mixed martial arts fighter, it may just be a morning warmup.

Crisis Management

Crisis management, then, is a function of responding to such an unexpected, uncertain, urgent, and important event in order to preserve or enhance the organizational reputation as a result. Researchers generally recognize three stages of crisis management: *pre-crisis, crisis,* and *post-crisis*. The importance of *pre-crisis* is highlighted by an old adage that the best crisis is the one that never happens. As a result, public relations professionals conduct *issues management*: actively monitoring the environment and identifying issues that may eventually evolve into crises. Early detection may allow the company to work on preventing the crisis from ever happening. For example, a company may suspect that an activist group is planning to block access to the company's factory. Learning about this early may allow the company to start reaching out proactively to these activists to find out what the issues are and if negotiations and comprises are possible. If a crisis is all but inevitable, early detection may help the company get a jump-start on preparing the most effective response possible and mobilizing the resources needed for such a response. In pre-crisis, organizations should work on developing such crises resources, including the most important ones: a *crisis response team* and a *crisis response plan*. Creating a crisis team and a crisis plan helps establish a proper chain of command to ensure a fast and effective response once the crisis hits. It is also beneficial to train the people on the response team on what to do during a crisis situation – practice makes perfect!

For example, in the state of Connecticut all owners of the high hazard and significant hazard class dams must develop an Emergency Action Plan (EAP). These EAPs provide detailed instructions on what must be done in case the dam breaches (see Figure 5.2). EAPs also provide a detailed flow chart of responsibilities and communications specifying who will contact whom and who will be responsible for what action, including the dam owners, emergency responders, local municipalities, and state officials. Having all these plans in place in advance should ensure a fast and decisive response in case any dam in the state experiences a failure (DEEP, 2023).

Once in a *crisis stage*, all efforts must be focused on the actual response – the crisis team and all the crisis plans must be activated. An important part of the crisis stage is the actual *crisis recognition* – sometimes it takes an effort to recognize that what is

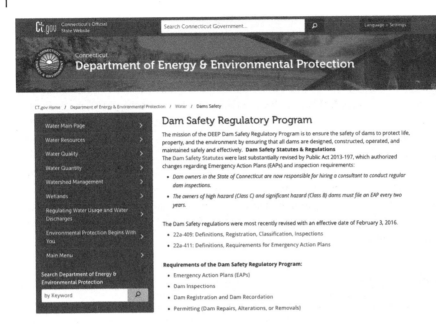

Figure 5.2 State of Connecticut Dam Safety Regulatory Program. *Source:* Department of Energy & Environmental Protection, https://portal.ct.gov/DEEP/Water/Dams/Dams-Safety/ last accessed August 04, 2023.

happening is a crisis. It took some time for Samsung to recognize that phone batteries catching fire is not just a minor manufacturing defect of early products, but a full-blown crisis.

Finally, the *post-crisis stage* should focus on the lessons learned and evaluating the effectiveness of the response. It is also beneficial, based on new information, to update crisis plans and perhaps the crisis team. It is also beneficial to work on restoring the reputation of the company or brand if it took a hit during the crisis. Samsung, for example, realizing that it lost a lot of public trust, opened up its factories and technologies to outside auditors, relying on their independence and reputation to bolster its own – hundreds of engineers tested thousands of batteries to ensure the phones were safe to use.

International Perspectives

Since crisis is perception based, it may be affected by the expectations of different publics. When these expectations are violated, the organization may find itself dealing with a crisis situation. In another words, perceptions are important both within and outside of the organization. However, we know that expectations may differ from country to country. In different countries organizational publics may have very different expectations about how organizations should act – and these expectations may affect the products organizations sell, services they provide, messages they broadcast, causes they support, and so on.

As a result, it becomes important for organizations to incorporate international perspectives into their reputation management activities. When it comes to international public relations and reputation management activities, they all may be categorized into four large groups: *regional, cross-national, international,* and *global* (Molleda & Laskin, 2005).

Regional Public Relations

Regional public relations refers to the efforts of the organization to adjust and adopt to different countries or regions the organization operates in. McDonald's, for example, offers different menu items in different countries of the world taking into account local customs (see Figure 5.3). For example, in India McDonald's does not sell beef but has extra-large selections of vegetarian options, including popular McAloo Tikki Burger that uses a potato and green pea patty instead of traditional beef. In addition to the whole new menu items or different promotional campaigns, even the same sandwiches may taste differently in different countries because of variations in cooking procedures designed once again to take into account local customs.

Of course, it is no easy task for organizations to adjust their operations for different countries around the world. Previous research identified key differentiators that organizations must take into account when operating in a country other than their own: political environment, economic development, legal system, and local culture (Hill, 2021). Thus, to be successful, organizations must learn about all of these variables and adjust their actions accordingly to be successful in a foreign country.

Figure 5.3   Poster in a McDonald's Restaurant Window in Costa Rica.

One way to achieve this is to hire local employees or local communication agencies to help organizations match the local environment and give them autonomy to function in their local market. This creates another challenge for the organization – to what extent those local subsidiaries can make their own decisions about what products to sell, what marketing campaigns to communicate, and what type of employee benefits to implement. This challenge is known as the problem of *coordination and control* (Martinez & Jarillo, 1989): to what extent could the decision-making across transnational organizations be centralized to achieve consistency and to what extent could it be regionalized to better adopt to local demand? Finding a perfect balance is a constant effort, as the world changes constantly as well, and depends on the specific organization and even specific message – thus, there is no uniform prescription for the proper coordination and control formula (Molleda & Laskin, 2009).

Cross-National Public Relations

Cross-national public relations refers to activities that, while limited to a specific country or region, affect the organization in another country or region. For example, during FIFA's World Cup in Moscow, Russia, Burger King launched a campaign in the Russian market that promised a free lifetime supply of Whoppers to any Russian woman who could get impregnated by any foreign football (soccer) player competing in the World Cup (Burger King Russia, 2018). The campaign asked Russian women to try to acquire "best football genes" in order to "lay down the success of the Russian national football team" (Rogers, 2018). Within Russia the campaign was generally successful as it related to the Russian tradition of making fun of bad Russian footballers and the national football (soccer) team because, as the saying goes, they were genetically bad at playing the game. In addition, it connected to Russia's recent historic events, when during the Olympic Games of 1980 in Moscow, Russian women were trying to get impregnated by foreign Olympic athletes in order to escape from behind the Iron Curtain of the Soviet Union.

However, when the word of this campaign reached the United States of America, where the Burger King headquarters are located, it caused a significant uproar as American audiences saw this advertising as sexist. As a result, Burger King had to apologize and cancel the campaign immediately. In other words, the reaction of publics in one country, the United States, forced the global corporation to cancel a marketing campaign intended for customers in a completely different country across the world, the Russian Federation (see Figure 5.4).

The situation where a crisis can shift from one country to another is called a cross-national conflict shifting (CNCS) (Molleda, Connolly-Ahern, & Quinn, 2005). Sometimes this cross-national conflict shifting may affect an organization's reputation not just in the country where the crisis happened or the country where the organization's headquarters are located but in a third country. For example, Mercedes-Benz Group, a German maker of Mercedes cars (as well as Maybach), was caught bribing local government officials in China, Turkey, Nigeria, Turkmenistan, and a few other countries in order to secure lucrative government contracts. In addition to reputational damages Mercedes suffered in those countries, it also faced court cases and negative publicity in its home country of Germany. What's more, Mercedes received a lot of negative publicity in the United States, a country unrelated to the scandal. In fact, the US Securities and Exchange Commission and US Justice Department

Figure 5.4   Burger King Restaurant. *Source:* Sunshine Seeds / Shutterstock.

launched an investigation in the Mercedes bribery case, which led to even more reputational damages for the organization (Pelofsky & Margolies, 2010). Of course as the globalization speeds up and the world shrinks, it is reasonable to expect that the effect of CNCS will happen more and more often – one social media post or an ad in one country can instantaneously be shared around the world with a click of a button. Even language is becoming less of a barrier as Google and other online services can now translate texts between languages in real time. The Burger King campaign mentioned above was posted in Russian language and on a Russian social media network, VK. Yet, it did not prevent the screenshots of that promotion to be widely shared on Twitter and Facebook in the United States within hours.

International Public Relations

International public relations refers to the activities of the organization specifically targeted at publics in another country. In other words, unlike regional public relations, where the communications stay within a country's border, or cross-national communications, where they are designed for a specific country but escape to other countries outside of the organization's desire, international public relations communications are deliberately planned to cross the borders of a country. A good example of international public relations is *public diplomacy* where governmental organizations of one country communicate directly to the citizens of another country.

For example, Radio Free Europe/Radio Liberty broadcasts to people living in Eastern Europe, Central Asia, Caucasus, and the Middle East in order to share the US government's view on the events around the world. In some countries, Radio Liberty is even labeled as US propaganda and banned (Voice of America, 2021). Of course, international public relations are not limited to just governments; they may be conducted by non-profits and corporations as well. Radio Free Europe/Radio Liberty mentioned above is registered as a non-profit organization 501(c)(3) sponsored and supervised by the US Agency for Global Media, an independent federal agency reporting to six house and senate committees.

Global Public Relations

Finally, *global public relations* refers to the strategic communication and reputation management activities on the global scale. These activities consider national borders irrelevant as their focus is the whole planet. These activities are usually associated with the largest organizations operating on the global scale – those may be quasi-governmental organizations such as the United Nations or World Bank; large corporations such as Microsoft or Coca-Cola; and large non-profits such as the Red Cross or Doctors Without Borders. National differences become irrelevant at this level as the organizations try to communicate with the whole world; or, another way to look at it is that all national peculiarities and customs must be taken into account at the same time in order to maintain the organizational reputation at this global scale, and to avoid offending and alienating a subset of the world population.

Being Ethical

One of the prerequisites of developing and maintaining a positive reputation at the global level is being an ethical organization. Ethical principles transcend national borders and unify all people into global humanity. Thus, ethics can be viewed as unifying principles of how humans ought to act (Singer, 1994). Ethical requirements are different from legal requirements, as some legal actions may be unethical and some unethical actions may be quite legal.

In the context of reputation management, when the organization follows ethical principles, it creates an opportunity for the organization to explain and rationalize its choices. "For example, if a stakeholder group is angered by an organization's policy, the public relations professional can discuss that policy with them in a defensible and logical manner. In this way, ethical decisions can be understood, if not agreed upon, and creating understanding reduces uncertainty" (Bowen, Moon, & Kim, 2017, p. 78).

For many years, the field of moral philosophy studied the concept of ethics. Among many different approaches to ethics, five are most commonly mentioned: *deontology, virtue, consequentialism, hedonism,* and *moral skepticism.*

Deontology

In *deontology*, ethics are based on the moral obligation, a *duty* to act, based on universal ethical principles making people and organizations rational, logical, consistent, and, as a result, predictable. Immanuel Kant (1785/1994) explained that deontology asks three questions to determine if the action is ethical or not: Would all rational decision-makers want the option they are about to take to become a universal law for all similar situations for all time? Will the action maintain the dignity of and respect for all involved stakeholders? Is the decision made from a basis of good intention alone? If the answer is yes to all three questions, then the action is ethical; otherwise, it is not.

Virtue

Virtue ethics refers to the works of ancient Greek philosophers Aristotle and Socrates who believed that the focus of ethics should be the actor and not the action. In other words, we should consider the actual person or the organization behind the action. Any action that makes them better, meaning more virtuous, is ethical. Thus, instead of following set, guiding, moral principles, an ethical action from the standpoint of virtue ethics is the one that makes the person or organization more virtuous.

Consequentialism

In *consequentialism,* the focus shifts to the consequences of any action instead of the action itself as in deontology or the actor as in the *virtue* ethics. What matters here is the end result – if an organization has to break the law or do something bad in order to make something good, then it is considered worthwhile and ethical from the standpoint of consequentialism. For example, while murder in general is wrong, consequentialists would consider murdering a terrorist to be an ethical act because it makes the world a safer place overall. In consequentialism, the end justifies the means.

Hedonism

Hedonism as a moral philosophy declares that all humans (and by extension, the organizations) may act in a way that increases the amount of pleasure and reduces the amount of pain. This has parallels with deontology as there is a universal guiding principle and with consequentialism as the account of pleasure/pain is usually judged in the result of the action rather than in the action itself. However, because of its unique focus on pleasure, it is commonly noted as a standalone type of ethics.

Moral Skepticism

Finally, *moral skepticism* claims that nobody has moral authority or even moral knowledge sufficient enough to decide what makes something ethical or unethical. German philosopher Friedrich Nietzsche explained that morality and ethics are nothing more than a herd instinct that limits freedom to enjoy life: "By morality the individual is taught to become a function of the herd, and to ascribe to himself value only as a function" (Nietzsche & Kaufmann, 1974). Thus, subscribing and following any ethical guidelines is essentially dehumanizing and, since no one can know what is truly ethical, meaningless. The challenge, then, arises: How would one know what to do and how to act without any ethical guidance? One answer to this problem may be to act as a professional.

Professionalism

Professionalism would suggest that for the organization to build and maintain a positive reputation it needs to make sure that everyone in the organization acts with the highest standards of their profession. Accountants act how accountants should act, engineers act how engineers should act, and public relations and communication professionals act how they are supposed to act from a professional standpoint. In fact, most professions develop and uphold professional codes of conduct that specify what a member of this profession should aspire to do.

For example, International Public Relations Association (IPRA) has the "IPRA Code of Conduct" for people working in the field of public relations that states the following:

In the conduct of public relations practitioners shall:

1. Observance.
   Observe the principles of the UN Charter and the Universal Declaration of Human Rights;
2. Integrity.
   Act with honesty and integrity at all times so as to secure and retain the confidence of those with whom the practitioner comes into contact;
3. Dialogue.
   Seek to establish the moral, cultural and intellectual conditions for dialogue, and recognize the rights of all parties involved to state their case and express their views;
4. Transparency.
   Be open and transparent in declaring their name, organization and the interest they represent;
5. Conflict.
   Avoid any professional conflicts of interest and to disclose such conflicts to affected parties when they occur;
6. Confidentiality.
   Honor confidential information provided to them;
7. Accuracy.
   Take all reasonable steps to ensure the truth and accuracy of all information provided;
8. Falsehood.
   Make every effort to not intentionally disseminate false or misleading information, exercise proper care to avoid doing so unintentionally and correct any such act promptly;
9. Deception.
   Not obtain information by deceptive or dishonest means;
10. Disclosure.
    Not create or use any organization to serve an announced cause but which actually serves an undisclosed interest;
11. Profit.
    Not sell for profit to third parties copies of documents obtained from public authorities;
12. Remuneration.
    Whilst providing professional services, not accept any form of payment in connection with those services from anyone other than the principal;
13. Inducement.
    Neither directly nor indirectly offer nor give any financial or other inducement to public representatives or the media, or other stakeholders;
14. Influence.
    Neither propose nor undertake any action which would constitute an improper influence on public representatives, the media, or other stakeholders;

15. Competitors.
Not intentionally injure the professional reputation of another practitioner;
16. Poaching.
Not seek to secure another practitioner's client by deceptive means;
17. Employment.
When employing personnel from public authorities or competitors take care to follow the rules and confidentiality requirements of those organizations;
18. Colleagues.
Observe this Code with respect to fellow IPRA members and public relations practitioners worldwide.

Similarly, CFA Institute, a professional association for financial analysts from around the world, has seven principles in its Standards of Professional Conduct (CFA Institute, 2023):

1. Professionalism.
This includes knowledge of the law, independence and objectivity, and avoiding misrepresentation and misconduct.
2. Integrity of Capital Markets.
This includes avoiding any kind of market manipulation and benefiting from material nonpublic information.
3. Duties to Clients.
This includes working with loyalty, prudence, and care, deal fairly and objectively, suiting the client's needs, disclosing performance information, and preserving confidentiality.
4. Duties to Employees.
This includes loyalty, fair compensation, and being good supervisors.
5. Investment Analysis, Recommendation, and Actions.
This includes being reasonable and diligent, providing honest information to clients and prospective clients, and saving the records of communication.
6. Conflict of Interest.
This principle focuses on the requirement to disclose any conflicts of interests, fee structure, including referral fees, and prioritizing clients' transactions.
7. Responsibilities as a CFA Institute Member or CFA Candidate.
This includes avoiding any conduct that may harm the reputation of the CFA Institute and avoiding any misrepresentation and aggeneration of CFA Institute and its membership.

Some professional associations label their codes of professional conduct as codes of ethics. For example, the Public Relations Society of America (PRSA) that we mentioned before has a professional code for its members but calls it the *PRSA Code of Ethics* (2023). Society of Professional Journalism (SPJ) also calls its principles an *SPJ Code of Ethics* (2014). This, however, is not accurate. As what is considered professional may be considered unethical. In fact, scholars suggest that it is important to distinguish between legal, professional, and ethical. Some actions may be illegal in some countries, unethical from a standpoint of some ethical approach, but would be considered professional according to the code of conduct of that profession.

One study (Laskin & Danner, 2007), for example, discusses the case of an American journalist, Judith Miller, who spent three months in jail for refusing to reveal her sources of information to the US Federal Court because as a journalist she promised confidentiality to the sources and as a result she was required to uphold her promise to the source. This is one of the key principles in the journalistic codes of conduct. However, the federal judge ruled that it was illegal, as failure to cooperate with the investigation adds a contempt of court charge. From the standpoint of deontological ethics, the action would seem to be unethical as well – as it is unlikely that most people would like all witnesses to withhold information about crimes from prosecutors and courts as a universal principle. Thus, the authors argued Miller's actions were professional but, at the same time, both illegal and unethical (Laskin & Danner, 2007).

In fact, the study concluded that professional, legal, and ethical dimensions can be represented as a Venn diagram called PLE (professional, legal, and ethical) with circles overlapping to some degree. In the end, such PLE diagram would create areas in which any action may be placed. Only area one, however, would contain actions that meet all three criteria: actions that are ethical, legal, and professional at the same time (see Figure 5.5).

The authors later suggested adding a fourth dimension (and a fourth overlapping circle) of culture and societal expectations because different countries may have their unique histories, cultures, religions, and social norms, and all these differences may affect what would be considered appropriate or inappropriate actions in different societies. Thus, it also becomes important to discuss how to build and maintain reputations in different countries, cultures, and societies.

Cultures and Societal Expectations

A large part of managing an organizational reputation involves managing strategic and tactical issues for the organization. As we discussed earlier in this chapter, the issues may be quite different across different countries the organization operates in. In fact, many reputational threats stem from the incongruence between organizational expectations and the expectations of various stakeholders of the organization. Thus, it is essential for organizations to adapt to the cultures and societies they operate in and, at the very least, develop an understanding of these cultures and societies in order to be able to identify the issues that may affect the organization. Such a process is known as *issue management*.

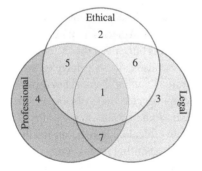

1 – Actions that are professional, legal, and ethical
2 – Actions that are ethical, but not professional or legal
3 – Actions that are legal but not professional or ethical
4 – Actions that are professional but not ethical or legal
5 – Actions that are ethical and professional but not legal
6 – Actions that are ethical and legal but not professional
7 – Actions that are professional and legal but not ethical

Figure 5.5 PLE Framework: Professional, Legal, and Ethical.

Issue management is commonly defined as the anticipatory strategic management process of identifying and responding to issues facing an organization. The issues are not static – they grow or shrink, the number of publics involved changes, and the issues increase or decrease in importance for those publics. Heath (2018) identified the life cycle of issues: early stage, emerging stage, current stage, crisis stage, and dormant stage; and types of issues: issues of fact, issues of value, issues of policy, and issues of identification. For example, an issue of policy for Walmart was its treatment of its hourly employees. For years, it was a dormant issue not attracting much attention from anybody except from those involved: Walmart hourly employees. However, the issue grew beyond the organization and spilled into the mass media. The issue turned into a full-blown crisis when Human Rights Watch began an investigation of Walmart's treatment of its employees. With customers boycotting the stores, employees leaving, class action lawsuits piling up, constant media coverage keeping the issue at the top of the agenda, and government pressure mounting, Walmart had to respond and modify its policies, but at this point the price of the response was significantly higher than it would have been if Walmart had been able to identify and manage the issue before it became a crisis.

Issue management is built on the idea that the best crisis is the one that never happens.

Predicting and managing issues to avoid future crises can save an organization from monetary and reputational losses. Issue management, however, is not only about avoiding losses; it is also about identifying opportunities. A new emerging technology or a change in customer preferences may allow a company to capitalize on the opportunity before its competitors seize this chance. This makes issue management an important part of the organizational process that involves all divisions and all employees. Although in different countries of the world with various historical and cultural backgrounds, societal expectations may be very different and thus the specific issues that may affect organizations would also greatly differ. These multitude of issues that may face organizations can usually be classified into three broad categories represented by the abbreviation ESG (Environmental issues, Social issues, and Governance issues). However, while originally used just for corporations, the ESG abbreviation is relevant for all types of organizations.

Environmental Sustainability

Since the United Nations raised the profile of sustainability and sustainable development in political, economic, and social agendas in the 1980s, corporations have been expected to publicly disclose their impact on the environment and avoid or minimize the harm they may be imposing on their environment. The term sustainable development is generally traced back to the United Nations report, Our Common Future. The Secretary General of the United Nations, Javier Perez de Cuellar, established the World Commission on Environment and Development chaired by Gro Harlem Brundtland in 1983. The result of the work of this Commission was the Our Common Future report, unofficially also known as a Brundtland Report. The report provides a well-recognized definition of the concept: "Sustainable development is development that meets the needs of the present without compromising the ability of future generations to meet their own needs" (World Commission, 1987, Chapter 2). The foundational principle of this definition is preserving our habitat while improving our standard of living – a noble desire, yet often called impossible, as improving standards of living for the ever-increasing number of people demands ever-increasing amounts of resources and thus invariably leads to the depletion of natural capital.

Several attempts have been made over the years to make the concept of sustainability more meaningful by developing a precise framework for measuring and operationalizing the concept. These frameworks were developed from a variety of standpoints and approaches. Among those frameworks are the Triple Bottom Line, the Natural Step, the Ecological Footprint, the Sustainability Hierarchy, and many more. Yet, the challenge endured as the concept remained elusive. For example, Norman and MacDonald (2004), having reviewed one of these conceptualizations, the Triple Bottom Line, concluded that it may be just a "good old-fashioned single bottom line" (p. 258) with the addition of some vague environmental promises.

Yet, despite this vagueness, many publics demand environmental disclosures from organizations. Sustainability reporting as part of broader corporate reporting is a function of investor relations (Laskin & Nesova, 2022). One of the key purposes of investor relations is to provide full and timely disclosure in order to enable investor and shareholders as well as other relevant stakeholders to better understand the business model and the fair value of the company (Laskin, 2022). Sustainability activities have an effect on a company's valuation and, as a result, are part of such disclosures (see Table 5.1).

More and more companies produce sustainability reports. For example, a recent study by Governance & Accountability Institute (2020) showed that 65% of all companies in the Russell 1000 Index produce sustainability reports; if the sample is limited to the 500 largest companies, the number of companies producing those reports increases to 90%. The growth in sustainability reporting is commonly celebrated, as it is suggested that such an increase has a correlation with the increased importance of the role sustainability plays in the corporate world.

Social Responsibility

In addition to the issues of environmental impact, many publics also consider how the organization addresses large societal issues. The organization's impact on society has long been a topic of debate in the academic and professional community. In fact, since the introduction of the term *corporate social responsibility* (CSR) arguments around its meaning have not subsided. Among the most accepted definitions is the one by Davis (1973): "The firm's considerations of, and response to, issues beyond the narrow economic, technical, and legal requirements of the firm to accomplish social benefits along with the traditional economic gains which the firm seeks" (p. 312). More recently, Kotler and Lee (2005) added that CSR is "a commitment to improve community well-being through discretionary business practices and contribution of corporate resources" (p. 3).

Even large investment organizations, which are usually thought of as primarily profit driven, often consider societal issues. For example, some investors may avoid investments in companies involved with the tobacco industry, weapons, or gambling. These stocks are known as *sinful stocks*. Even at the end of the nineteenth and the beginning of the twentieth centuries, certain investors, for example Quakers, avoided any investment in sinful stocks or doing any business with sinful companies.

Table 5.1   100 Most Sustainable Companies of 2023.

2023 Rank	Name	Industry	Location	Revenue, USD PPP
1	Schnitzer Steel Industries Inc.	Metals & mining	Portland, USA	2,758,551,000.0
2	Vestas Wind Systems A/S	Electrical equipment	Aarhus, Denmark	22,655,523,255.8
3	Brambles Ltd	Commercial services & supplies	Sydney, Australia	5,558,900,000.0
4	Brookfield Renewable Partners LP	Independent power and renewable electricity producers	Hamilton, Bermuda	4,071,000,000.0
5	Autodesk Inc.	Software	San Francisco, USA	4,386,400,000.0
6	Evoqua Water Technologies Corp	Machinery	Pittsburgh, USA	1,464,429,000.0
7*	Stantec Inc.	Professional services	Edmonton, Canada	3,679,099,678.5
7*	Schneider Electric SE	Electrical equipment	Rueil-Malmaison, France	42,013,081,395.3
8	Siemens Gamesa Renewable Energy SA	Electrical equipment	Zamudio, Spain	14,822,409,883.7
9	Taiwan High Speed Rail Corp	Transportation infrastructure	Taipei City, Taiwan	1,986,194,033.8
10	Dassault Systemes SE	Software	Velizy-Villacoublay, France	7,064,098,837.2
12	Xinyi Solar Holdings Ltd.	Semiconductors & semiconductor equipment	Wuhu, China	2,738,604,671.0
13	Orsted A/S	Electric utilities	Fredericia, Denmark	11,636,404,494.4
14	Sims Ltd	Metals & mining	Mascot, Australia	6,200,267,379.7
15	Banco do Brasil SA	Banks	Brasilia, Brazil	52,591,137,549.4
16	Rockwool A/S	Building products	Hedehusene, Denmark	4,488,372,093.0
17	Johnson Controls International PLC	Building products	Cork, Ireland	23,668,000,000.0
18	Chr Hansen Holding A/S	Chemicals	Hoersholm, Denmark	1,472,143,895.3

(Continued)

Table 5.1 (Continued)

2023 Rank	Name	Industry	Location	Revenue, USD PPP
19	Kone Oyj	Machinery	Espoo, Finland	15,282,122,093.0
20	Cascades Inc.	Containers & packaging	Kingsey Falls, Canada	3,180,064,308.7
21	Atlantica Sustainable Infrastructure PLC	Independent power and renewable electricity producers	Brentford, United Kingdom	1,211,749,000.0
22	McCormick & Company Inc.	Food products	Hunt Valley, USA	6,317,900,000.0
23	Novozymes A/S	Chemicals	Bagsvaerd, Denmark	2,239,850,187.3
24	Iberdrola SA	Electric utilities	Bilbao, Spain	56,851,744,186.0
25	BT Group PLC	Diversified telecommunication services	London, United Kingdom	30,564,516,129.0
26	Alphabet Inc.	Interactive media & services	Mountain View, USA	257,637,000,000.0
27	Vitasoy International Holdings Ltd	Food products	Hong Kong, Hong Kong	1,108,287,589.5
28	City Developments Ltd	Real estate management & development	Singapore, Singapore	3,214,018,359.9
29	Neste Oyj	Oil, gas & consumable fuels	Espoo, Finland	22,017,441,860.5
30	Ecolab Inc.	Chemicals	Saint Paul, USA	12,733,100,000.0

*Note: Tied for seventh place.
Source: Corporate Knights. https://www.corporateknights.com/rankings/global-100-rankings/2023-global-100-rankings/2023-global-100-most-sustainable-companies

On the other hand, *positive screening funds*, instead of avoiding doing business with sinful companies, actively seek out organizations that contribute positively to society – focusing on education, medicine, or elimination of poverty and hunger. Some financial organizations introduced the concept of *impact investing* – looking to bring about positive change through the companies they invest in. One of the earliest socially responsible investment funds, PaxWorld, dates back to 1971, when two United Methodist Church ministers, Luther Tyson and Jack Corbett, looked to use investments not just to make profits but also to affect peace, housing, and employment opportunities, and to allow investors in their fund to align their investments with their religious values.

The financial industry in general is investing in DEI causes: *diversity, equity*, and *inclusion*. In fall 2020, for example, JPMorgan Chase committed to invest $30 billion to eliminate the wealth gap between White and Black Americans. Specifically, the bank announced a goal to allocate $14 billion for housing loans for Black and Latino borrowers, $8 billion for affordable housing projects, $4 billion for refinancing,

$2 billion for small business lending, and the final $2 billion for related philanthropic causes. The CEO of JPMorgan Chase, Jamie Dimon, stated, "We can do more and do better to break down systems that that have propagated racism and widespread economic inequality, especially for Black and Latinx people. It's long past time that society addresses racial inequalities in a more tangible, meaningful way" (Rabouin & Witherspoon, 2020, p. 1).

A particular subset of social issues involves doing business in or with certain countries. For example, in the past, financial organizations sold their investments in corporations located in South Africa or involved with the apartheid regime and avoided doing any business with South Africa. This became known as the *protest divestment campaigns*. The South African protest divestment campaign started on college campuses. As students protested apartheid, they discovered that their own colleges invested in companies doing business with the apartheid regime. Although initially colleges ignored students' demands, by 1988 over 100 colleges had pledged to stop investing in companies working with South Africa. Eventually, the movement spilled from college endowments to pension funds and mutual funds, and then to the US Congress, which enacted sanctions against South Africa. In more recent years, similar protest divestment campaigns have focused on Sudan, Syria, and Russia.

Of course, other publics find societal issues important, too. For example, when Russia invaded Ukraine many consumers around the world proclaimed that they would never buy Russian vodka again. Even some store owners posted on social media pictures and videos of them destroying bottles of Russian vodka. For example, Evel Pie pizza in Las Vegas poured out all of its Russian vodka bottles (Hurley, 2022).

Corporate Governance

Corporate governance is necessary because management is separated from ownership in modern corporations. In other words, the people who own the company are not the same as people who run it on a daily basis. In a small family business, for example, the managers and the owners are often the same people. However, if ownership is separated from management, it is important for owners to make sure that managers act in the best interests of the company's owners; this requires knowledge about what's happening with the corporations and what decisions managers are making.

Adam Smith was famously pessimistic about the separation of managers and owners. He worried that corporate executives

> being the managers rather of other people's money than of their own, it cannot well be expected that they should watch over it with the same anxious vigilance with which the partners in a private counter party frequently watch over their own. Like the stewards of a rich man, they are apt to consider attention to small matters as not for their master's honor, and very easily give themselves a dispensation from having it. Negligence and profusion, therefore, must always prevail, more or less, in the management of the affairs of such a company. It is upon this account, that joint-stock companies for foreign trade have seldom been able to maintain the competition against private adventurers. (Smith, 1776/2007, pp. 574–575)

Thus, the system of modern corporations requires a system of control over the managers. This system provides an oversight process that allows the shareholders to ensure that managers act in the best interests of owners rather than in their own self-interest. This oversight system is called *corporate governance*.

The key theory that focuses on this interaction between managers and shareholders is the *Agency Theory*. In the agency theory, shareholders are *principals*, and managers are *agents*. The principal provides money or other resources, and the agent uses these resources to advance the interests of the principal. Principals employ agents to act on their behalf and to represent principals in day-to-day operations. In order to achieve this, agents are authorized to make decisions in place of principals. However, the theory posits that people may have disagreements and different perspectives on the same events, and, as a result, may prefer different courses of action, especially if the self-interests are different for different groups of people.

Thus, the agency theory proposes to align the *incentives of agents* with the *interests of principals* to ensure the agents always act in the best interests of the principals. For example, managers of corporations may receive bonuses if the share price of the corporation increases during a particular time period. Elon Musk, CEO of Tesla, famously does not take a salary from the company, but Tesla created an incentive plan for him to align his interests with the interests of Tesla shareholders.

In its 2018 proxy statement, Tesla confirmed: "The basic premise is simple – Elon's compensation will be 100% aligned with the interests of our stockholders." Under the plan, Musk was asked to increase the share price of Tesla stock by more than 10 times, raising the total value of Tesla to above $650 billion. When he reached the target, he was scheduled to be awarded $56 billion, making him the highest-paid CEO of any company on the planet. Of course, since his incentive package was based on the Tesla stock price, the total value of the award was even higher, when Tesla stock was trading above $850 per share.

Part of the agency theory also focuses on *risk* – specifically, it studies the interesting paradox that principals carry all the risk since they can lose all the resources they provided, but make no decisions; at the same time, agents carry virtually no risk, but make all the decisions. This situation may encourage risky behavior as managers seem to be more open to taking chances than owners would be. Thus, it becomes important to develop corporate governance mechanisms that can mitigate the risky behaviors of agents and introduce the incentives that could also control the risk.

A key component of governance in the corporate environment is the Board of Directors. The directors on the Board are representatives of shareholders and are tasked with protecting and advancing shareholders' interests. Coca-Cola's 2020 proxy statement describes the important role of its Board of Directors:

> The Board is elected by the shareowners to oversee their interests in the long-term health and overall success of the Company's business and financial strength. The Board serves as the ultimate decision-making body of the Company, except for those matters reserved to or shared with the shareowners. The Board oversees the proper safeguarding of the assets of the Company, the maintenance of appropriate financial and other internal controls and the Company's compliance with applicable laws and regulations and proper governance. The Board selects the Chief Executive Officer and oversees the members of senior management, who are charged by the Board with conducting the business of the Company.

Overall, the Board of Directors is the key instrument of corporate governance. It is responsible for creating corporate governance mechanisms that would align the interests of the company's management with the interests of shareholders, the company's owners. The Board is also responsible for providing constant oversight to ensure that these mechanisms are functioning properly, and the management is following all procedures developed. Of course, shareholders, in addition to being represented through the Board of Directors, also have their own voice and direct input into corporate governance. As part of the governance process, corporations are required to conduct an annual shareholder meeting. At the meeting, each common share of stock gives its holder one vote. In other words, a shareholder with 1,000 shares will have 1,000 votes, while a shareholder with one share will have just one vote.

Of course in many democratic countries citizens also vote for their representatives in various levels of governments – their representatives on city council, mayor, state representatives, governors, federal representatives, and presidents. Thus, the issue of governance is also important in political contexts. Are the elections fair? Does everyone have equal access to be on the ballot or to participate in the voting process? The White House of the United States (2021), for example, recently passed an Executive Order on access to voting to support and enhance Americans' ability to vote to address some of challenges in the US process of governance.

Governance issues are relevant to non-profit organizations as well. Especially relevant for non-profit organizations are the issues of properly spending the donations and the disclosure about the non-profit expenses. After all, nobody wants to donate to a non-profit organization that instead of advancing its mission spends money on luxury retreats for its staff or rewards for the CEO. For example, the Friends of the VA Connecticut Fisher House, a non-profit that promised to help veterans undergoing treatments at Veteran Affairs hospitals by providing them with free housing, instead had its CEO use the money for his personal needs. After it was discovered that he embezzled about $1.4 million of donations, the non-profit lost the support and trust of its donors and the public at large, and had to close for good. The former CEO of the former non-profit was sentenced to a combined total of 62 months in prison (Division of Criminal Justice, 2021). Thus, failure to install proper governance mechanisms destroyed the organization and, most likely, hurt the overall perception of non-profits, making it more difficult for other non-profits to advance their missions.

Chapter Summary

For an event to raise to a level of a *crisis*, several key requirements must be present: a crisis is typically important, unexpected, urgent, and, at the same, produce uncertainty about what to do next. An organizational process of responding to a crisis, known as crisis management, involves three stages: pre-crisis, crisis, and post-crisis. Since the best crisis is the one that never happened, an important part of the organizational crisis preparedness is issues management – identifying and preemptively resolving issues facing the organization before they could develop into a full-blown crisis. For many organizations, most issues can be described by the ESG abbreviation: *Environmental* sustainability, *Social* responsibility, and *Governance* of the organization. In addition, for organizations that operate across different cultures, countries, and continents, it is important to take into account international perspective, as issues may differ across the country's borders. Whatever the organization's operational environment is, however, the organization's conduct must be *legal, professional, ethical*, and *culturally appropriate*.

Five Key Terms to Remember

Crisis
Crisis Management
Ethics
Professionalism
ESG

Discussion Questions and Activities

1 Discuss what makes crisis a crisis. Can you share about some crisis events you were a part of?

2 If a crisis is unexpected, explain why crisis preparation is the most important part of the crisis management. How can one prepare for the unexpected?

3 Compare and contrast four types of international public relations activities – regional, cross-national, international, and global. Can you think of any examples for each of these types?

4 In managing reputations, it is important to consider ethical, legal, and professional influences. Discuss what is the best course of action when these influences point the organization in different directions. Can you think of examples when ethical, legal, and professional requirements were at odds with each other?

5 ESG (Environmental, Social, and Governance) issues have a very strong effect on the organizational reputation. Discuss some recent examples when organizations damaged or enhanced their reputations based on how they responded to an ESG challenge.

References

Bowen, S. A., Moon, W. K., & Kim, J. K. (2017). Ethics in financial communication and investor relations: Stakeholder expectations, corporate social responsibility, and principle-based analyses. In A. V. Laskin, Ed., *The handbook of financial communication and investor relations* (pp. 71–85). Hoboken, NJ: Wiley.

Burger King Russia (2018). Home [VK page]. VK.com. https://vk.com/burgerking

CFA Institute (2023). Code of ethics and standards of professional conduct. https://www.cfainstitute.org/en/ethics-standards/ethics/code-of-ethics-standards-of-conduct-guidance

Coombs, T. (2012). *Ongoing crisis communication* (3rd ed.). Los Angeles: Sage.

Davis, K. (1973). The case for and against business assumption of social responsibilities. *Academy of Management Journal, 16*, 312–322 https://doi.org/10.2307/255331

DEEP: Department of Energy and Environmental Protection (2023). *Dam safety regulatory program*. https://portal.ct.gov/DEEP/Water/Dams/Dams-Safety

Division of Criminal Justice, Connecticut State (2021, May 12). *Litchfield attorney sentenced for embezzling almost $1 million from charity for military veterans and their families*. https://portal.ct.gov/DCJ/Press-Room/Press-Releases/05122021KevinCreedSentencing

Governance & Accountability Institute (2020, October 26). *G&A institute's 2020 research report shows 65% of Russell 1000® published sustainability reports in 2019, up from 60% in 2018*. https://www.ga-institute.com/press-releases/article/ga-institutes-2020-research-report-shows-65-of-russell-1000R-published-sustainability-reports.html

Heath, R. L. (2018). Strategic issues management: organizations operating in rhetorical arenas. In *The handbook of organizational rhetoric and communication* (pp. 383–399).

Hill, C. (2021). *International business: competing in the global marketplace* (13th ed.). McGraw Hill.

Hurley, B. (2022, February 27). Bars and liquor stores removing Russian drinks in protest at Ukraine invasion: "I guess this is our sanction." *Independent* (U.S. edition). www.independent.co.uk/news/world/americas/russia-vodka-removed-usa-bars-ukraine-invasion-b2024050.html

Kant, I. (1785/1994). In T. E. Hill, & A. Zweig, Eds., *Groundwork for the metaphysics of morals*. New York: Oxford University Press.

Kotler, P., & Lee, N. (2005). *Corporate social responsibility: doing the most good for company and your cause*. Wiley.

Laskin, A. V. (2022). *Investor relations and financial communication: Creating value through trust and understanding*. Malden, MA: Wiley-Blackwell.

Laskin, A. V., & Danner, B. A. (2007, October). *Refining the boundaries of professional, legal, and ethical obligations*. Paper presented to the 72nd Annual Convention of the Association for Business Communication, Washington, DC.

Laskin, A. V., & Nesova, N. M. (2022). The language of optimism in corporate sustainability reports: A computerized content analysis. *Business and Professional Communication Quarterly*, *85*(1), 80–98. https://doi.org/10.1177/23294906211065507

Martinez, J. I., & Jarillo, J. C. (1989). The evolution of research on coordination mechanisms in multinational corporations. *Journal of International Business Studies*, *20*(3), 489–514.

Molleda, J. C., & Laskin, A. V. (2005). Global, international, comparative and regional public relations knowledge from 1990 to 2005: A quantitative content analysis of academic and trade publications. Institute for Public Relations.

Molleda, J. C., & Laskin, A. (2009). Coordination and control of global public relations to manage cross-national conflict shifts: A multidisciplinary theoretical perspective for research and practice. In *International media communication in a global age* (pp. 327–352). Routledge.

Molleda, J. C., Connolly-Ahern, C., & Quinn, C. (2005). Cross-national conflict shifting: expanding a theory of global public relations management through quantitative content analysis. *Journalism Studies*, *6*(1), 87–102.

Nietzsche, F. W., & Kaufmann, W. (1974). *The gay science: with a prelude in rhymes and an appendix of songs* (1st ed.). New York: Vintage Books.

Norman, W., & MacDonald, C. (2004). Getting to the bottom of the "triple bottom line." *Business Ethics Quarterly*, *12*, 243–262.

Pelofsky, J., & Margolies, D. (2010, March 24). U.S. charges Daimler with violating bribery laws. *Reuters*. https://www.reuters.com/article/us-daimler-bribery/u-s-charges-daimler-with-violating-bribery-laws-idUSTRE62M3TK20100324

PRSA (2023). *PRSA Code of Ethics*. https://www.prsa.org/about/ethics/prsa-code-of-ethics

Rabouin, D., & Witherspoon, A. (2020). JP Morgan commits $30 billion to fight the racial wealth gap. Axios (October 8). https://www.axios.com/2020/10/08/jpmorgan-commits-30-billion-racial-wealth-gap

Rogers, M. (2018, June 21). Burger King apologizes for offensive Russian World Cup pregnancy ad. *USA Today*. https://www.usatoday.com/story/sports/soccer/worldcup/2018/06/21/burger-king-apologizes-offensive-russian-world-cup-pregnancy-ad/720668002

Singer, M. (1994). Discourse inference processes. In M. A. Gernsbacher, Ed., *Handbook of psycholinguistics* (pp. 479–515). Academic Press.

SPJ, Society of Professional Journalists (2014, September 6). *SPJ Code of Ethics*. https://www.spj.org/ethicscode.asp

Smith, A. (1776/2007). *An inquiry into the nature and causes of the wealth of nations*. MetaLibi.

Ulmer, R. R., Seeger, M. W., & Sellnow, T. L. (2007). Post-crisis communication and renewal: expanding the parameters of post-crisis discourse. *Public Relations Review*, *33*, 130–134.

Voice of America (2021, April 6). Moscow ramps up pressure on Radio Free Europe/Radio Liberty. https://www.voanews.com/a/moscow-ramps-up-pressure-on-radio-free-europe-radio-liberty-/7005385.html

White House (2021, March 7). *Executive order on promoting access to voting*. https://www.whitehouse.gov/briefing-room/presidential-actions/2021/03/07/executive-order-on-promoting-access-to-voting

World Commission on Environment and Development (1987). *Our common future*. United Nations. http://www.un-documents.net/wced-ocf.htm

6

Employees and Other Internal Publics: Close to Heart

LEARNING OBJECTIVES

1. *After reading this chapter, students will be able to define employees as one of the organizational publics.*
2. *After reading this chapter, students will be able to identify key points in the organization-employee relationships.*
3. *After reading this chapter, students will be able to develop strategic public relations programs aimed at employees in order to enhance the organizational reputation.*

Define the Public

Any organization is first and foremost its people. In fact, many organizations in a variety of sectors of the economy claim that employees represent the organization's most valuable asset. Traditionally, *employees* are defined as those who work for another in return for financial or other compensation. Although the legal definition of an employee may be more complex: "a person in the service of another under any contract of hire, express or implied, oral or written, where the employer has the power or right to control and direct the employee in the material details of how the work is to be performed" (Black, 1991, p. 363).

The societal views on employment are not static and are constantly changing. What was considered a common employer–employee relationship just 100 years ago may be unacceptable today. In the past, an employee may have been viewed as a person who worked 40-hour work weeks for an organization year after year and in exchange was reliably paid a good salary, often with health, retirement, and other benefits. Today, however, more and more employees are part of the so-called *contingent work force* – "independent contractors, leased employees, temporary employees, on-call workers, and more" (Muhl, 2002, p. 3). In other words, they do not have a long-term contract with their employer and, as a result, do not see their work arrangement as long-term.

Whether traditional employees or contingent workers, they are the ones who actually represent and act on behalf of the organization and they are the ones who project an organizational image to the outside world. When you order an Uber, that Uber

Organizational Reputation Management: A Strategic Public Relations Perspective,
First Edition. Alexander V. Laskin.

Figure 6.1 Uber Driver. *Source:* Tero Vesalainen / Shutterstock.

driver represents Uber, and whether you have a good or bad experience on that ride will reflect your perception of Uber and, as a result, will affect Uber's reputation (see Figure 6.1). As we discussed in Chapter 1, organizational reputation is based upon the reflection of the organization in the minds of various publics. But if employees are the ones who actually work on projecting and creating the image of the organization, this poses a question – can we really consider employees as part of the reputation measurement? Can they really project and reflect the organizational image at the same time?

On the other hand, employees are not just cogs in the organizational machine – even when they are working on building an organizational identity and representing their organization, they also simultaneously reflect this identity by processing it through the prism of their own relationships and experiences with the organization.

As a result, some scholars proposed to include employees into the calculations of reputation but developed a special terminology for their views on the organization: *internal reputation* (Helm, 2011; Kang, 2022) because employees are considered the *internal public*, as opposed to *external reputation* that would include perspectives of various *external publics*. In fact, the term *The Employer Brand* was proposed to describe the efforts the employers invest in their branding efforts among employees in order to develop a positive image for their workplace environment (Ambler & Barrow, 1996, p. 185).

Others noted that employees' views on the organization may be even more important than views of any other publics because the organizational image among the employees may itself influence the reputation of the organization among external publics (Kim & Rhee, 2011; Lee, 2021; Lee & Kim, 2020). In other words, employees who have negative views about the organization and openly voice their dissatisfaction with the organization may affect what other publics think about the organization as much as the official communications from the organizations. A disgruntled employee may really hurt an organizational reputation among other external publics.

Kang (2022) concluded that "employee testimonials about negative experiences in their work especially can lead to a significantly damaging blow to how external constituents view the organization" (p. 3). The reason that external publics place such significant value on communications from the employees is because employees are seen as insiders who pose in-depth and credible knowledge about the inner workings of the organization whether it is actually the case or not. As a result, it is quite common for organizations to monitor what their employees are saying about the organization and even interfere, if necessary, by asking the employees to modify or retract their public comments or even terminating employees based on their communications.

Value of the Relationship

As a result, it is difficult to overestimate the importance of investments in relationships with employees for the organization. If employees feel motivated and supported, they will perform their tasks better and would be a better representation for the organization in formal and informal settings. Such employees are engaged and happy to be at work – they are also more likely to go an extra mile in fulfilling their duties. Being known as a great place to work also makes it easier for the organization to attract top talent; and, reversely, if the employer's brand is negative, the organization may have to put extra efforts to attract employees and may have to offer them high salaries to compete with other organizations with better reputations. Table 6.1 shows 30 Best Companies to Work For, according to *Fortune*. Thus, this relationship has a direct impact on the organizational bottom line.

The same is true for retention. If an organization manages to develop a strong, positive relationship with its employees, they are more likely to stay with the organization for the long haul. This also has a strong effect on the organization – hiring and training new employees costs a lot of money.

Finally, as already mentioned earlier, employees are representatives of the organization. As a result, a bad relationship with the employees is likely to affect how the organization is perceived by other publics as well – customers, investors, local community, government, and so on. So, what could organizations do to build and maintain relationships with their employees?

Maintaining and Building Reputation through Relationship Management Strategies

Paycheck

A key way for the organization to show its appreciation to employees is salary and other compensation packages. It is unlikely that organizations would be able to maintain their workforce if they stopped providing a paycheck. Employees expect to be paid for their work in order to support themselves – buying groceries, paying rent or mortgage, enjoying travel and entertainment, and so on. As a result, announcing salary

Table 6.1 30 Best Companies to Work For.

2023 Rank	Company	Location	Industry
1	Cisco	San Jose, CA, US	Information technology
2	Hilton	McLean, VA, US	Hospitality
3	American Express	New York, NY, US	Financial services & insurance
4	Wegmans Food Markets, Inc.	Rochester, NY, US	Retail
5	Accenture	New York, NY, US	Professional services
6	NVIDIA	Santa Clara, CA, US	Information technology
7	Atlassian, Inc.	San Francisco, CA, US	Information technology
8	Salesforce	San Francisco, CA, US	Information technology
9	Comcast NBCUniversal	Philadelphia, PA, US	Telecommunications
10	Marriott International	Bethesda, MD, US	Hospitality
11	Rocket Companies	Detroit, MI, US	Financial services & insurance
12	Slalom Consulting	Seattle, WA, US	Professional services
13	Power Home Remodeling	Chester, PA, US	Construction
14	Intuit	Mountain View, CA, US	Information technology
15	Capital One	McLean, VA, US	Financial services & insurance
16	Plante Moran	Southfield, MI, US	Professional services
17	Deloitte	New York, NY, US	Professional services
18	Orrick	San Francisco, CA, US	Professional services
19	World Wide Technology	St. Louis, MO, US	Information technology
20	Synchrony Financial	Stamford, CT, US	Financial services & insurance
21	Nationwide Mutual Insurance Company	Columbus, OH, US	Financial services & insurance
22	David Weekley Homes	Houston, TX, US	Construction
23	Baird	Milwaukee, WI, US	Financial services & insurance
24	Pinnacle Financial Partners	Nashville, TN, US	Financial services & insurance
25	Protiviti	Menlo Park, CA, US	Professional services
26	Target Corporation	Minneapolis, MN, US	Retail
27	Box, Inc.	Redwood City, CA, US	Information technology
28	Kimley-Horn and Associates, Inc.	Raleigh, NC, US	Professional services
29	Veterans United Home Loans	Columbia, MO, US	Financial services & insurance
30	PricewaterhouseCoopers, LLP	New York, NY, US	Professional services

Source: Fortune 100 Best Companies to Work For, 2023 https://www.greatplacetowork.com/best-companies-to-work-for

increases is often linked with a positive response from employees, leading to an improved organizational reputation among employees, while salary cuts are likely to be met negatively. In fact, managing compensation for years has been "the bedrock of HR activity" when it comes to managing the organizations' internal reputation (Ambler & Barrow, 1996, p. 199).

Over the years, organizations, especially corporations, learned to be very creative with their employee compensation strategies – moving away from flat salaries to *performance-based* payments. For example, employees in sales may be awarded a commission or a certain percent of sales they could generate; the top salesperson of a month may be awarded an additional bonus or award on top of their commission. This helps organizations align the interests of employees with the interests of the organization – the more sales an employee can generate the higher their compensation will be, and the more revenues are generated for the organization.

Senior-level executives may have their compensations tied to a share price appreciation, being awarded billions of dollars if the company performs well. For example, when Elon Musk joined Tesla as its CEO, he agreed to work without any base salary for 10 years. However, if after 10 years, he manages to increase Tesla's share price to make the overall value of the company's stock above $650 billion (a 1000% increase!), he would be awarded a bonus of $55.8 billion – the world's largest corporate bonus ever paid. According to some media publications, the deal was designed not just to align the interests of the company with Musk's interests, but also to guarantee to investors that Musk is with Tesla for the long term and keep him focused on electric cars and away from his many other projects, such as colonizing Mars (Neate, 2018).

The plan seemingly worked as Musk stayed with the company for all this time and drove the Tesla's market capitalization to $1.2 trillion at the start of 2022 – significantly more value than any other car manufacturer (see Figure 6.2). In 2022, however, Elon Musk, who had become the richest person in the world thanks in large part to his Tesla bonus, announced a bid to purchase Twitter and, as a result, caused a significant concern that his attention will now be taken away from Tesla (Zahn, 2022). Perhaps because of this, Tesla share price plummeted and at the start of 2023 the total market valuation of Tesla is down to less than $450 billion – a loss of about 60% in its corporate value.

Appreciation

While a paycheck is definitely important, employees often expect more than just a transactional relationship with their employers. Employees also want to feel valued and appreciated. In fact, research shows that employees are looking for "trust, commitment, shared values, and longevity of relationships" as well as empathy from the management (Ambler & Barrow, 1996, p. 199). These values must be communicated by the organization to its employees. As a result, many organizations develop sophisticated communication programs that may involve daily updates, weekly or monthly newsletters, blogs or vlogs, in-person or virtual town hall meetings, anonymous feedback channels, and so on.

One of the best ways to maintain good relationships with employees is by making them feel valued: "Making employees feel valued builds trust, raises productivity, increases morale and reduces turnover" (Gillen, 2022). Part of this are big and

Figure 6.2 Tesla Cars at Tesla Charging Station.

important decisions – giving employees autonomy, paying fair salaries, recognizing challenges and helping to overcome them. But some, maybe little things are also nevertheless important: having an open door for the employees, chatting with employees from time to time, and even celebrating personal and professional milestones.

Such celebrations may range from a birthday cake during the lunch break to a mention in the organization's email newsletter, but whatever the organization does often leaves a positive mark on the organization-employee relationship. Some of these recognitions may be based on various performance criteria and some on longevity of employment. For example, Quinnipiac University has an annual event where the university recognizes employees' longevity milestones, celebrating employees with 5 years of tenure at the university, 10 years, 15 years, 20 years, and so on. As part of this "End-of-the-Year Celebration featuring Employee Milestones and Retiree Recognition" the university displays a slide show of the employees recognized and presents them with university mementos that increase in value as the time of service increases as well (see Figure 6.3).

Thus, it is essential for organizations to invest in building and maintaining an environment in which employees feel like an important part of the organization. Such organizational culture must be based on principles of *diversity, equity,* and *inclusion* (DEI). One of the first steps in advancing an organization's DEI agenda is developing a shared understanding of what the concept of DEI actually means for the organization and its employees (Kamezaki, 2022). The same abbreviation, DEI, may mean different things on different continents, in different countries, and for different organizations. The efforts should reflect what the organization and its employees value and

Figure 6.3 Quinnipiac University's Annual Employee Milestone Celebration.

find important to work on, at the same time taking into account the outside reality of the current societal expectations. In other words, such organizational culture works best when it is rooted in the overall purpose of the organization.

Organizational Purpose

One of the best ways to build strong, long-term relationships with employees is to hire employees who are a good match for the organization and its mission from the get-go. Southwest Airlines was once asked how they train their employees to act so friendly and happy in their customer interactions. Southwest responded that they simply hire happy people in the first place! But there is more to Southwest success than this – since its founding the company declared itself as a people-first company. The company is known for sharing a large portion of its profits with the employees, investing in workplace culture, and encouraging employees to think and act like owners of the company. The founder of the airline, Herb Kelleher, was quoted as saying: "Profitsharing is an expense we want to be as big as possible so our people get a greater reward" (Dahl, 2017).

Whether it is being people-focused, or environment-focused, or technology-focused, companies develop unique spots among others that becomes a company's purpose. But such purpose is nothing without employees' buy-in: executives may develop a corporate purpose but only employees can actually activate it. And once the company articulates a purpose that employees can believe in, good things are bound to happen. A recent study, *Company Purpose in Practice*, reported that corporations with purpose are more likely to be financially successful, have better employee retention, enjoy more positive reputation, and, finally, recruit better employees (Neumeier, 2022).

Yet, many organizations still fail on building a purpose-driven workforce. In fact, only 40% of employees strongly feel being motivated by their company's purpose (Zemke, 2022).

Professionalism

While aligning employees' paycheck with the company's overall performance and showing appreciation for the employees' work are important contributors to the organizational reputation among employees, the process of how both of these things are defined and achieved is also important. Employees want to be treated like the professionals that they are, and appreciate autonomy in performing their tasks and inclusion in the larger organizational decision-making process. For example, it is nice when a CEO of a corporation rents a large restaurant for the company's Christmas party, but this gesture may also backfire if employees would rather use the money spent on the party for their Christmas bonuses. Lack of employees' involvement in the decision-making process may lead to unexpected results and hurt the organization's reputation despite the best of intentions.

Employees are also experts in what they do, and they appreciate the opportunity to do their work in the best possible way. Yet, some supervisors may default to micro-managing their employees, trying to control every aspect of the work to the detriment of the organization and its reputation. For example, as the COVID epidemic subsided, many employees learned that they can perform remotely as well or even better than in the office, while also saving hours on the commute. Some organizations even saw this as a profitable opportunity – they need to pay for less office space, save on the office expenses and utilities, and still enjoy the same or even higher level of productivity from their remote employees. However, other organizations were less flexible and decided to demand their employees return back to the office no matter what. For those employees who can perform their work remotely as well as they can in the office and who proved it during COVID's remote work period, such demands may create unnecessary dissatisfaction with their employers.

Whenever a decision like this needs to be made, it is vital for organizations to empower employees to do their best work and consult with them on how to achieve such a goal. This includes offering flexible schedules, avoiding micro-management, allowing more autonomy in the decision-making: in other words, letting employees decide "where, when, and how they work" (Zemke, 2022, p. 2).

This also helps employees take more ownership in their work and develop a stronger connection with the overall organizational purpose; employees essentially get to decide on the best and most productive ways to advance the company's mission in their own role. The organization then can use their compensation system to guide employees in their choices: "This helps culture grow organically from within as employees shift behavior to meet what's being rewarded and recognized" (Zemke, 2022, p. 4). This also helps to keep, maintain, and develop employees in the organization year after year as they feel their value, their unique contribution to the overall organization, and can adjust their day-to-day schedules and processes to their changing personal lives outside of the organization.

Unionization

Employees are also unique in their relationship with the organization because they can choose a third party to represent them in this process. In recent years, employees' demands for joining a union has increased. For example, Starbucks had its first store employees file a petition for union elections on August 30, 2021. Less than a year later, by April 2022, 250 other stores decided to do the same. The soaring demand for labor unions that can negotiate on wages, benefits, and other conditions and policies of employment indicates that management itself is either failing to understand what employees want or failing to meet their demands. In fact, an NPR article suggests that unionization is growing exceptionally fast at companies that represent accommodation and food services – a sector of the economy that was hit especially hard by the pandemic. In fact, employees at Starbucks and Amazon "cited the pandemic as a major impetus for organizing, saying their companies did not do enough to protect them from the risks of COVID or reward them for carrying on with the work that has made their companies highly profitable over the past two years" (Hsu, 2022, p. 3).

The issue of unionization became important in the United States since the 1935 passage of the National Labor Relations Act. The Act developed in response to one crisis, the Great Depression, once again showed its importance in the time of current crisis – when the pandemic led workers to feel overwhelmed, exhausted, unappreciated, and often without a say in decisions about their own safety and workplace changes needed (Fisher, 2022).

Crisis Management Strategies

During any crisis situation, employees are among the most important audience. The organizations count on their employees to support the organization during the difficult times and help lead the organization out of the crisis.

One of the largest crises that hit employee relationships in recent years was the sudden and quite unexpected shift to remote and hybrid work in response to the COVID-19 pandemic. Many organizations made a decision about the shift to remote work seemingly overnight, some even without consulting with their workforce. Such an approach in part contributed to the so-called *Great Resignation* of workers who decided to leave their organizations in the midst of the pandemic. American workers resigned from their jobs in record numbers, with the record being set in September 2021. By the end of 2021, however, the Great Resignation turned into the *Great Reshuffle* as many of those people who previously resigned returned back to work at a new or even the same organizations they had previously resigned from (Whittington, 2022).

As a result, many organizations learned their lessons and treated return to in-person work with more care. Organizations surveyed or interviewed their team members to better understand their comfort level and their preferences about returning to the office. Some organizations even provided a flexible approach: giving their employees a chance to return to in-person work for only one day of the week or two days of the week, and then slowly increasing the numbers of in-office days as time went on and people felt more accustomed to being in the office again.

But even returning to the very same old work had consequences for both employees and employers. Many employees realized what sacrifices they made for their employers – the peak resignation month, September, coincided with the start of the school year that in 2021 was mainly remote or hybrid, thus, requiring parents, whose jobs by that time often returned to in-person settings, to make a difficult choice between work and family. In addition, many employees during the pandemic realized that many of the tasks can actually be done without having to drive to the office and back, or having to sit for hours in various meetings. On the other hand, employers were losing expertise and having to invest in recruiting and training a new labor force – and this was at the time, when labor was in short supply, forcing the organization to offer higher pay and benefits.

All of this led to renewed appreciation for building and maintaining relationships with the employees, especially in the time of crisis. Employee communication became one of the key priorities and attracted additional organizational resources – namely, people and money. "Leadership has a renewed interest in communicating to their employees – likely on a weekly basis, if not daily. Employees are hungry for content within their organization and looking for connections, especially if they are now remote or hybrid" (Whittington, 2022, p. 1).

Amanda Fisher (2022) proposed five guidelines for maintaining relationships with employees:

1. *Create a culture of transparency.* This requires management to be honest, transparent, and forthcoming about good news and bad news.
2. *Practice active listening.* It is not enough to speak to employees; it is also important to listen to what employees have to say. Management should establish formal and informal avenues for collecting employees' feedback and be ready to make changes based on the feedback received.
3. *Give a voice to the most vulnerable workforce segment.* This can apply to those who are at the lowest end of the pay scale, or those who are just starting at the company, or even simply those who rarely share any feedback because they do not feel valued at the organization no matter what their official title or pay scale would suggest.
4. *Lean into employee socialization.* Managing relationships is not only about formal processes and functions but also about informal. Employees may go to the local bar after a hard work week or have a birthday celebration in a break room. These informal events are also important for maintaining employee relationships – such horizontal and informal relationships may be a better motivator for employees than formal events like a company's picnic.
5. *Talk to every employee.* It is easy to think about employees in multiples, but each employee is a person with their own hopes, fears, and relationships with the organization. Thus, management should take an effort to speak to each person on a periodic basis, at least once a year, as well as talk to people individually when an issue that needs addressing arises. "Through these one-on-one conversations, leaders can learn more about what motivates employees and make their work experience better. In turn, leaders can make informed changes that improve their holistic employee experience – and, ultimately, earn employees' loyalty and commitment" (Fisher, 2022, p. 4–5).

It is also important to never set up the relationships between the organization and the employees as adversarial – after all, employees are the organization. Many employees actually missed some elements of the in-person work such as sharing a lunch with a co-worker – thus, it was important for the organizations to emphasize and promote such relationship-building activities: "Time may be tight on the days you are back in the office so make sure you are prioritizing opportunities for the team to be together and build community" (Castellini, 2022).

Layoffs

Probably the most stressful event in the employee communication practice is announcing layoffs. Announcing to employees that their positions are being terminated is an easy way to destroy any goodwill the company developed with their employees and, as a result, can hurt the overall organizational reputation.

One of the recent examples of layoff announcements going horribly wrong was the CEO Vishal Garg's announcement about elimination of 900 jobs at http://Better.com. In addition to the poor timing of the announcement – between Thanksgiving and Christmas holidays – Mr. Garg chose to do it in a mass Zoom call. The content of the announcement itself was also quite disrespectful as the CEO stated: "If you're on this call, you are part of the unlucky group that is being laid off" (Wanderellaco, 2021). While this was obviously a very stressful and emotional time for the employees on the call being laid off, the CEO managed to make it about himself somehow by saying "the last time I did this, I cried. This time, I hope to be stronger" (Wanderellaco, 2021).

Needless to say, the recording of this three-minute Zoom call ended up on TikTok, YouTube, and other social media sites, as well as, eventually, in mainstream media, damaging the reputation of http://Better.com and its CEO. In fact, Mr. Garg was forced to step down from his position as the CEO at the request of the board of directors of http://Better.com shortly after the news of layoffs became public. While Mr. Garg returned as the CEO later, the damage to the company's relationships with its employees is more difficult to restore. Several executives that were key to http://Better.com's success resigned in addition to other employees looking for jobs elsewhere. http://Better.com also had to delay its plans to go public and is now faced with several lawsuits (Azevedo, 2022).

Does it mean that any layoffs mean a disaster for a company? Not necessarily. But it is important to manage layoff communications in an honest and transparent manner. Ken Scudder, a crisis communication consultant, lists several guidelines for proper layoff communications:

1. Explain why this is happening
2. Show some compassion
3. Explain how it will be handled
4. Take questions
5. Do not make it about you
6. Do not ask for secrecy
7. Keep your door open (Scudder, 2022, p. 2–4)

In fact, no matter what kind of crises the organization finds itself in, employees must be treated and positioned as allies, not as adversaries. Thus, it is important to make sure that employees are well informed and understand what is going on. Employees will talk on social media or to the mass media no matter how many times the management will request for them not to. And when employees do talk, they are usually perceived to be more trustworthy and more authentic than any official corporate statement. Thus, having employees on the side of the organization is quite beneficial for everyone involved.

It might also be beneficial in addition to sharing all the relevant information in a timely and transparent manner with the employees to enable and encourage them to represent the organization to the outside world. Some organizations create the *Organization Ambassadors* who talk to the media or on their own social media pages about the organization during regular times and in crisis. If there is a chemical-reaction-gone-wrong type of crisis, one of the company's chemists may be an appropriate ambassador to talk about the events. If there is a train derailment, a train engineer may be an appropriate person to discuss what happened. Such an approach of openness and reliance on front-line employees builds trust between the organization and its employees as well as helps the organization maintain or even improve its reputation among many external publics in the face of challenging events.

Future Proofing Your Strategies

The key trend that is affecting employees today and is likely to continue and even grow in the future is the increased demand for flexibility in the employer-employee relations. This trend has two sides. On one side, employees want more flexibility – in terms of working remotely or on-site, commitment in terms of work hours, ability to customize their schedules, and even having a say in how they are compensated and how their performance is evaluated. For any organization strategizing about their employee relations programs, offering such flexibility, of course, taking into the account the demands of the job, is a must.

The other side of this coin, however, is the increased flexibility that employers themselves create in their workforce through contingent labor. Employers are likely to continue increased reliance on the contingent workforce in the future – this allows employers greater flexibility in managing their payroll. They can easily cut their expenses if there is a downturn in the economy and they need less labor; the employers can also quickly ramp up their workforce, if needed. For building and maintaining employee relations, contingent workers present additional challenges – they may require more communication and more training to be effective at representing the organization. Taken into account that these contingent workers are easier to hire and to dismiss may also lead to a lack of organizational loyalty and increased turnover. In this situation, it is important to preserve and support your best performers.

Increased data collection and accountability – another trend in the future of employee relations – is likely to help with the task of evaluating full-time, part-time, and contingent workers. Employers are consistently increasing their monitoring and data collection on employees' performance. Such data collection does not always have to be focused on just deciding who gets promoted and who gets laid off – the data could be used to develop individualized training plans or modify tasks for specific employees to make sure they perform to their best abilities. Of course, this can also help with personalization of employee communications.

Such personalization is likely to rely on artificial intelligence. It is impossible for a single human resources employee to develop personalized messages for thousands of employees, taking into account their individual strengths and weaknesses. However, the generative AI chat bots can help draft such personalized communications in a matter of seconds. Already today, AI tools may help HR with many basic communication tasks – from explaining changes in health insurance coverage to analyzing resumes of job applicants.

It is also important for maintaining good relationships with employees to be transparent about news, good and bad. Employees do not want to learn from news media that their company is declaring bankruptcy or going through layoffs. Employees must be the first to know, as such news affects their life.

There is no doubt that the reliance on the remote collaboration tools such as Zoom, Teams, or Slack will continue to grow. These tools open additional possibilities for employee relationship management. A company-wide town hall for an organization with thousands of employees spread over many countries would be impossible without remote collaboration, but on Zoom the CEO can work on building the unified organizational identity across countries and continents (of course, taking into the account the time difference!). Making sure employees are all on the same page is going to be more and more important as the world gets progressively smaller and employees become more and more open to sharing their views on social media. Let us not forget that employees are often viewed as credible sources about their employers – thus, it is important to make sure the employees represent their organizations well. Plus, employees may communicate about the organization on anonymous review sites such as Glassdoor, making it easier or more difficult for the organization to attract and maintain the best workforce.

Chapter Summary

Employees are considered internal publics for the organization. As a result, they have a double function when it comes to reputation – they communicate on behalf of the organization and they also reflect the organization's communication. This makes employee relations highly important. Some propose to have a separate measure of reputation just for the internal publics – internal reputation. Employees obviously need the paycheck they get from the organization, but for many the employer–employee relationship is more than just a monetary transaction. Employees seek recognition and appreciation, want to see the purpose in their work and in the overall organization's mission, and desire to be treated as professionals with proper autonomy and flexibility.

Five Key Terms to Remember

Employee
Contingent workforce
Internal reputation
Organizational purpose
Unionization

Discussion Questions and Activities

1 Explain what it means that the most important part of any organization is its people.
2 Discuss what benefits and drawbacks an organization may expect by enabling its employees to speak about and on behalf of the organization on social media and to the mass media.

3 Analyze the concept of internal reputation. Compare internal and external reputation, and discuss the relationships between the two.

4 Make a list of your priorities for an organization in which you would like to have a job after graduation. Compare your priorities with those of your classmates. What similarities and differences can you identify? How would you explain these similarities and differences?

5 Choose any company on the Glassdoor site. Read the reviews of this organization. How does it make you feel about applying for a job at this organization? If you were in charge of employee relations at this organization, what would you do about those reviews?

How to Learn More

Verhulst, S.L. and DeCenzo, D.A. (2021). *Fundamentals of human resource management*, 14e. Hoboken, NJ: Wiley.

Schein, E.H. and Schein, P.A. (2016). *Organizational culture and leadership*, 5e. Hoboken, NJ: Wiley.

Locker, K., Mackiewicz, J., Aune, J.E., and Kienzler, D. (2023). *Business communication*, 13e. McGraw Hill.

Case Study

Activision Blizzard: Can Microsoft Weather the Blizzard?

Figure 6.4

1. Summary of the Case

On July 20, 2021, the California Department of Fair Employment and Housing filed a lawsuit against Activision Blizzard. The suit contained accusations of gender discrimination, sexual misconduct, and promoting a "frat boy" workplace culture. On November 16, 2021, there was an employee walkout demanding that Bobby Kotick be immediately replaced as the CEO of Activision Blizzard. Employees organized a walkout, and a petition was signed by over 2,000 staff members demanding changes at the company. Since then, Activision Blizzard has been in a whirlwind of backlash. By not removing Kotick as CEO, the company is facing a hard task ahead in proving that they are serious about changing the inhospitable work environment, and that harassment and discrimination will no longer be tolerated at Activision Blizzard. As Microsoft is closing in on the acquisition of Activision Blizzard, it raises an interesting question: how would Microsoft, commonly ranked among best companies to work for (Drapkin, 2022), address the employment issues at Activision Blizzard moving forward in order to maintain the company's success in the gaming industry and, furthermore, what precedent will it establish for the whole gaming industry? This case highlights the importance of employee relations for the organizational reputation.

2. Organization's Background and Historical Development

Activision was founded in 1979 by David Crane, Alan Miller, and Jim Levy (Ray, 2022). Their goal was to create a company "where designers would be an essential part of the brand identity" (Ray, 2022) and where game developers would receive their proper credit. The company was responsible for the creation of numerous Atari 2600 games that were well received by gamers, making the company a profitable enterprise and allowing it to acquire many other video game companies (Lerner, 2018). Vivendi Games was founded in 1996 and was an American video game publisher and holding company based in Los Angeles. Blizzard Entertainment was founded in 1991 by Allen Adham, Michael Morhaime, and Frank Pearce. The company started out by converting existing electronic games to computer-friendly versions (Ray, 2022).

The companies merged in 2008 to form Activision Blizzard, a large computer game producer with hundreds of millions of active users all over the world. Activision Blizzard creates games for gaming consoles, computers, phones, etc. and is responsible for some of today's most popular games like *Candy Crush, Call of Duty, World of Warcraft*, and more (Activision Blizzard, 2023). Activision Blizzard is divided into five different sections including Activision, Blizzard Entertainment, King Digital Entertainment, Major League Gaming, and Activision Blizzard Studios (Lerner, 2018).

3. Operational Environment and Main Publics

The video gaming industry was going through consolidation and Activision was no exception. One of these acquisitions was Raven Software, another was Infinity Ward, which provided Activision with the essential and important franchise *Call of*

(Continued)

Case Study (Continued)

Duty. By 2009, the *Call of Duty* franchise brought in $3 billion in revenue for Activision (5 Companies Owned by Activision Blizzard, n.d.). The merger of Activision with Blizzard provided the company with access to the multiplayer online gaming market, with the *World of Warcraft* franchise, as well as the promotion of subscription-based models. Then, the company acquired King Digital, a major mobile game developer. This acquisition brought the *Candy Crush* saga and a new market demographic. The core market for *Candy Crush* is predominantly women within the 21–35 age bracket as opposed to mainly male players in other Activision franchises. In fact, there has been a rise in female gamers in recent years that has altered the statistics within the gaming industry. The changing customer demographics also contributed to changing demographics in the gaming industry employees. Yet, Activision Blizzard may have been behind on adjusting to these changes.

In fact, Activision Blizzard was involved in several lawsuits regarding toxic workplace environment and sexual misconduct over the years. Employees have consistently called out the company for sexism and workplace misconduct. Activision Blizzard also struggled with diversity and inclusion in the workplace, as only 20% of its 9,500 employees are women and its top leadership executives are all white men. There have also been several reports that the company pays and promotes women much less than men, and female employees are subject to "constant sexual harassment," including unsolicited sexual comments, advances, and groping. The work environment has been referred to as a "frat boy" culture (Murphy, 2021). Additionally, there have been complaints of low wages, with rates as low as $12 an hour. Many employees also noted that during peak times they would be forced to work up to seven days a week for at least 10 hours a day, which made it especially difficult on employees with families (Carpenter, 2021). While the CEO has made promises to make changes to the company's toxic culture, employees expressed doubt since they see the senior management team as a part of the problem and not of a solution (Murphy, 2021).

4. The Issue Development

On July 20, 2021, California concluded a two-year investigation and announced that it was suing Activision Blizzard over allegations of a "frat boy culture" and sexual harassment. Activision Blizzard released a heavily criticized official statement in response to the lawsuit on the same day. Several days later, there were conflicting internal emails regarding the scandal. Blizzard President J. Allen Brack said that he would work to root out the frat boy behavior and that it has no place at their company. Shortly thereafter, a different executive vehemently disagreed with the president in his letter (the letter that was wildly believed to be written by the CEO Kotik himself) and said that there was no problem at the company.

Many employees believed that Activision CEO Bobby Kotick knew about the harassment allegations for years. Kotick stated that he would "consider" stepping down if he cannot solve the problems quickly. A week after the initial announcement, over 2,000 current and former employees (20% of employees at the company) signed an open letter criticizing the company's response to the discrimination lawsuit where they called the Activision Blizzard position abhorrent and insulting: "Our company executives have claimed that actions will be taken to protect us, but in the face of legal action – and the troubling official responses that followed – we no longer trust that our leaders will place employee safety above their own interests. To claim this is a 'truly meritless and irresponsible lawsuit,' while seeing so many current and former employees speak out about their own experiences regarding harassment and abuse, is simply unacceptable" (Carpenter, 2021).

Activision Blizzard employees also staged a walkout to protest the company's lack of real actions and voiced demands to revamp the established company's practices for recruiting, hiring, and promoting employees. Problems mounted as several key employees responsible for important game franchises left Activision and investors sued the company over the failure to disclose internal problems.

The Activision Blizzard CEO, Bobby Kotick, issued a response, calling the company's initial statement tone deaf and promising swift actions. The company hired a former Disney Executive to oversee its human resource and employee communication operations, and began the process of rebuilding trust within the company. Activision Blizzard then took the step of creating a "Workplace Responsibility Committee."

Following the lawsuits, Activision reached an agreement with the US Equal Employment Opportunity Commission (EEOC) to settle claims and correct its policies to prevent harassment and discrimination in the workplace. The company committed to an $18 million fund to compensate those who made the harassment and sexual assault claims. They also promised that any funds not used to compensate the victims would be donated to charities that advance women in the video game industry or promote awareness around harassment, gender equality, or diversity and inclusion initiatives. Activision also agreed to upgrade its policies, practices, and training to prevent any harassment and discrimination in the future. In a statement following the agreement, Kotick said "There is no place anywhere at our company for discrimination, harassment, or unequal treatment of any kind, and I am grateful to the employees who bravely shared their experiences. I am sorry that anyone had to experience inappropriate conduct, and I remain unwavering in my commitment to make Activision Blizzard one of the world's most inclusive, respected, and respectful workplaces" (Activision Blizzard, 2021, p. 1). In mid-October, Activision Blizzard made a statement that it had fired 20 employees related to the harassment allegations. Activision Blizzard also canceled its annual convention, BlizzCon to "reimagine future events."

The company invested $250 million toward hiring more women, nonbinary, and people from underrepresented communities. CEO Bobby Kotick said his goal was to increase the percentage of employees who are women or nonbinary from its current 23% to 50% or more over the next five years. Activision is responding to requests of waving its policy of mandatory arbitration for sexual harassment and discrimination claims, which is a way of settling disputes outside of the court system. The company is also adopting a zero-tolerance harassment policy where those who have violated the terms will be fired rather than being written up or given a warning, as they were previously. To guarantee his personal commitment

(Continued)

Case Study   (Continued)

to meeting these goals, Kotick has taken a reduction in his salary until the board decides that Activision reached its diversity goals.

Many company employees still remained hesitant to trust these promises of change, as the company is still run by the same people who were at the center of the scandal. Even people in the gaming industry were skeptical. Jim Ryan, president and CEO of Sony Interactive Entertainment, seemed unsatisfied with Activision's response: "We do not believe their statements of response properly address the situation" (Campbell, 2021). New lawsuits were also filed against the company and additional investigations were launched. Nevertheless, in a somewhat surprising move, Microsoft, one of the largest global corporations, announced that it intended to acquire Activision Blizzard to expand its gaming business!

5. What's Next?

Microsoft's acquisition seems like a great opportunity for Activision Blizzard. In fact, its share price jumped 40% on the acquisition announcement showing the market's appreciation for the move. It will provide the company with access to vast resources of Microsoft, one of the largest global corporations. It will also integrate Activision employees into well-managed Microsoft's human resources system and the company that is commonly considered among the best companies to work for (Drapkin, 2022). At the same time, the deal seems to guarantee Kotick the position of CEO of Activision Blizzard, but for many employees who see him as the main culprit of the previous problems, it is unacceptable. Even some Microsoft executives voiced their concerns with Kotik's staying in power. CEO of Microsoft, Satya Nadella, faces a difficult task – he needs the acquisition to go well, making sure Activision Blizzard continues producing highly popular games targeting a variety of demographics. For this to happen, it is important to maintain a proven leader like Kotik who demonstrated his ability to deliver great games, but it is also important to maintain talented and high-quality game engineers, writers, and designers as well as be able to attract new talent to join Activision as the business grows. To ensure that Activision Blizzard is a great acquisition for Microsoft, Nadella would have to respond to these demands. These demands, however, seem contradictory, forcing Nadella to make a difficult choice. But what is the right choice in this situation?

References

5 Companies Owned by Activision Blizzard. (n.d.). *Investopedia.* https://www.investopedia.com/5-companies-owned-by-atvi-5093046#:~:text=After%20several%20years%20of%20rapid

Activision Blizzard (2021, September 27). *Activision Blizzard commits to expanded workplace initiatives, reaches agreement with the EEOC.* https://investor.activision.com/news-releases/news-release-details/activision-blizzard-commits-expanded-workplace-initiatives

Activision Blizzard (2023). Who we are. https://www.activisionblizzard.com/who-we-are

Ambler, T., and Barrow, S. (1996). The employer brand. *The Journal of Brand Management* 4 (3): 185–206.

Azevedo, M. A. (2022, June 21). Better.com loses three more senior executives, including SVP and VP of sales. *TechCrunch.* https://techcrunch.com/2022/06/21/better-com-loses-three-more-senior-executives-including-svp-and-vp-of-sales

Black, H. C. (1991). *Black's law dictionary.* Employee, 363. St. Paul, MN: West Publishing Co.

Campbell, K. (2021). *Playstation CEO Jim Ryan left "stunned" over Activision Blizzard's response to allegations.* https://ftw.usatoday.com/2021/11/playstation-jim-ryan-activision-blizzard

Carpenter, N. (2021). Activision Blizzard employees call leadership response to harassment suit "abhorrent and insulting." Polygon. https://www.polygon.com/22594765/activision-blizzard-open-letter-harassment-lawsuit

Castellini, B. (2022, April). Improving the daily flow of the hybrid workplace. *Strategies & Tactics.* https://www.prsa.org/article/improving-the-daily-flow-of-the-hybrid-workplace?_zs=nVu6m&_zl=7akA2

Dahl, D. (2017, July 28). Why do Southwest Airlines employees always seem so happy? *Forbes.* https://www.forbes.com/sites/darrendahl/2017/07/28/why-do-southwest-airlines-employees-always-seem-so-happy/?sh=61b111ba59b0

Drapkin, A. (2022, May 6). Microsoft is the world's best company to work for, report says. Tech.co. https://tech.co/news/microsoft-worlds-best-company-work-for-report

Fisher, A. (2022, April). How to strengthen relationships with frontline workers. *Strategies & Tactics.* https://www.prsa.org/article/how-to-strengthen-relationships-with-frontline-workers?_zs=nVu6m&_zl=CakA2

Gillen, G. (2022, April). 5 ways to connect with virtual staff. *Strategies & Tactics.* https://www.prsa.org/article/5-ways-to-connect-with-virtual-staff?_zs=nVu6m&_zl=8akA2

Helm, S. (2011). Employees' awareness of their impact on corporate reputation. *Journal of Business Research* 64 (7): 657–663.

Hsu, A. (2022, May 1). Starbucks workers drive nationwide surge in union organizing. NPR. https://www.npr.org/2022/05/01/1095477792/union-election-labor-starbucks-workers-food-service-representation

Kamezaki, E. (2022, April). 4 ways to ensure that your DE&I efforts resonate with employees. *Strategies & Tactics.* https://www.prsa.org/article/4-ways-to-ensure-that-your-de-i-efforts-resonate-with-employees?_zs=nVu6m&_zl=4akA2

Kang, M. (2022). Employees' dissenting voices via testimonials and their impact on corporate hypocrisy perception and reputational damage via narrative transportation. *Journal of Public Relations Research* https://doi.org/10.1080/1062726X.2021.2023020

Kim, J. N., and Rhee, Y. (2011). Strategic thinking about employee communication behavior (ECB) in public relations: Testing the models of megaphoning and scouting effects in Korea. *Journal of Public Relations Research* 23 (3): 243–268.

Lee, Y. (2021). Employees' negative megaphoning in response to organizational injustice: The mediating role of employee–organization relationship and negative affect. *Journal of Business Ethics* 1–15.

Lee, Y., and Kim, K. H. (2020). De-motivating employees' negative communication behaviors on anonymous social media: The role of public relations. *Public Relations Review* 46 (4): 101955.

Lerner, S. (2018, May 1). *12 interesting facts about Activision Blizzard that you probably didn't know*. *Tech Times*. https://www.techtimes.com/articles/226092/20180501/12-interesting-facts-about-activision-blizzard-that-you-probably-didnt-know.htm

Muhl, C. J. (2002). What is an employee? The answer depends on federal law. *Monthly Labor Review* 3–11.

Murphy, M. (2021, July 28). Activision Blizzard Workers walk out over toxic workplace culture. *MarketWatch*. https://www.marketwatch.com/story/we-will-not-return-to-silence-activision-blizzard-workers-walk-out-over-toxic-workplace-culture-11627515690

Neate, R. (2018, January 23). Elon Musk lines up $55 bn payday – the world's biggest bonus. *The Guardian*. https://www.theguardian.com/technology/2018/jan/23/elon-musk-aiming-for-worlds-biggest-bonus-40bn

Neumeier, M. (2022, April). The path to creating meaningful organizational purpose. *Strategies & Tactics*. https://www.prsa.org/article/the-path-to-creating-meaningful-organizational-purpose?_zs=nVu6m&_zl=EakA2

Ray, M. (2022). Activision Blizzard, Inc. *Encyclopædia Britannica*. https://www.britannica.com/topic/Activision-Blizzard-Inc

Scudder, K. (2022, April). Better approaches to communicating layoffs. *Strategies & Tactics*. https://www.prsa.org/article/better-approaches-to-communicating-layoffs?_zs=nVu6m&_zl=DakA2

Wanderellaco (2021, December 3). Better.com CEO lays off 15% of employees right before the holidays. *TikTok*. https://www.tiktok.com/@wanderellaco/video/7037405156564176174

Whittington, E. (2022, April). Building relationships with new employees. *Strategies & Tactics*. https://www.prsa.org/article/building-relationships-with-new-employees?_zs=nVu6m&_zl=2akA2

Zahn, M. (2022, November 11). A timeline of Elon Musk's tumultuous Twitter acquisition. *ABC News*. https://abcnews.go.com/Business/timeline-elon-musks-tumultuous-twitter-acquisition-attempt/story?id=86611191#:~:text=Tesla%20CEO%20Elon%20Musk%20completed,cost%20of%20roughly%20%2444%20billion

Zemke, A. (2022, April). How to retain talent through organizational culture. *Strategies & Tactics*. https://www.prsa.org/article/how-to-retain-talent-through-organizational-culture?_zs=nVu6m&_zl=9akA2

7

Investors and Shareholders: Money Talks

LEARNING OBJECTIVES

1. *After reading this chapter, students will be able to define who investors are and explain different types of investors.*
2. *After reading this chapter, students will be able to understand the importance of managing relationships with investors and shareholders.*
3. *After reading this chapter, students will be able to develop strategic plans for building and maintaining relationships with investors and shareholders to enhance organizational reputation.*

Define the Public

An important public for organizational reputation management is investors. In fact, several scholars even claim that investors can be considered the most important external public for corporations because they have tremendous power over the organization and can even influence the dismissal of the top managers of the organization (Kelly et al., 2010; Laskin, 2018a, b; Ragas et al., 2014). *Investors* are organizations and people who invest their money into a corporation – in exchange, they become owners of a certain share of stock of that corporation (hence, they are also called *shareholders* or *stockholders*), receive a right to vote about certain corporate matters, and get a claim on the corporate profits (Laskin, 2021, 2022).

Modern corporations are so large that their financial appetites are virtually unlimited. If Apple wants to increase the production of its iPhones, it needs money to design, produce, market, and sell these phones. What is important, Apple needs the money before it can sell the iPhones because customers will not pay for the phone until it is made. Thus, it has to raise funding to implement its plans into life. And many investors are happy to provide such financing to Apple for an opportunity to gain from future profits of sales of the new iPhones.

At the dawn of modern society, much of the production was concentrated on individual workers, such as blacksmiths, carpenters, masons, or weavers. They were the managers of their enterprises, as well as employees and investors. They did it all.

At best, their families helped with their work, especially if the work involved farming, beekeeping, or winemaking – something, that is extremely difficult to do for just one individual.

Eventually, as societies developed, demands for production, in terms of both quantity and quality, outgrew what individual or even family businesses could satisfy. It became essential to organize enterprises that could pull together resources from many people. When many people came together to establish an enterprise, they contributed a certain share of their resources and their work to these enterprises – thus, these enterprises became known as shareholding companies and these individuals as shareholders (Laskin, 2022).

The earliest shareholding company is believed to be *Stora Kopparberg Bergslags Aktiebolag*, the copper mine in the Swedish town of Falun. On June 16, 1288, the ownership of the Stora Kopparberg was divided into eight shares, each representing 12.5% of the company's stock. Mining operations are extremely complex, labor- and capital-intensive, and thus it is no surprise that the oldest shareholding company was the copper mine. Stora Kopparberg is an example of what today is called a private shareholding company – this means that nobody is allowed to purchase stock in the company. The shareholders had to meet certain requirements – primarily, the ownership was restricted to a few rich noble people who could provide significant funding. This is why only eight shares were needed (Laskin, 2018b) (Figure 7.1).

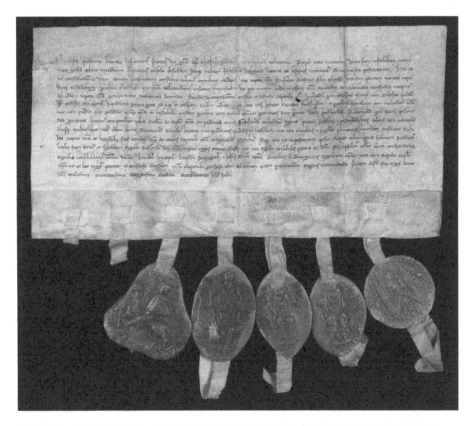

Figure 7.1 The Oldest Known Share of Stock: Stora Kopparberg Original Share, June 16, 1288. *Source:* National Archives of Sweden.

Many largest modern-day shareholding corporations are public companies – meaning anyone can buy a share in the company's stock. Absolutely anyone can buy shares in Apple, Tesla, Amazon, Microsoft, Johnson & Johnson, Visa, Coca-Cola, General Electric, and many more. Instead of dividing their stock into just eight shares like Stora Kopparberg did hundreds of years ago, they typically issue millions of shares because instead of targeting just a few wealthy and noble shareholders, they want to attract millions of diverse shareholders – individual investors of all incomes and all kinds of institutional investors, such as pension funds, mutual funds, and others. Apple, for example, issued over 16 billion shares that are currently owned by 23,502 shareholders according to its 2022 *annual report* on *Form 10-K*. For public companies, building and maintaining relationships with their shareholders becomes an important priority in the reputation management process (Laskin & Koehler, 2012). The first step in this relationship management process is knowing who their shareholders are. Generally, all shareholders are divided into two large groups – *retail shareholders* and *institutional investors*.

Retail Shareholders

Once the company is a *public shareholding company*, all restrictions for share ownership are removed and anyone can buy and sell its stock. Any private individual can buy shares of publicly traded companies like Microsoft, Netflix, or Disney, and then hold them or sell them whenever they want – if the share price increases by the time the shareholders sell the stock, they make a profit; if the price decreases, they lose money. These private individual investors are called *retail shareholders*. They may buy shares because they see a good investment opportunity, or they may like and actively use the products of the company, or they may support the company's mission. Tesla stock is a great example of the former. Many Tesla shareholders believe in the mission of the company and want to support the green company building electric cars and solar panels. It does not matter much to them if the company misses its earnings estimate or falls behind on its delivery schedule – they are very loyal investors. One such retail investor, Brandon Smith, invested about US$90,000 in Tesla stock and so far has never sold a single share. As of 2021, his investment is worth more than US$1 million. Another Tesla millionaire, or *Teslanaire* as they are known, Basel Termanini, has been driving Tesla cars since 2012 and is passionate about the brand – as a result, he also bought Tesla stock and his investment in 2021 is worth US$2.5 million (Hull, 2020). The CEO of Tesla, Elon Musk, consistently shows his appreciation for retail investors and values their direct experience with the company's products.

Another type of retail investor is a company's own employees who want to invest in the shares of their employer. As these investors also work at the company, they have significant knowledge about what the company does. Some of these investors are called *insiders* – these are usually senior-level employees who have access to information not available to other investors; such information is called *nonpublic information*. For example, the CEO of a company is likely to find out good or bad news about the company or its products before anybody else. As a result, the CEO would have a chance to buy or sell the stock before the price changes based on this new information. This practice of using nonpublic information to benefit from stock trades is called *insider trading*. Since this would be unfair to all other investors, insider trading is illegal, and insiders must report their trading activity to the Securities and Exchange Commission (SEC) – thus, making such activity public knowledge.

Some employees also receive shares of the company as part of the *stock compensation* or *stock bonus*. For example, an employee may receive a certain number of shares if the company meets a specific sales benchmark – this encourages all employees to put their best efforts toward reaching the corporate goal as they know they will be rewarded for that. In other cases, stock may be given to employees based on their longevity; for example, employees who have worked at the company for 5, 10, or 20 years may receive company stock as a reward.

It is also quite common for corporations to encourage their employees to buy their stock – it essentially aligns the interests of employees with the interests of the company at large. As a result, many companies add stock to various retirement saving programs or develop special stock purchase programs for employees. For example, in 2020, Sanofi, one of the largest global pharmaceutical companies, introduced "Action 2020," a stock program where Sanofi employees can buy shares of the company at only 80% of the market price. In addition, for every five shares purchased, Sanofi was adding one extra share for free. According to Sanofi, the goal of this program is "to better associate its employees, who are key contributors in this value creation, to the future development and results of the company" (Sanofi, 2020).

Institutional Investors

On the opposite side from the retail shareholders, there are *institutional investors* or *professional investors*. There are many types of professional investors, with the main ones being pension funds, mutual funds, hedge funds, endowments, and sovereign funds (Laskin, 2022).

Pension funds, also called *superannuation funds*, are designed to provide retirement income to their beneficiaries. The largest pension fund in the world is the Federal Old-Age and Survivors Insurance Trust Fund. To many people in the United States, this fund is known as *Social Security*. It manages assets exceeding US$2.7 trillion. Social Security, however, is different from most other pension funds because it is funded through taxes and the fund is not allowed to invest in shares of companies or any other marketable securities.

A typical pension fund, however, is funded by contributions from employees and employers. Then, these contributions are invested in various securities, including shares of publicly traded corporations. California Public Employees' Retirement System (CalPERS) is one such fund, with US$300 billion in investments. The value of investments may increase or decrease with fluctuations in the market. For example, it is estimated that in 2009 during the financial crisis, CalPERS lost about US$55 billion. The Australian National Superannuation Scheme manages more than US$1.7 trillion of assets funded by a 9.5% contribution from every employee in Australia. The scheme has about 500 funds with different investment strategies and management structures, with people being able to choose how to allocate their investments between these funds.

Mutual funds, similarly, accumulate funds from many individuals and organizations and then invest them on their behalf. For example, a retail investor may buy shares in Apple, Microsoft, Facebook, Tesla, and Walmart directly or, instead, such an investor may invest in the Vanguard 500 Index Fund, which automatically invests in the 500 largest US companies including Apple, Microsoft, and so on. This Vanguard 500 Index Fund has over US$620 billion in assets and, as a result, investing in such a fund creates more diversification and economies of scale. The funds typically charge a management fee for operating the investments on behalf of their clients. Mutual funds also have different investment strategies and an investor can align their investment philosophy with a particular fund. Vanguard, in addition to the 500 Index Fund, operates many other funds with different strategies; for example, the Vanguard FTSE Social Index Fund screens its investments based on environmental, social, and corporate governance criteria, and excludes stocks in alcohol, tobacco, weapons, adult entertainment, fossil fuels, and gaming companies (Figure 7.2).

Hedge funds are similar to mutual funds but usually involve more risks and use more complex investment strategies and investment instruments, such as derivatives. As a result, hedge funds tend to be limited to sophisticated investors and not open to the general public. One of such complex investment strategies that hedge funds use is *short selling*. Short selling essentially means selling securities that the hedge fund does not own. For example, a hedge fund may sell 100 shares of Microsoft stock without having any Microsoft shares on its balance sheet. The logic behind the short sale is the hedge fund expects the share price to decline soon, and the fund would be able to buy the shares in the future at a cheaper price than the price they are selling the shares for at this very moment. It is easy to make money when all the stock prices are going up, but short selling is a way to make money when the prices are going down. Short selling is essentially a bet against the company's success; it is an expectation that the company is going to fail. Since short sellers do not have to own the stock to sell it, theoretically they can even sell more stock than the company has issued. All this puts pressure on

Figure 7.2 Wall Street. *Source:* Matteo Colombo/Getty Images.

the stock price. In fact, by going on a selling spree, short sellers can push the stock price down even without any underlying reason – just because of a large *sell-off*.

Another type of professional investor is *endowments*. Many colleges and other non-profit organizations have financial endowments that manage investments in order to support the mission of the organizations. For example, the endowment of Harvard University is made up of 14,000 different funds with a combined value of almost US$50 billion in investments. Most Harvard investments are in hedge funds, followed by private equity and public equity investments.

Finally, *sovereign funds*, *sovereign investment funds*, or *sovereign wealth funds* are state-owned funds. Some consider Social Security as a sovereign fund, but since its primary purpose is retirement, most people treat it as a pension fund. An example of a sovereign fund is the Abu Dhabi Investment Authority from the United Arab Emirates, which has an estimated US$800 billion in assets. The fund has a variety of investments including Nestlé Skin Health, ThyssenKrupp Elevator, and Citigroup among others.

Value of the Relationship

Corporations want their investors to invest for the long term. Some investor relations professionals even introduced a special term for such long-term investors: *shareowners* as opposed to shareholders (Laskin, 2022). *Shareowners* can be individuals or institutional investors, but they tend to have a long-term focus on a specific stock. The reasons for this focus may be different, but typically it is somebody who really believes in the company and is hoping to make a very big return over the years. The term shareowners emphasizes the fact that they do not just hold the stock temporarily. Instead, they are owners of the stock for long periods of time – usually years – and they know and care about the company. These are the investors that every *investor relations officer* (IRO) wants to build long-term relationships with and these are the investors who want to know as much as possible about the company. They are also sometimes called *strategic investors*.

A certain subtype of these shareowners is *activist investors*. A typical investor tends to sell the stock of the company if they do not like what the company is doing or how it is managed. They are said to *vote with their feet* or *vote with their wallets*. Activist investors, however, instead of selling the shares, try to influence the management of the company through a variety of means to change whatever they do not like about the company and to improve the company's operations. While, on the one hand, both investors and management typically want what is in the corporation's best interest, on the other hand, such activist behavior tends to require significant effort from the investor relations personnel of the corporation as they work in the middle between the company's investors and the company's management. Disagreement may arise due to miscommunications or lack of communication, and extra effort may be required to maintain the relationship.

Warren Buffett is an example of such a strategic investor, who often uses activism to make the changes he deems necessary. One of the companies Warren Buffett invested in over the years was Salomon Brothers. In 1987, Buffett's Berkshire Hathaway became the largest shareholder of Salomon Brothers. As the years progressed and Buffett learned more about his new investment, he did not really like what he saw. The firm was frequently cited for violating the rules established for trading securities, over-stretching its resources to become one of the most leveraged companies, and taking too much risk in junk bond trading. But instead of cutting his losses and selling the stock, Warren Buffett used his shares to make himself a chairman of the board of Salomon Brothers, fired the existing leadership responsible for bad decisions, and made significant strategic changes at the company, including modifying its investment philosophy, making employees "owner operators," and demanding compliance with all rules and regulations (Loomis, 1997). In the end, Buffett's intervention and the changes he brought were extremely successful: Salomon Brothers' value increased and Buffett was able to record a profit of almost 100% on his investment in the company.

This example is, of course, as active as it gets – even activist investors typically do not start running the corporations themselves, but they tend to be very vocal about what they think should be done. Activist investors often meet with the company's management to discuss what they think and give their suggestions to the company's management, go public with their concerns to the press and social media, and often utilize annual shareholder meetings and other public events to make their concerns known to other shareholders and to try to persuade them to join forces against the management. Carl Icahn, a famous activist investor, at one point purchased about 1.4% of Motorola stock, and with that stock launched a campaign to get a seat on the Board of Directors, accusing current Board members of rubber-stamping everything the management proposed and not acting in the best interests of shareholders. Since his share of stock was not sufficient to get a seat on the Board, he launched a campaign to reach other shareholders trying to persuade them to vote for him. Although Icahn initially failed, with time he achieved his goal and forced Motorola to sell its cell phone business to Google with a huge premium for Motorola shareholders (Tonello, 2014).

Maintaining and Building Reputation through Relationship Management Strategies

For many small companies, the best way to find investors is through the *sell-side*, the organizations responsible for facilitating the sales of various securities such as shares or bonds. Sell-side organizations that include banks and brokers have large databases of clients, and if they recommend them to buy shares in a particular stock, many of their clients will at least take a look at the company, if not make the purchase outright. As a result, for many small companies and start-up companies, developing sell-side relationships is a vitally important task. These companies invest significant efforts into sell-side communications and also attend special events organized by the sell-side – investor conferences, roadshows, and investor field days.

Sell-side analysts tend to focus on a specific industry or industries – this makes them experts not just in finance but also in that particular industry – as a result, they tend to develop a good understanding of both the technology and the business. To be industry-level experts, financial analysts are interested in much more than just financial numbers. In fact, to properly evaluate the company it is not enough to look at the balance sheet alone. It is important to understand the company as a whole: What are its competitive advantages? What is unique about its products? How does it compare with others in the industry?

For example, one of the largest investment banks, UBS, recently tasked its analysts with studying battery technologies for the electric car market. The battery is one of the main components in an electric car and, thus, whoever has the lead in the battery technology is well positioned for the future as sales of electric cars are expected to grow. Financial results are based on what happened in the past; for financial analysts, however, it is of primary importance what is going to happen in the future. In order to answer this question, analysts must understand what is going to happen with the company and the whole industry. Tesla sells more electric vehicles than its competitors, but whether it will be able to maintain its leadership depends to a large extent on the developments in the battery technology by Tesla and by its competitors – Volkswagen, General Motors, and others. UBS financial analysts concluded that, although Tesla has an advantage in battery technologies, its reliance on battery suppliers like LG and Panasonic presents a weakness for the company versus having its own battery production. Financial analysts would then communicate that information to fund managers and other investors who make decisions on buying and selling stocks.

Of course, it is also important for organizations to establish direct relations with investors in addition to indirect relations through the sell-side. The investors are called the *buy-side* in stock market jargon because they are the ones who actually buy the shares of stock. Investor relations typically have a sophisticated annual schedule of special events when they meet with investors – this schedule is known as investor relations calendar. Key parts of such calendars are activities aimed at disclosure.

Disclosure is one of the most visible tasks of the investor relations profession because it is a regulatory mandate. In fact, some even equate disclosure with investor relations, calling investor relations professionals *disclosure officers* and citing disclosure as the main function of financial communicators. The foundation of the required disclosure is *periodic reporting*. In the United States, for publicly traded companies, it is centered on *Form 10-K*, the *annual report*, and *Form 10-Q*, the *quarterly report*. As the name suggests, 10-K focuses on the results of the past year, while 10-Q discusses what happened over the most recent three months (Schramm et al., 2022).

When a company submits its quarterly report or its annual report to the US SEC, the company typically also issues a public media release that summarizes the key points of the filing, with a strong focus on the financial results. The final line in the financial statement of the company is typically corporate *earnings*. As a result, the media release about quarterly or annual results is often called the *earnings release*. Earnings releases are usually accompanied by an *earnings call, earnings cast,* or *earnings conference*. Investor relations professionals are usually responsible for preparing for and managing these calls. The calls are often simulcast online and are also saved and stored on the investor relations section of a company's website, allowing investors to access them at a later date. The top company executives tend to speak at these calls, including the CEO and CFO; depending on the topics the company wishes to focus on, company experts from operations, sales, or research may also be invited to speak. The goal of the call, however, is typically to frame the most recent financial results and put them in the context of the long-term ambitions of the company and its mission. A crucial part of the call is the ability of investors and analysts to ask questions and receive clarifying information from management. Sometimes, these exchanges may get tense – if the company is not doing so well or if management is withholding information, for example. It is the job of an IRO to manage both sides of the call – the investment community and the management – to ensure fair, transparent, and full disclosure of all relevant information.

The most significant event IROs manage is the *annual shareholder meeting*, or *annual general meeting* (AGM). The AGM is typically a large-budget event at a company's headquarters or at a large fancy hotel's conference center, where shareholders of the company can gather together to hear reports from management and the Board of Directors, and vote on the key issues facing the corporation. The key issue in requiring a vote is election of the new Board of Directors, who would represent the shareholders between the annual meetings and perform oversight over the company's management in the best interests of all shareholders.

The shareholders also vote on electing a new auditor, an organization that certifies financial disclosure of the corporation, to ensure accuracy of all the financial statements the company produces. The executive compensation must also be presented at the AGM for a shareholders' vote – this process is known as *say on pay*. The vote on executive compensation is *nonbinding*, or *advisory*, meaning that even if shareholders do not approve the compensation package for a CEO, the company can still proceed with the payment. Although nonbinding, no CEO wants to have shareholders publicly express disagreement with the proposed compensation, as it often shows a lack of satisfaction with the work the CEO is doing. Finally, in addition to the required bylaw items, shareholders can propose additional items for discussion at the AGM – these are known as *shareholder proposals*. The shareholder proposals may focus on absolutely any issue related to the company – employee practices, sustainability, management diversity, the structure of the Board of Directors, or anything else (Figure 7.3).

Prior to the annual meeting, whether it is conducted in person or online, a *proxy statement*, or simply, *proxy*, is prepared. The proxy statement is also called *Form 14A*. The goal of the proxy is to provide information to the shareholders about the matters they are expected to vote on. The proxy includes all the annual financial information as well as management's discussion and analysis of these results. Since shareholders elect the members of the Board of Directors, there is also detailed information on each candidate for the Board. The form also provides key details about the meeting with instructions on how to submit questions, how to vote, and how to attend the meeting.

In addition to these quarterly and annual documents, IROs are responsible for disclosing information that may materially affect the valuation of a company as it happens. Such information is called *material information* and such reporting is called *current reporting*. One of the ways IROs provide such disclosure is through US SEC's *Form 8-K, current report*. The SEC explains that companies are expected to file Form 8-K in order "to announce major events that shareholders should know about" (SEC, 2012).

The Web homepages of publicly traded corporations usually have a section labeled *Investors* or *For Investors* where information relevant for shareholders, investors, and financial analysts is posted. IROs are primarily responsible for managing the content of this section of the corporate website, of course working in collaboration with other corporate functions responsible for external communications.

One of the most effective tactics IROs use for building and maintaining relationships with the financial community is *one-on-one meetings*, or simply *one-on-ones*.

NOTICE OF 2023 ANNUAL MEETING OF STOCKHOLDERS

TO BE HELD ON MAY 16, 2023

Dear Tesla Stockholders:

We are pleased to inform you that our 2023 Annual Meeting of Stockholders (the "2023 Annual Meeting") will be held on Tuesday, May 16, 2023, at 3:00 p.m. Central Time, both virtually via the Internet at www.meetnow.global/TESLA2023 and in person for a limited number of stockholders at Tesla's Gigafactory Texas located at 1 Tesla Road, Austin, TX 78725. For your convenience, we will also webcast the 2023 Annual Meeting live via the Internet at www.tesla.com/2023shareholdermeeting. The agenda of the 2023 Annual Meeting will be the following items of business, which are more fully described in this proxy statement:

Agenda Item	Board Vote Recommendation
Tesla Proposals	
1. A Tesla proposal to elect three Class I directors to serve for a term of three years, or until their respective successors are duly elected and qualified ("Proposal One").	"FOR EACH COMPANY NOMINEE"
2. A Tesla proposal to approve executive compensation on a non-binding advisory basis ("Proposal Two").	"FOR"
3. A Tesla proposal to approve the frequency of future votes on executive compensation on a non-binding advisory basis ("Proposal Three").	"EVERY THREE YEARS"
4. A Tesla proposal to ratify the appointment of PricewaterhouseCoopers LLP as Tesla's independent registered public accounting firm for the fiscal year ending December 31, 2023 ("Proposal Four").	"FOR"
Stockholder Proposals	
5. A stockholder proposal regarding reporting on key-person risk, if properly presented ("Proposal Five").	"AGAINST"

All stockholders as of the close of business on March 20, 2023 are cordially invited to attend the 2023 Annual Meeting virtually via the Internet at www.meetnow.global/TESLA2023. We will also accommodate a limited number of stockholders in person at Gigafactory Texas.

We are providing our proxy materials to our stockholders over the Internet. This reduces our environmental impact and our costs while ensuring our stockholders have timely access to this important information. Accordingly, stockholders of record at the close of business on March 20, 2023 will receive a Notice of Internet Availability of Proxy Materials (the "Notice of Internet Availability") with details on accessing these materials. Beneficial owners of Tesla common stock at the close of business on March 20, 2023 will receive separate notices on behalf of their brokers, banks or other intermediaries through which they hold shares.

> **Your vote is very important.** Whether or not you plan to attend the 2023 Annual Meeting, we encourage you to read the proxy statement and vote as soon as possible. For specific instructions on how to vote your shares, please refer to the section entitled *"Questions and Answers About the 2023 Annual Meeting and Procedural Matters"* and the instructions on the Notice of Internet Availability or the notice you receive from your broker, bank or other intermediary.

Thank you for your ongoing support of Tesla.

Elon Musk

Robyn Denholm

Figure 7.3 Tesla's Notice of 2023 Annual Meeting from its Proxy Statement.

One-on-one meetings with investors or analysts have long been considered a cornerstone of investor relations. These one-on-ones are individual meetings, typically with an institutional investor or a sell-side financial analyst. The meetings show respect and appreciation to the investor, who gets a chance to ask questions about the company and receive direct and immediate responses. It is common to have a team of top company representatives at such meetings. In addition to the IRO, the meeting may be attended by the CEO, CFO, COO, CMO, and other executives depending on the topic of conversation and how important the investor is.

For example, if a pharmaceutical company is promoting its new chemical compound, a research scientist who developed the compound may be invited to the meeting to help investors understand the potential of the medicine. Or if a company talks about new ways to sell its products, for example, switching to a subscription model, marketing and sales leadership may be invited. Investors and analysts also cherish one-on-one meetings as these meetings provide an opportunity to get all their questions answered, while at the same time, they can analyze the nonverbal cues and body language of the top management.

Strategically, the focus of all investor relations activities is on building and maintaining relationships with current and prospective shareholders as well as other financial publics. These relationships are the foundation on which understanding of the company and its business, as well as trust in the management team and its decision-making are built. A fair evaluation of the company's securities is impossible without such understanding and trust.

Crisis Management Strategies

One of the unique crisis scenarios for investor relations is *shareholder activism*. When a shareholder is unhappy with the direction the company is going, a common response is a sale of securities. The shareholder sells their shares in the company and invests money in something else. However, in some cases, instead of selling the stock, the shareholder turns into an activist. An *activist shareholder* is one who attempts to influence the company's decision-making and bring about change on an issue or multiple issues of concern (Laskin, 2022).

Declining share prices and poor operational results are common reasons for shareholders to turn activist because shareholders are the ones losing money in this situation. In some cases, the price of the share can get so low that it makes more sense for shareholders to try to improve the company's performance rather than just sell the stock, as the investors will not recover the losses in the case of a sell. Declining share price also creates an opportunity for an activist investor to band together with other shareholders, as no shareholders want to see the price of the stock they are holding go down. Thus, activist investors have a chance to gain wider support for their shareholder proposals if they communicate with other company shareholders.

A decline in prices and revenues is a common but not the only reason for shareholder activists to target a corporation. Many shareholder activists focus on ESG (environmental, social, and governance) issues. Investors are especially interested in the corporate *governance* issues. A common issue for shareholder activism is the *Board of Directors' composition*. Another common reason for shareholder activism is *disclosure*. Investors are looking for information that goes beyond what is required by law so that they can better understand the company's business model. If they cannot get that information, they may turn to shareholder activism.

For example, climate change is an important issue that affects people around the world – floods, droughts, snowstorms, forest fires, and similar. This presents a real risk for future operations at many corporations. As a result, investors demand corporations provide additional information about how they are planning for the risks triggered by *climate change*. To make their voices heard, large investors banded together into the Climate Action 100+ coalition. At the start of 2021, the coalition included more than 500 investors with over US\$52 trillion in assets under management. One of the top requirements these investors impose on the corporations they invest in is to provide enhanced corporate disclosure "to enable investors to assess the robustness of companies' business plans against a range of climate scenarios, including well below two degrees and improve investment decision-making" (Climate Action 100+, 2023).

Environmental and social issues are becoming more and more important to society and to investors as well (Laskin, 2018a; Laskin & Kresic, 2021). Already today, many shareholders evaluate the work leaders of the corporations are doing by using some of the ESG metrics. A recent report on executive compensation by *IR Magazine* showed that three out of four investors expect the compensation of senior management to be linked also to some ESG metrics. On the other hand, most companies still do not use ESG indicators in their executive compensation performance measurements (Bevan, 2022). This shows a significant disconnect between what investors want and what the corporations are doing.

Some investors specifically focus on ESG issues as the cornerstone of their investment strategy. Global ESG assets are growing every year and are expected to exceed US$53 trillion, which is more than a third of all assets under management (Heilbuth, 2022). In addition, the *Financial Times* reports that assets under management of these *ESG funds* are expected to triple in the near future. If the prediction is true and over the next five years this number grows to more than half of all the investment funds, it will have a significant effect on the investment landscape and will put publicly traded companies under scrutiny related to their ESG actions and ESG reporting. If a particular company fails to act on its own regarding ESG, investors are likely to take action. AGMs in 2020 saw a record number of proposals from shareholders on issues related to various ESG issues.

As a result, it is not a surprise that corporations that want to attract those ESG investments may overexaggerate their "greenness" – a phenomenon known as *greenwashing*. Various investment funds may also engage in greenwashing to attract investors looking for ESG investment vehicles. A recent analysis by *Morningstar* led to a removal of ESG denomination from more than 1,200 funds (Schwartzkopff, 2022) that overpromised on their ESG commitment (Table 7.1).

In fact, recent research identified four types of greenwashing:

1. *Wokewashing*, when corporations or their leaders take a public stance on an issue usually at the top of society's agenda, but do not act in accordance with their public stance behind closed doors. For example, oil companies may be publicly promising investments in renewable energy, while lobbying behind the scenes to remove environmental regulations.
2. *Evidence-free ESG reporting*, when corporations boast their environmental record without any substantial evidence. Many ESG reports are not regulated or audited – this allows companies to use generic language and promotional communications rather than providing facts about what they are doing.
3. *Competence washing*, when corporations do not hire or promote experts in ESG issues, instead assigning it to the marketing department or giving it as an extra responsibility to executives who already have other responsibilities.
4. *Dubious net-zero goals*, when corporations use their creative interpretations of what net-zero actually means. Since this area is not strictly regulated, organizations can make claims that use different interpretations of how much carbon the corporation emits and how much it absorbs (Heilbuth, 2022).

Historically, shareholder activism was associated with professional investors and hedge funds. Recently, however, we have seen the revival of retail shareholders – regular individuals who may own just a couple of shares of stock. However, these small retail shareholders can combine their efforts and their resources together. One of the best examples of retail shareholders' power was the story of GameStop. While professional hedge fund investors were short-selling the stock of GameStop, regular retail investors banded together to buy and hold these shares. Many of the GameStop retail shareholders originated on Reddit, more specifically on the WallStreetBets subreddit. All these investors had access to trading through free and easy-to-use apps like Robinhood. When hedge funds expected GameStop stock to go down in price even to the point of GameStop going out of business, they started short-selling the stock. Retail investors noted this short-selling and started buying the stock, sharing information

Table 7.1 Morningstar's 15 Top Funds Leading the Way on ESG.

Fund	Ticker	Morningstar Analyst Rating	Strategy ESG Commitment Level	Morningstar Sustainability Rating	Asset Manager
Parnassus Core Equity	PRILX	Silver	Leader	*****	Parnassus
Parnassus Mid Cap	PFPMX	Silver	Leader	*****	Parnassus
Parnassus Mid Cap Growth	PFPRX	Bronze	Leader	*****	Parnassus
Pax Global Opportunities	PXGOX	Bronze	Leader	*****	Impax
TIAA-CREF Core Impact Bond	TSBIX	Bronze	Leader	—	Nuveen, A TIAA Company
PIMCO Total Return ESG	PTSAX	Gold	Advanced	—	Pimco
Brown Advisory Sustainable Growth	BAFWX	Silver	Advanced	****	Brown Advisors
iShares ESG MSCI USA Leaders ETF	SUSL	Silver	Advanced	*****	BlackRock
iShares MSCI USA ESG Select ETF	SUSA	Silver	Advanced	*****	BlackRock
PIMCO Low Duration ESG	PLDIX	Silver	Advanced	—	Pimco
BlackRock Advantage ESG US Equity	BIRIX	Bronze	Advanced	****	BlackRock
iShares MSCI KLD 400 Social ETF	DSI	Bronze	Advanced	*****	BlackRock
TIAA-CREF Social Choice Equity	TISCX	Bronze	Advanced	****	Nuveen, A TIAA Company
Vanguard Global ESG Select Stock	VESGX	Bronze	Advanced	*****	Wellington Management
Xtrackers MSCI USA ESG Leaders Eq ETF	USSG	Bronze	Advanced	*****	DWS

Source: Morningstar. https://www.morningstar.com/funds/15-top-funds-leading-way-esg

about their buys on Reddit. This power of retail shareholders pushed the stock of GameStop from less than US$1 per share in 2019 to above US$450 per share in January 2021. Early reports indicated that professional hedge fund losses were in billions of dollars, while retail shareholders started talking about financial revolution, redistribution of wealth, and new fairness in the financial markets. Melvin Capital lost about US$7 billion on its GameStop short-bet due in large part to individual investors banding together on social media, primarily on r/wallstreetbets, to buy and hold GameStop stock. This caused the so-called short-squeeze pushing the stock price up – from under US$5 to over US$300.

Moreover, redditors on wallstreetbets are now spreading their influence to other stocks, such as AMC, Nokia, and Best Buy. AMC now has over 80% of its stock in the hands of retail shareholders. Those shareholders may have different demands on the company and its management. AMC is recognized as one of the *meme stocks* – stocks in which people invest not based on the company's fundamental value or expectations of future growth, but as a joke or part of the social media movement. The CEO of AMC seems to recognize this as the company recently announced a donation of US$50,000 to Dian Fossey Gorilla Fund in an apparent nod to these retail investors who are known on social media as *apes*. The joke made the full circle – from investing in a meme stock to the stock issuer recognizing its ape investors (Schultze, 2021, p. 1).

Future Proofing Your Strategies

Virtual Engagement

The COVID-19 pandemic forced many annual shareholder meetings and other in-person events to become virtual. This online environment has also proven beneficial for increased engagement. More shareholders participated in annual meetings in 2020 than ever before. *IR Magazine* reports that, in addition to higher attendance, *virtual shareholder meeting* participants stayed longer, voted more often, and asked more questions. Nili & Shaner (2020) suggested that virtual shareholder meetings helped reclaim shareholder democracy! IROs will have to take these trends into account. The future may require always having a remote option available even when the meeting is conducted primarily in-person for the benefit of shareholders who cannot travel or prefer to communicate virtually.

As remote technologies develop, it is possible future AGMs, investor conferences, or roadshows could be conducted in virtual reality (VR). Once the adoption of VR headsets becomes as widespread as smartphones and TVs, IROs will be able to seamlessly engage investors and analysts in the VR environment. This would combine the convenience of remote meetings with the face-to-face experience of in-person events. VR creates a virtual environment for users separate from the actual environment where the user is located and thus can place a user in any place and time in the world. For example, VR can show a new mining infrastructure without actually having shareholders go into the mine. Other technologies can enhance and build upon the reality. In-person events can be supplemented with augmented reality (AR) and mixed reality (MR) layers too; for example, allowing on-demand access in real time to additional data about a company's finances while in the meeting. AR could bring an artificial object into the investor meeting like an open-hearth furnace, and MR could allow investors to interact with it to better learn its operations.

In fact, in the future, in-person events are likely to become more sparse. Yet, this will also lead to an additional appreciation of in-person one-on-ones, small-group meetings, and roadshows. Adam Borgatti, senior vice president of Corporate Development and Investor Relations at Aecon, calls these in-person opportunities *touch and feel events* and proposes that those will be in significant demand. It is likely that even those in-person events will have a virtual component: investors and analysts now expect to be able to participate virtually, whether in live format or as a recording. Plus, at least for now, an ability to actually touch and feel depends significantly on the vaccination and the infection rates.

Technology

In addition to the increased usage of remote and online communication technologies, technological innovations will likely have an influence on every other aspect of investor relations as well. For example, IROs may have to learn how to connect with new kinds of investors: investors operating based on artificial intelligence (AI), neural networks, natural language processing, and alternative and niche data sets. The constantly growing amount of data generated and processed allows for identifying the most obscure connections between share price and other performance indicators. Deep mining algorithms may find a connection between, for example, a stock price and social media reviews on Yelp, and a fund may be created to invest based on this information with millions of retail shareholders pouring their cash into such a fund. IROs will have to be at the forefront of monitoring these trends and finding and analyzing such information themselves to educate investors and to educate the company's management. Of course, IROs will also have to understand how these new investment tools work and what effect they may have on the corporate stock.

On the other hand, IROs will gain access to many new technologies themselves; this may make the lives of IROs easier in some respects, but at the same time will no doubt place additional demands on the role of IROs. The investor relations profession will undoubtedly use more data. Some professional discussions already focus on the issue of automation and AI taking jobs away from IROs and financial analysts. There is little doubt that AI is more efficient than humans at crunching the numbers; however, the relationship-building aspect and nonfinancial information may give the advantage back to humans. So, although it seems unlikely that technology will replace IROs, IROs will be able to use technology to their advantage: letting AI process quantitative data, identifying investors to target, analyzing trading patterns, and so on, while IROs can focus on qualitative data and producing insights based on all the data combined. And, of course, and most importantly, IROs are the ones who will be acting based on those insights. Even if AI can prepare an excellent financial statement, it would still require the company executives to put their signatures on these statements.

Shareholder Activism

The growing numbers of retail shareholders, increased market volatility, amplified voices arguing for social justice and wealth redistribution, technological innovation, improved access to corporations, and mounting pressure on companies to demonstrate ESG commitments will continue to lead to more shareholder activism. As it is reasonable to expect more shareholder activism in terms of pure numbers, it is likely that qualitatively shareholder activism will grow, too, involving more and more issues, especially focusing on the issues of *diversity*, *equity*, and *inclusion*, which will become more and more relevant.

Chapter Summary

Investors and shareholders provide resources for corporate organizations to operate. In exchange, they receive shares of corporate stock, get access to organizational information through corporate disclosures, and often receive a right to vote on organizational matters. For publicly traded corporations, in which everyone can invest, public disclosure is a legal requirement – all material information must be publicly available. Corporations, in addition to retail shareholders and institutional investors, collectively known as buy-side, must invest resources into managing relationships with the sell-side, the intermediaries of the financial markets. Many corporations appoint designated professionals for building and maintaining relationships with the buy-side and sell-side, IROs. IROs are responsible for releasing periodic and current disclosure, producing annual shareholder meetings with accompanying proxy statements, organizing roadshows and securities offerings, managing investor-focused Web sites and social media, and even engaging in one-on-one meetings with key investors and financial analysts – all of this, for the purpose of building and maintaining relationships with the financial community to enhance the reputation of the organization they work for.

Five Key Terms to Remember

Buy-side
Sell-side
Publicly traded corporation
Disclosure
Periodic and current reporting

Discussion Questions and Activities

1 Compare and contrast various types of financial publics. What are their main priorities and how will knowing those priorities help organizations build and maintain relationships with them?
2 Since retail shareholding is growing, what should companies do, if anything, to better connect with retail shareholders? Do you expect companies will focus more on retail shareholders in the future? Why or why not?
3 Discuss how the COVID-19 pandemic has affected investor relations. What changes do you expect will go away and which ones are here to stay for a long time?
4 Visit the SEC website. What new or proposed regulations are being discussed on the Web site? What do you think are the reasons behind these regulations?
5 Pick a large publicly traded corporation of your choice. Listen and analyze the most recent conference call of this corporation. Identify the speakers, the topic discussed, and the questions asked at the call.

How to Learn More

Laskin, A. V. (2022). *Investor relations and financial communication: Creating value through trust and understanding.* Malden, MA: Wiley-Blackwell.

Lev, B. (2012). *Winning investors over: Surprising truths about honesty, earnings guidance, and other ways to boost your stock price.* Harvard Business Press.

Whitehouse, M. (2023). *Transdisciplinary in financial communication: Writing for target readers.* Springer Nature.

Case Study

WeWork: Will It Work After All?

Figure 7.4

1. Summary of the Case

WeWork was founded by Adam Neumann and Miguel McKelvey in New York City in 2010. The company promised to revolutionize the business real estate market in a way similar to how Uber revolutionized transportation and AirBnB revolutionized vacations. WeWork rented unused real estate and converted it into upscale

(Continued)

Case Study (Continued)

coworking spaces for startups, companies, and independent workers. The charismatic CEO of WeWork, Adam Neumann, led rapid, massive growth, selling lofty promises of a radically improved work experience. Investors loved the CEO and the company reached a shocking US$47 billion valuation in 2019. The same year, WeWork began preparations for going public and started the IPO process in hopes of raising even more money at an even higher valuation. Yet, the required pre-IPO disclosure, the *S1 filing*, allowed investors and analysts to finally see what was behind the charisma, vision, and promises – the actual data of WeWork's business operations. Investors and analysts concluded that the business was running on fumes. The IPO failed, the company lost US$40 billion in value, Neumann was ousted, and WeWork's biggest investor, SoftBank, took over control as a result. Thus, this case highlights how valuable and consequential relationships with investors may be for the organizational reputation.

2. Organization's Background and Historical Development

In 2008, Adam Neumann was creating baby clothes for his own company, Krawlers, in a partially empty office building in Brooklyn. Things were not going well. In those early days of the great recession, the market for knee-padded baby garments was not quite paying the bills. So, he sublet part of his office space to other businesses to make rent – and an idea was born. Neumann enlisted the help of Miguel McKelvey, who worked as an architect in the same building. They saw an opportunity in the vacant space around them and launched GreenDesk, the precursor to WeWork, in 2008. They rented empty space from their landlord and furnished coworking spaces to rent out to independent entrepreneurs. The hook was sustainability, featuring recycled furniture and wind-powered energy. The team eventually sold the company to their landlord and took what they had learned to the next level.

Neumann and McKelvey launched WeWork in 2010, offering coworking spaces that combined the best of green office design, the amenities of a health club, and the community of an entrepreneurial fraternity house. Design and amenities evolved with the times, but glass walls, beer and cold-brew on tap, game tables, and hammocks were emblematic of these spaces. Through design and communication, WeWork invited customers to make a life, not just a living. Sustainability was the baseline; the community was the hook. The brand promise was aspirational – ideal office space, minimal overhead, freedom to work remotely or independently around like-minded creative geniuses and ride the technology wave into the future.

Neumann's charisma hooked powerful funders including Bruce Dunlevie of Benchmark Capital and JPMorgan's Jamie Dimon. With Dunlevie's direction, Benchmark led a Series A funding round of US$17 million. Deep in growth mode, "WeWork shot up to 1.5 million square feet of space and 10,000 members by 2014" (Aydin, 2019). By the fall of 2015, business media was hailing WeWork as "The Most Valuable Startup in New York City" (Kasoff, 2015). With a US$10 billion valuation, WeWork became the 11th most valuable startup in the world (Kasoff, 2015). Coverage lavished Neumann with praise, depicting a visionary leading a limitless organization. WeWork was growing at a rapid but reasonable startup pace. Then, Masayoshi Son came into the picture.

Korean–Japanese investor Son backed e-commerce giant Alibaba back in 2000, making a US$20 million investment that eventually grew into a US$200 billion business (Aydin, 2019). Son's firm, SoftBank, invested big in tech startups, chasing another massive success. For most of the 2010s, that seemed like a smart bet. This was the age of tech unicorns – billion-dollar companies growing out of Silicon Valley garages. SoftBank was not the only one backing disruptors like Uber, which seemed to promise nothing but growth. Son was attracted to novelty, focusing "investments on capital intensive, low-margin, mature businesses wrapped in a patina of technology that, for all the hype, don't fundamentally improve weak operating economics" (Sherman, 2019b).

So when Neumann caught Son's eye in 2018, he had every reason to throw his money into WeWork. Within a year of meeting Neumann, Son invested his first US$4.4 billion in WeWork. SoftBank would eventually provide US$11 billion in funding, paving the way for outsize growth and influence from Son.

Neumann pressed on and led expansion beyond real estate. In January 2019, WeWork officially rebranded as the We Company. Under the We umbrella, the organization would reach beyond commercial real estate and into "all aspects of people's lives, in both physical and digital worlds" (Brooker, 2019a). New business branches included residential co-living (WeLive), and WeGrow, the conscious entrepreneurial school created by Rebekah Neumann (Aydin, 2019). And that was supposed to be just the start: Neumann envisioned "everything from WeSleep to WeSail to WeBank" (Brooker, 2019a). Despite logistical and technical issues, WeWork's star was still rising. Going into the summer of 2019, WeWork had "466,000 members working out of 485 locations in more than 100 cities in 28 countries" (Wiedeman, 2019). The company was valued at US$47 billion and ready to float an IPO (Campbell, 2019).

3. Operational Environment and Main Publics

WeWork growth was based on the foundations of the 2008 recession. Once-thriving businesses could no longer afford rent, much less fill their existing office footprints. Qualified professionals found themselves out of steady work and ready to take on one job at a time, launching freelance careers and independent endeavors. This was the beginning of the gig economy and, as it seemed, the end of the office as we knew it. In the recession, "Neumann had the foresight to bet landlords would need tenants, and that legions of underemployed professionals would pay for an appealing alternative to working from a Starbucks while they got back on their feet" (Sherman, 2019a). WeWork came on the scene as people were figuring out how to work on their own, businesses were scaling back, and a wave of tech-driven disrupters was about to fill the economic void of the Great Recession.

In simple terms, WeWork just rents coworking office space to individuals and teams on a short- and long-term basis. One freelancer can rent a desk in a common space for a day. An organization can contract an office suite for a year or even design a custom buildout. Whatever you need an office to be, WeWork promises to meet that need. WeWork is a real estate business, but Neumann sold more – energy,

(Continued)

Case Study (Continued)

community, and aspiration. As early funder Bruce Dunlevie put it to Neumann, "you're not selling coworking, you're selling an energy I've never felt" (Sherman, 2019a).

The company's stated mission is to "Create a world where people work to make a life, not just a living" (WeWork, n.d.). They declare that from the inception, "we wanted to build more than beautiful, shared office spaces. We wanted to build a community. A place you join as an individual, 'me,' but where you become part of a greater 'we.' A place where we're redefining success measured by personal fulfillment, not just the bottom line. Community is our catalyst" (WeWork, n.d.). The company describes its value-based approach as: inspired, entrepreneurial, authentic, tenacious, grateful, and collective (WeWork, n.d.).

Flexibility is a cornerstone of WeWork's value proposition. As their website advertises, "Free your balance sheet and future-proof your real estate portfolio by tapping into the space you need, when you need it" (WeWork, n.d.). WeWork takes on that future risk and balance-sheet obligation. The business model is renting out lots and lots of empty space, mainly on long-term leases, then dividing it up into short-term, marked-up rentals.

By the summer of 2018, Neumann had won over publics in every corner: investors, renters, employees, and reporters.

Employees loved working for Neumann. The company made big promises and the potential for growth seemed limitless. But employees did not have to make any sacrifices as they were waiting for future rewards. WeWork lavished employees with luxury travel, live inspiration from the likes of Deepak Chopra, and a concert by music star Lorde on one fancy and mandatory retreat (Widdicombe, 2019).

Customers loved WeWork as well. The company actually understood the needs of its customers and offered an excellent solution for the clear market need. Independent workers of the growing gig economy needed the coworking spaces and the fact that the spaces offered featured luxuries of a large Silicon Valley corporation was a great bonus. One of the key features of WeWork spaces was unlimited beer on tap as part of its "work hard, party hard" motto (Molla & Ghaffary, 2019). Plus, WeWork office spaces were offered at extremely competitive pricing, taking into account all the amenities provided. In order to give its customers a good deal on rent the company was losing money at an unprecedented rate – in 2019 WeWork reported US$1.6 billion losses on US$1.8 billion in revenues (Molla & Ghaffary, 2019). But WeWork was always more than just a good deal; it was more than an office space – WeWork sold a lifestyle of success that many entrepreneurs wanted to be a part of.

While WeWork had a general admiration of the world, nobody loved WeWork more than its early investors. The startups that promised to disrupt the world were shooting to billion-dollar valuations seemingly overnight and investors did not want to miss their chance to make it big. Making a profit was not the requirement for any of these startups – Facebook, Uber, AirBnB – all were losing money while their valuations were growing. Even business media could not get enough of WeWork and its CEO. Coverage lavished Neumann with praise, depicting a visionary leading a limitless organization. While WeWork was not really a tech company, Neumann acted like a tech CEO – the coverage discussed his lavish lifestyle, his habit of walking barefoot around the office, and his ambitions to become either a first trillionaire, or a president of the world, or both (Brown, 2019).

4. The Issue Development

In this environment, WeWork was on top of the world admired by all. It was time to go public and offer its shares to the world! The We Company's S1 filing prospectus went public on August 14, 2019. Analysts and journalists quickly discovered the man in front of the curtain was putting on a big, expensive show, and there was not actually anyone behind him making sure it all worked.

The prospectus revealed countless weaknesses and liabilities within the We business plan and operations. The company had lost US$900 million in the first half of 2019 alone. Neumann held nearly all the voting power, and his wife Rebekah was appointed to select his successor in the event of his demise. Neumann and WeWork's reputations also tanked as analysts discovered that SoftBank's bankroll had artificially inflated the promising valuation (Brooker, 2019b).

Things might have gone differently for We Company earlier in the age of disruption. But, the memories of the Uber IPO disaster are still fresh in many investors' minds. The ride-sharing company "lost more money faster than just about any startup in history" and shed more than a third of its value in its first five months as a public company (Sherman, 2019a). Med-tech marvel Theranos had fallen apart the prior year when the SEC discovered that founder Elizabeth Holmes had raised more than US$700 million in funding for non-existent technology (Securities and Exchange Commission, 2018). Neumann's IPO attempt came at "precisely the wrong time to be the visionary leader of a company with imperial dreams and obscure finances" (Campbell, 2019). In the fall of 2019, investors were not falling for the hype.

Rampant conflicts of interest were among some of the most damning details in the prospectus. WeWork was renting spaces in buildings Neumann partially owned and bankrolled his lavish lifestyle. He had repeatedly taken loans (in the hundreds of millions of dollars) from the company on extremely favorable terms. When it rebranded as the We Company, the organization had paid US$5.9 million to license the "We" trademark. The prospectus revealed Neumann owned the holding company that owned the trademark. He would eventually return that US$5.9 million under pressure.

Just as troubling as the details the prospectus did disclose were those it tried to hide. One expert analyst called the report a "masterpiece of obfuscation" in the week following its release (Singer, 2019). Dates and budgets for WeWork locations were missing. The report did not follow generally accepted accounting principles and used made-up metrics to spin numbers. Expenses like sales, marketing, and even salaries were reported inconsistently in different categories, artificially lowering reported operating costs (Singer, 2019).

The prospectus essentially revealed a flawed business model that, if it continued on this path, would continue losing money. WeWork "was on the hook for US$47 billion in future lease payments to building owners while having committed revenue of only US$4 billion. Last year's loss jumped to US$1.9 billion on revenue of US$1.8 billion – for every dollar it made, it was spending two" (Campbell, 2019).

(Continued)

Case Study   (Continued)

With its grand ambitions and ideas, the We Company was not concerned about its losses: "We have a history of losses and, especially if we continue to grow at an accelerated rate, we may be unable to achieve profitability at a company level for the foreseeable future" (Campbell, 2019). Bankers, media, and analysts could not back up WeWork's value, forcing the stock from a rising star to junk territory as the share price dropped.

In the midst of the storm, Neumann appealed to his team with humility, admitting in an internal webcast that the way he had run WeWork as his own would not translate to running a public company. He knew he had to adapt, and he still believed he could.

Then, on September 18, a *Wall Street Journal* article connected the dots between Neumann's wild side and inability to responsibly run a company. The article detailed his alcohol and drug use on company time, "and of a layoffs discussion followed with tequila shots and a performance by a member of Run-DMC" (Campbell, 2019). Neumann officially lost the luminary status that had been the key to his success. Even his closest advisors and biggest supporters decided it was time for him to go. Neumann resigned on September 24, and WeWork withdrew its initial public offering on September 30 (Eavis & de la Merced, 2019).

The goal now shifted from raising billions in the IPO to saving WeWork as a viable business. The largest investors stepped in to save the company and, as a result, their investments. Neumann was paid around US$3 billion to walk away. That included a US$1.7 billion severance payment, US$1 billion to buy out his stocks, and a US$500 million credit line (Kelly, 2019). A team of SoftBank executives took the helm and began hard work to refocus the We Company "on its core business of renting office space, and getting rid of side businesses such as Rebekah Neumann's school to control costs and – perhaps – restore investor confidence" (Campbell, 2019).

What Is Next?

The future of WeWork is far from certain. SoftBank hopes to rescue the firm with continued funding and new leadership, either for a profitable sale or at least mitigation of losses.

Although growth has slowed significantly, WeWork is still in the business of renting coworking space, and the company indicates it will continue to do so. WeWork must now closely review everything that was built in a hurry. Through restructuring, cost-cutting, and a narrowed focus on profitable pursuits, it will work toward a sustainable business model. New leadership is now tasked with honoring lease commitments, not taking on more debt, and turning a profit.

Investors are framing the failed IPO as a setback and a learning experience: "We paid too much valuation for WeWork, and we did too much belief in the entrepreneur. But I think even with WeWork, we're now confident that we put in new management, a new plan, and we're going to turn it around and make a decent return" (Konrad, 2020).

New Executive Chairman Marcelo Claure has experience turning around SoftBank's investments. He previously managed critical improvements before a profitable sale of SoftBank-backed Sprint (Edgecliffe et al. 2019). Now he needs to bring the same level of improvement to WeWork and "prove that a company that has never made a profit can do so, and avert the need to keep raising fresh funds" (Konrad, 2020). Although new management is confident that WeWork can turn a profit, they are contending with investor belief that "the fundamental business model of taking on long-term leases and signing up short-term tenants isn't sustainable" (Sherman, 2019b). Whether or not the team will effectively wield every tool in their operational and communication arsenal to regain investor confidence, employee loyalty, and media respect in a changing world and shrinking economy remains to be seen....

References

Aydin, R. (2019). The history of WeWork—from its first office in a SoHo building to pushing out CEO and cofounder Adam Neumann. *Business Insider* (22 October). https://www.businessinsider.com/wework-ipo-we-company-history-founder-story-timeline-adam-neumann-2019-8

Bevan, L. (2022). Investors expect senior management pay to be linked to ESG. *IR Magazine* (19 May). https://www.irmagazine.com/careers/investors-expect-senior-management-pay-be-linked-esg

Brooker, K. (2019a). Exclusive: WeWork rebrands to the We company; CEO Neymann talks about revised SoftBank Round. *Fast Company* (18 January). https://www.fastcompany.com/90289512/exclusive-wework-to-rebrand-to-the-we-company-in-wake-of-disappointing-funding-news

Brooker, K. (2019b). WeFail: How the doomed Masa Son-Adam Neumann relationship set WeWork on the road to disaster. *Fast Company* (15 November). https://www.fastcompany.com/90426446/wefail-how-the-doomed-masa-son-adam-neumann-relationship-set-wework-on-the-road-to-disaster

Brown, E. (2019). How Adam Neumann's over-the-top style built WeWork. 'This is not the way everybody behaves.' *The Wall Street Journal* (18 September). https://www.wsj.com/articles/this-is-not-the-way-everybody-behaves-how-adam-neumanns-over-the-top-style-built-wework-11568823827?shareToken=st3fcd4c5c55d94ffc80b5721a8aa6ffa2

Campbell, D. (2019). How WeWork spiraled from a $47 billion valuation to talk of bankruptcy in just 6 weeks. *Business Insider* (28 September). https://www.businessinsider.com/weworks-nightmare-ipo

Climate Action 100+ (2023). About climate action 100+. https://www.climateaction100.org/about/

Eavis, P., & de la Merced, M. J. (2019). WeWork IPO is withdrawn as investors grow wary. *The New York Times* (30 September). https://www.nytimes.com/2019/09/30/business/wework-ipo.html

Edgecliffe, J., Platt, E., Inagaki, K., & Evans, J. (2019). WeWork rescue: the winners and the losers. *Financial Times* (23 October). https://www.ft.com/content/d32c8526-f555-11e9-b018-3ef8794b17c6

Heilbuth, L. (2022). Four common signs of greenwashing. *IR Magazine* (5 May). https://www.irmagazine.com/reporting/four-common-signs-greenwashing

Hull, D. (2020, December 18). *Elon Musk has made millionaires out of his most loyal fans.* Bloomberg. https://www.bloomberg.com/news/articles/2020-12-18/tesla-s-tsla-stock-price-an-army-of-millionaire-retail-traders-hold-on

Kasoff, M. (2015). How WeWork became the most valuable startup in New York City. *Business Insider* (22 October). https://www.businessinsider.com/the-founding-story-of-wework-2015-10

Kelly, J. (2019). WeWork was a $47 billion unicorn—now it plans to layoff up to 6,000 employees. *Forbes* (18 November). https://www.forbes.com/sites/jackkelly/2019/11/18/wework-was-a-47-billion-unicornmonths-later-it-now-plans-to-layoff-up-to-6000-employees/#29b2358392c5

Kelly, K. S., Laskin, A. V., & Rosenstein, G. A. (2010). Investor relations: two-way symmetrical practice. *Journal of Public Relations Research, 22*(2), 182–208.

Konrad, A. (2020). Masayoshi Son talks WeWork, Vision Fund, and SoftBank under Siege. *Forbes* (5 April). https://www.forbes.com/sites/alexkonrad/2020/04/05/exclusive-interview-masayoshi-son-talks-wework-vision-fund-softbank/#798affbf7f41

Laskin, A. V. (2018a). The third-person effects in the investment decision making: a case of corporate social responsibility. *Corporate Communications: An International Journal, 23*(3), 456–468.

Laskin, A.V. (2018b). Investor relations and financial communication: The evolution of the profession. In A.V. Laskin (Ed.) Handbook of Financial Communication and Investor Relations (pp. 3–22). Malden, MA: Wiley-Blackwell.

Laskin, A. V. (2021). Measuring investor relations and financial communication: An empirical test of scales of public relations. *Organicom, 18*(35), 95–115.

Laskin, A. V. (2022). *Investor relations and financial communication: Creating value through trust and understanding.* Malden, MA: Wiley-Blackwell.

Laskin, A. V. and Koehler, K. (2012). Investor relations: The state of the profession. *19th International Public Relations Symposium BledCom*, 115–129.

Laskin, A. V., & Kresic, K. M. (2021). Inclusion as component of CSR and a brand connection strategy. In D. Pompper, Ed., *Public Relations for Social Responsibility: Affirming DEI Commitment with Action* (pp. 149–164). Bingley: Emerald Publishing.

Loomis, C. J. (1997). Warren Buffett's wild ride at Salomon. *Fortune* (27 October). https://fortune.com/1997/10/27/warren-buffett-salomon

Molla, R., & Ghaffary, S. (2019). The WeWork mess, explained. *Vox* (22 October). https://www.vox.com/recode/2019/9/23/20879656/wework-mess-explained-ipo-softbank

Nili, Y., & Shaner, M.W. (2020). Back to the future? Reclaiming shareholder democracy through virtual annual meetings. Harvard Law School Forum on Corporate Governance. https://corpgov.law.harvard.edu/2020/10/21/back-to-the-future-reclaiming-shareholder-democracy-through-virtual-annual-meetings

Ragas, M. W., Laskin, A. V., & Brusch, M. (2014). Investor relations measurement: An industry survey. *Journal of Communication Management, 18*(2), 176–192.

Sanofi (2020). Sanofi to launch action 2020. https://www.sanofi.com/en/media-room/press-releases/2020/2020-06-03-16-00-00-2043122

Schramm, M. E., Place, K. R., & Laskin, A. V. (2022). Framing the strategic R&D paradigm shift in big pharma: A content analysis of pharmaceutical annual reports. *Journal of Communication Management.* https://doi.org/10.1108/JCOM-05-2021-0052

Schultze, G. (2021). Are the apes now running wall street? *Forbes* (15 June). https://www.forbes.com/sites/georgeschultze/2021/06/15/are-the-apes-now-running-wall-street/?sh=4f6bc4635e88

Schwartzkopff, F. (2022). ESG funds managing $1 trillion are stripped of sustainable tag by Morningstar. *Bloomberg* (10 February). https://www.bloomberg.com/news/articles/2022-02-10/funds-managing-1-trillion-stripped-of-esg-tag-by-morningstar

SEC (2012). Form 8-K. https://www.sec.gov/answers/form8k.htm

Securities and Exchange Commission. (2018). Theranos, CEO Holmes, and former president Balwani charged with massive fraud. U.S. Securities and Exchange Commission. https://www.sec.gov/news/press-release/2018-41

Sherman, G. (2019a). Inside the fall of WeWork. *Vanity Fair* (21 November). https://www.vanityfair.com/news/2019/11/inside-the-fall-of-wework

Sherman, L. (2019b). WeWork's failure is SoftBank's day of reckoning. *Wired* (19 October). https://www.wired.com/story/weworks-failure-is-softbanks-day-of-reckoning

Singer, D. (2019). WeWork analyst warns IPO filing a 'Masterpiece of Obfuscation.' *Bloomberg* (20 August). https://www.bloomberg.com/news/articles/2019-08-20/wework-analyst-warns-ipo-filing-a-masterpiece-of-obfuscation

Tonello, M. (2014). The activism of Carl Icahn and Bill Ackman. Harvard Law School Forum on Corporate Governance. https://corpgov.law.harvard.edu/2014/05/29/the-activism-of-carl-icahn-and-bill-ackman

WeWork (n.d.). Our Mission. https://www.wework.com/mission

Widdicombe, L. (2019). The rise and fall of WeWork. *The New Yorker* (6 November). https://www.newyorker.com/culture/culture-desk/the-rise-and-fall-of-wework

Wiedeman, R. (2019). The I in we: How did WeWork's Adam Neumann turn office space with "community" into a $47 billion company? Not by sharing. *New York Magazine Intelligencer* (10 June). https://nymag.com/intelligencer/2019/06/wework-adam-neumann.html

8

Customers and Subscribers: More Than Making a Sale

LEARNING OBJECTIVES

1. *After reading this chapter, students will be able to define who customers and subscribers are as the organizational public.*
2. *After reading this chapter, students will be able to understand the importance of managing relationships with customers and subscribers.*
3. *After reading this chapter, students will be able to develop strategic plans for building and maintaining relationships with customers and subscribers to enhance organizational reputation.*

Define the Public

It is difficult to imagine a public more important than customers and subscribers. These are the people who keep the organization in business by using the goods and services the organization creates. And, what is important, customers buying the products and the subscribers purchasing the services are paying for them with cash! This generates the cash flow organizations need to pay salaries to their employees, issue dividends to their investors, and cover invoices from their suppliers. As a result, customers and subscribers are also called *buyers*.

There are different ways to classify customers but perhaps the most important type of classification is by types of buyer. In this classification, all buyers are divided into two large groups: *Businesses* and *Consumers*. Consumers, also called *retail*, are regular individuals and families who buy products and services for their personal consumption. Businesses, on the other hand, purchase products and services to use in their business. As a result, when organizations think about their relationships with their customers, the first step is to understand if their customers are businesses, then these relationships are called *B2B* (business-to-business), or consumers, then these relationships are called *B2C* (business-to-consumer). These different types of customers may have very different demands on the organizational products and services and without understanding these demands a successful relationship may be difficult to maintain. For example, if a car manufacturer seeks to target retail consumers, they

Organizational Reputation Management: A Strategic Public Relations Perspective, First Edition. Alexander V. Laskin.
© 2024 John Wiley & Sons, Inc. Published 2024 by John Wiley & Sons, Inc.

may need to invest in their car design, beautiful paint colors, and a selection of features available. However, if the same car manufacturer would target their business customers, paint colors and designs may be irrelevant as the businesses would be more interested in oil change intervals and other maintenance and repair procedures.

Of course, for some types of products, the buyer is predetermined. For example, typical retail consumers do not have electric arc furnaces in their basement, and thus if the organization builds electric arc furnaces, it would have to focus on B2B communications. But, for many organizations and their products, both B2B and B2C relationships are important. For example, if you are selling phones, retail and business consumers are among your target publics as phones can be used for personal and business purposes. With different demands of B2B and B2C relationships, however, it would require almost two separate communication and relationship-management programs. Apple, for example, runs a separate program called *Apple at Work* that specifically focuses on relationship management with small businesses and large enterprises providing solutions that are important for their business users, such as Apple Business Manager. Apple explains that their B2B solutions are "Apple hardware, software, and services work together to give you and your employees the power and flexibility to do whatever needs doing – whether you're a small business or enterprise" (Apple, 2023).

It is also important to note that although it is customary to talk about B2B, as in business-to-business, these customers and subscribers can be other types of organizations in addition to business. For example, B2B would also include governments and non-profit organizations. In fact, in many places, governmental organizations are among the largest employers and, as a result, among the largest buyers of goods and services. They need paper, office furniture, computers and peripherals, cleaning supplies, and much more. Thus, relationships with these governmental agencies become quite important for organizations who want to sell all these products and services to the government. The same can be true for non-profit organizations. For example, the two largest employers in the city of Cambridge, MA, are Harvard University and the Massachusetts Institute of Technology – both not-for-profit universities. A local supplier of printing paper would be quite lucky to get an account with any of these two non-profits and would definitely want to maintain this B2B relationship for a long time.

Value of the Relationship

Developing and maintaining relationships with customers and subscribers has a very strong effect on the organizational reputation. In the past, an unhappy customer would mean a loss of a repeat sale from that customer. Today, an unhappy customer may mean a loss of thousands of sales. For example, a study of Seattle restaurant reviews on http://Yelp.com compared the Yelp rankings with the Washington State Department of Revenue data on restaurant sales and found that a difference of one star in restaurant ranking is equal to 5%–9% of restaurant revenues (Luca, 2016). With a continued growth in the volume of social media posts, comments from customers can spread across Facebook, Instagram, TikTok, and Twitter almost instantaneously bringing with it positive or negative effects on the organizational reputation and on the organizational sales and profits.

Some social media platforms allow customers and subscribers to create communities dedicated to specific brands, products, or services. For example, a community dedicated to iPhones on Reddit, r/iphone, was among the first places where the slowing down of older iPhones was reported by users who banded together to share and analyze information from their devices in order to understand the reasons behind such a decrease in performance on their phones. This led to #BatteryGate scandal that spread to other social media platforms and eventually to mass media and the courts. While Apple initially denied their deliberate manipulation of older phones, they later admitted responsibility, apologized to their customers, and agreed to pay $113 million to settle the legal case (Clayton, 2020).

Such online communities are also homes to an organization's most dedicated customers and supporters. Tesla Motors Club online forum (http://teslamotorsclub.com) is the largest independent online community for Tesla owners and enthusiasts founded in 2006. Today, it is the premier destination for any news about Tesla as well as for troubleshooting any issues with operating Tesla vehicles.

Building and Maintaining Reputation through Relationship Management Strategies

The process of building and maintaining relationships with customers and subscribers is known as *Customer Relationship Management* (CRM). This process is one of the key components of the discipline of *marketing*. The leading professional association of marketing, the American Marketing Association (AMA), defines marketing as "the activity, set of institutions, and processes for creating, communicating, delivering, and exchanging offerings that have value for customers, clients, partners, and society at large" (AMA, 2017). CRM includes several stages of relationship development with customers.

1. *Awareness.* A person or business must first become aware of the organization's product or service and how their needs can be met with such product or service. Without awareness, no relationship can begin.
2. *Initial purchase.* An organization acquires the first-time customer.
3. *Repeat customer.* If the first-time customer is happy with the product or service, they are likely to buy it again. For example, if you like a meal at a restaurant, you are likely to return to that restaurant again, becoming a repeat customer.
4. *Client.* At this stage in relationship development, an organization tries to move from occasional interactions to steady the relationship. A customer may sign a catering contract with a restaurant or a restaurant may be added to the list of approved vendors by a local university allowing students to pay with their student ID cards.
5. *Community.* Create a community of customers where business bonds and relationships will be supplemented with personal bonds and relationships. For example, Google created a community for users of Pixels, Google's outstanding smartphone brand, and named the community Pixel Superfans.

6. *Advocacy.* The last step in the CRM progression is building a bond between the product and the customer so strongly that the customer sees the product as part of their personality or their business identity. Think about the cult of Lululemon and the people who would never wear any other brand to their yoga classes. Or imagine the community of Porsche drivers who cannot imagine replacing their classic 911s or sporty Panameras with other car brands.

Of course, each of these stages requires significant investments of time and money to move customers along the relationship ladder.

Relationship Marketing

CRM became the foundation of what is now known as *relationship marketing.* Relationship marketing as opposed to more traditional *transactional marketing* focuses on building mutually beneficial relationships between buyers and sellers. Since both sellers and buyers derive value from the transactions, their interactions tend to mutually satisfy relationships that last for long periods of time. In fact, in theory, such relationships would grow stronger and deeper as the sellers would learn more and more insights about their customers and their needs, helping the organization to develop products and services better suited for their customers. In return, customers would be happier and happier with those products and services and more likely to pay higher prices for such perfect products, allowing the sellers to increase their profits year after year. Higher profits lead to more research, innovations, and improvements, making products even better and customers even happier, which feeds the cycle indefinitely. This is known as a win-win scenario.

In order to achieve and sustain such win-win relationships, one of the most effective yet underutilized approaches is listening to the customers. Organizations tend to create a lot of opportunities for employees to share their perspectives, and investors have legally mandated annual shareholder meetings where they can voice their opinions, but consumers often are talked to and rarely listened to (Figure 8.1).

One of the most advanced programs focused on listening is run by Haleon, a maker of consumer health products such as Advil, Excedrin, Centrum, Tums, and more. Daniel Gardner, the head of social intelligence its Haleon explains that social intelligence is like listening with a purpose – in other words, insights from listening and monitoring conversations inform organizational decision-making. Haleon focuses its social intelligence on its own brands, its competitors' brands, broad categories in which the organization competes (such as headache medications or multivitamins), and the macro and cultural trends that may affect the brands and consumers (Wood, 2023).

Customers also value when organizations practice stewardship strategies: if customers feel appreciated, they are more likely to become repeat loyal supporters of the organization. Tesla, for example, has a network of Tesla Owner Clubs. Tesla Owner Club (TOC) is "a community of owners and enthusiasts committed to advancing Tesla's mission to accelerate the world's transition to sustainable energy" (Tesla, 2023). Members of TOC get access to exclusive merchandise, participate in TOC-only events, and even receive insider information from Tesla headquarters. Tesla, in return, gets access to a group of loyal supporters who, from time to time, "help advocate for Tesla" (Tesla, 2023). The TOC of Connecticut has a news section that updates owners on

You hear the phrases *consumer obsessed* or *consumer centric* a lot these days and for good reason, consumers can make (e.g., online communities) or break your brand (e.g., de-influencing). Whether it's a raving positive review on Amazon or a viral video on TikTok complaining about the misleading benefits of a product, consumers voice their opinions everywhere all day long. It's never been more important to meet your consumers where they are, on the digital frontlines of social media.

Now that's easier said than done, social listening and its more advanced form (social intelligence) requires specialized expertise. Social listening is a simple concept at face value but it's actually a multidisciplinary skill that borrows elements from data analytics, market research, marketing, anthropology, psychology, linguistics, and more!

Running searches or what's known in the profession as Boolean queries is far from a Google search. The social listening manager at Subway has to distinguish everyone talking about the NYC subway from their actual stores or take a brand like Band-Aid that's used as a catch-all for the word "bandage" even though it's technically a brand name. An innovation team might be looking at CBD, which is an acronym that has many different definitions. These are just a few of the caveats and exclusions that social listening professionals work through in their tools to collect and tidy their data, which is half the battle.

Data quality is everything, *garbage in garbage out* definitely applies here, but once you have good quality data you can start digging for insights; likes, dislikes, behaviors, hacks, unexpected mentions, comparisons to alternative brands, PR opportunities, threats to brand equity, viral moments, etc.

Every company in the world is trying to operationalize their social listening, from internal tech stacks, to use cases, to buy-in, to always-on access; it's a race to the insights & analytics finish line.

Daniel Gardner
Head of Social Media Insights and Analytics, North America
Haleon

Figure 8.1   Social Listening and Social Intelligence.

supercharging network development in the surrounding area and updates on service centers and future sales facilities, events and calendar section that provides updates on monthly meetups known as Kilowatts "*n*" Coffee or periodic group drives and picnics, or even testifying before state legislature. The Web site also has a resources page where Tesla owners share their tips on service and ownership. Finally, the site features the Miles High Club, a list of Tesla cars owned by club members with more than 100,000 miles on the odometer.

One of the challenges of managing relationships with customers is understanding who the customers are in the first place. For example, for B2B relationships, it may be a challenge to identify who is the actual decision-making person. And without knowing who your actual customer is, it becomes difficult to listen and to maintain relationships with them. For example, if Google wants a large organization to switch from Apple iPhones to Google Pixel phones, it may be a challenge to identify the individual (or a group of individuals) responsible for making such a decision. The same challenge can also happen in B2C scenarios. For example, Can/Am Hockey company organizes youth hockey tournaments across the United States and Canada. Hockey teams sign up for those tournaments and Can/Am provides lodging, meals, and a tournament schedule to compete. However, these tournaments are extremely expensive, Can/Am Hockey demands high down payments, and athletes and families do not even get information on what hotels they would be staying in or what meals they will be getting until after they pay for the tournament. One would think that Can/Am Hockey is not doing a very good job in building their relationships with their customers. However, closer investigation suggests that perhaps they realize that kids playing hockey are not the decision-makers in this scenario. Even their parents are not the ones who make the decision to join the tournaments. Instead, their customer relationship focus is better aimed on the coaches of those youth teams. Coaches are the ones who make the decision about what tournament to participate in. Thus, such organizations may pretty much ignore the players and their parents as long as they maintain good relationships with coaches. In this scenario, giving free lodging or other perks to the coaches will provide a better return on investment than trying to please the youth athletes or their parents.

Market Segmentation

Over the years, the marketing discipline developed very sophisticated research approaches to understanding who their customers are. The foundation of such customer understanding is *market segmentation*. Market segmentation is the process of dividing all the customers into homogeneous groups based on the criteria relevant to the product, service, or brand. Such groups are known as *market segments*. Indeed, organizations may have customers with different needs and wants who may use even the same type of products differently. There is a reason Toyota sells different types of cars despite their fact that it would have been more efficient to sell only one type. Some Toyota consumers need to haul heavy equipment and Toyota offers them Tacoma and Tundra trucks. Other customers may need extra cabin space for passengers and Toyota offers them Sequoia and Highlander SUVs. And yet other customers may have a need for speed and Toyota offers them Supra and GR86 coupes.

One of the approaches to market segmentation is based on *demographics*. Demographic information includes variables such as age, gender, race and ethnicity, income, education, occupation, and similar. An 18-year-old college student may want to buy a bright red GR86 coupe to make sure he stands out on campus, but may want to switch to a Tacoma truck after graduation as he may get a job that requires driving around with lots of equipment. Yet, even later, he may want to trade that truck in for a Sequoia SUV after he gets married and has children to make sure there is enough cabin space for children and perhaps family dogs.

A more sophisticated approach to market segmentation goes beyond pure descriptive demographics to try to understand the effects of these demographics on consumers' decision-making. This approach is known as *psychographics*. In the psychographic approach, the organization segments their customers based on their psychological traits. While related to demographics, psychographics also accounts for *motivation* and *resources*. The motivation category includes ideals, achievement, and self-expression. As a result, if consumers' motivations are driven by their ideals, they would make decisions based on principles and knowledge. If consumers are motivated by achievement, they would choose the products that could demonstrate their success to others. Finally, if motivations are the result of self-expression, consumers would be more open to risk, social interactions, and physical activities. The consumer resources category includes more than disposable income a person can spend on the organization's products. This category also takes into account the customer's energy level, self-confidence, level of intellect, and even impulsiveness (Table 8.1).

Strategic Business Insights (2020), a global research and consulting services firm, segments all US adult consumers into eight psychographic types, known as VALS™ Types. These types include

1. Innovators
2. Thinkers
3. Believers
4. Achievers
5. Strivers
6. Experiencers
7. Makers
8. Survivors

Yet, another market segmentation approach is called *behavioral segmentation*. Behavioral segmentation, as the name suggests, is based on the behaviors of customers. For example, some customers may be buying Jeep Wranglers as a second vehicle in order to use it for off-roading on the weekends. Another group of customers may be purchasing Wranglers because it snows heavily where they live and they need a reliable car that can handle deep snow. And yet another group of consumers may be buying Wranglers because they look sexy and they use them as a daily vehicle in sunny Florida with no choice for snow and never taking their Jeeps off the road. Understanding these customer behaviors around their product can help Jeep better market to these customer segments and build better long-term relationships with them.

Customer Metrics

Finally, it is important for an organization to closely monitor their successes and failures in building and maintaining relationships with their customers. One of the most common metrics in customer management is *Lifetime Value of a Customer* (LTV). LTV is a summary of all revenues generated by the customers over the years. Of course, the larger the value, the better making the customer more and more valuable for the organization. Another important relational metric is the *Customer Retention Rate* (CRR) that measures how many first-time customers return to buy more of an organization's products and services. While ideally organizations would want to achieve 100% CRR, it is impossible to please everyone. A typical retention rate for the retail organization is about 63%; for banking where costs of switching are higher, the average retention rate reaches 75%; and insurance companies and media companies exceed 80% (Statista, 2022).

Table 8.1 VALS™ Types by Strategic Business Insights.

Innovators	• Are always taking in information (antennas up) • Are confident enough to experiment • Make the highest number of financial transactions • Are skeptical about advertising • Have international exposure • Are future oriented • Are self-directed consumers • Believe science and R&D are credible • Are most receptive to new ideas and technologies • Enjoy the challenge of problem solving • Have the widest variety of interests and activities
Thinkers	• Have "ought" and "should" benchmarks for social conduct • Have a tendency toward analysis paralysis • Plan, research, and consider before they act • Enjoy a historical perspective • Are financially established • Are not influenced by what's hot • Use technology in functional ways • Prefer traditional intellectual pursuits • Buy proven products
Believers	• Believe in basic rights and wrongs to lead a good life • Rely on spirituality and faith to provide inspiration • Want friendly communities • Watch TV and read romance novels to find an escape • Want to know where things stand; have no tolerance for ambiguity • Are not looking to change society • Find advertising a legitimate source of information • Value constancy and stability (can appear to be loyal) • Have strong me-too fashion attitudes
Achievers	• Have a "me first, my family first" attitude • Believe money is the source of authority • Are committed to family and job • Are fully scheduled • Are goal oriented • Are hardworking • Are moderate • Act as anchors of the status quo • Are peer conscious • Are private • Are professional • Value technology that provides a productivity boost
Strivers	• Have revolving employment; high temporary unemployment • Use video and video games as a form of fantasy • Are fun loving • Are imitative • Rely heavily on public transportation • Are the center of low-status street culture • Desire to better their lives but have difficulty in realizing their desire • Wear their wealth
Experienc-ers	• Want everything • Are first in and first out of trend adoption • Go against the current mainstream • Are up on the latest fashions • Love physical activity (are sensation seeking) • See themselves as very sociable • Believe that friends are extremely important • Are spontaneous • Have a heightened sense of visual stimulation

(Continued)

Table 8.1 (Continued)

Makers	• Are distrustful of government
	• Have a strong interest in all things automotive
	• Have strong outdoor interests (hunting and fishing)
	• Believe in sharp gender roles
	• Want to protect what they perceive to be theirs
	• See themselves as straightforward; appear to others as anti-intellectual
	• Want to own land
Survivors	• Are cautious and risk averse
	• Are the oldest consumers
	• Are thrifty
	• Are not concerned about appearing traditional or trendy
	• Take comfort in routine, familiar people, and places
	• Are heavy TV viewers
	• Are loyal to brands and products
	• Spend most of their time alone
	• Are the least likely to use the internet
	• Are the most likely to have a landline-only household

Source: Strategic Business Insights. https://www.strategicbusinessinsights.com/vals/ustypes.shtml

Crisis Management Strategies

In the summer of 2021, customers of the Swedish grocery chain Coop were met with closed doors and a sign informing them that the store cash registers were hacked. As cybercriminals demanded ransom in order to re-enable the cash registers and Coop refusing to pay up, the shutdown lasted for almost a week. Camilla Nothhaft (2022) explained that for many neighborhoods, Coop was the only grocery store, which created significant customer relations issues, especially in thinly populated areas. Coop's strategy focused on being "exceptionally open and transparent" (Nothhaft 2022, p. 3) delivering all the information that the company had internally to their external audiences as well, namely, their customers. Customers appreciated the honesty and were on the side of their local store. In the end, Coop ran a billboard campaign to show appreciation for this support. The billboards read: "How does one get through a global IT attack? Together" (Nothhaft, 2022, p. 6).

The Coop's cybersecurity crisis response can be compared with one of the most famous crises in customer relations, the Tylenol crisis of 1982. In fact, some even claim that the Tylenol crisis set the stage for the whole discipline of crisis communication management (Fearn-Banks, 2011). The crisis developed when several deaths were reported in the Chicago area from ingesting Tylenol Extra Strength. Later, the investigation revealed the cause of death to be cyanide that somehow got into the Tylenol bottles. While Johnson & Johnson did not think it was an industrial accident but rather the work of a madman who tampered with the bottles after they left the factory, the company swiftly issued a recall of the affected batch of Tylenol in the Chicago area. Johnson & Johnson was also honest and forthcoming with the media and the customers. In fact, the company placed ads in the media to inform consumers not to use the affected drugs and exchange them free of charge for safe alternatives. As the company placed its customers first in this crisis, they were able to devise a solution to restore their trust in the product's safety. Instead of simply blaming a madman for poisoning and moving on to letting law enforcement deal with the issue, Johnson & Johnson invested efforts into redesigning their packaging to make sure customers knew that the products they were buying had not been tampered with. Thanks to that crisis response, today customers around the world have medicine bottles sealed securely. In fact, it took just 10 weeks for Johnson & Johnson to start selling Tylenol in tamper-proof and triple-sealed containers. The organization was able to turn the crisis into opportunity and because of its decisive actions and prioritizing its customers Johnson & Johnson was able to maintain its sales despite the seven reported deaths the incident had caused.

The previous two examples talk about crises caused by external forces attacking the organization. Sometimes, however, the organization itself and even its marketing efforts themselves can lead to a crisis instead of building or maintaining relationships with customers. For example, *Aqua Teen Hunger Force Colon Movie Film for Theaters'* promotional campaign placed electronic placards measuring 1 by 1.5 ft that contained a battery and wiring to display characters from the movie in order to entertain people and encourage them to go to movie theaters to watch Aqua Teen. The end result, however, was quite different. Many passers-by called the police after seeing boxes with wires placed around cities. In fact, Boston police dispatched a bomb squad as the initial investigation concluded that the device resembled an improvised explosive device. After the boxes were discovered to be just marketing devices, Turner Broadcasting and its marketing agency responsible for the stunt were absolved of any criminal wrongdoing but agreed to pay $1 million to the Boston Police Department and $1 million to the Department of Homeland Security. The movie itself, despite (or thanks to) the stunt, was a box office success generating over $3 million during its opening weekend on a modest $750,000 budget (Blakeman, 2009).

Future Proofing Your Strategies

Today and in the future, organizations would need to continue building and maintaining relationships with their customers. As we learned in the chapter, such relationships rely on knowing and understanding the organization's customers. Yet, customers and their needs and wants are not stable – they change and this requires organizations to continuously adjust to their changing customer base. For example, Victoria's Secret's annual fashion show was the premier television event for years, drawing up to 10 million viewers. Victoria's Secret Angels showcased the company's exclusive lingerie in the event that featured performances by leading musicians and attendance by top celebrities. Yet, in 2019 the show was canceled – the viewership was significantly down and sales of Victoria's Secret products were declining as well. Victoria's Secret customer expectations have changed – they demanded a shift from unrealistic body ideals and women's objectification to more inclusive events and product selections. Failure to include plus-size and transgender models was in contrast to customers' evolving demands focused on diversity, equity, and inclusion (DEI). This divide shattered the brand connection between the organization and its customers (Laskin & Kresic, 2021).

Over the years, organizations started embracing the concept of *corporate social responsibility* (CSR) as customers and other publics demanded organizations take into account more than profits and actually focus on doing what is good for society (Frederick, 1960; Laskin & Nesova, 2022). Today, the idea of CSR evolved into three distinct duties – *environmental sustainability, social responsibility*, and *corporate governance* – collectively known as ESG (Laskin, 2022). Study after study shows that consumers are willing to reward organizations that practice ESG and punish those that do not (Cha et al., 2016; Golob & Podnar, 2019; Laskin, 2018; Yu, 2009).

While CSR and ESG focus on the way organizations perform in their industries, customers' expectations today are growing even outside of the organization's industries. In fact, a growing effect on consumers and their purchase decisions is being exhibited by Corporate Social Advocacy (CSA). In CSA, an organization places itself on one side in a controversial societal issue that can be completely unrelated to what the company is doing. Recent examples of CSA include Dick's Sporting Goods' support for gun reform, Nike's stance on racism, or Chik-fil-A's promotion of a Christian religion (Figure 8.2).

CSA is based on the idea that customers like to shop and support the brands that share the same values as them. When a customer perceives organizations to be on the same side of a controversial issue, they develop a close, almost personal, bond with the organization. As a result, CSA can have a direct effect on customers' behavior (Dodd & Supa, 2014; Kim et al., 2023; Overton et al., 2020). At the same time, as CSA by definition involves controversial issues, it can also alienate some of the organization's customers and even lead to product boycotts (Afego & Alagidede, 2021; Rim et al., 2020). Especially in the United States, in a society characterized by growing polarization on a variety of issues, taking a CSA stand almost always carries risks as well as benefits. For example, some Nike customers took it to social media to burn Nike products on camera and to announce the boycott of the brand, with #NikeBoycott becoming one of the top trending topics on Twitter. Bud Light was also criticized by some of its customers

← **Tweet**

KidRock ✓
@KidRock

⋯

11:17 PM · Apr 3, 2023 · **52.8M** Views

Figure 8.2 Kid Rock Records a Video Shooting at Cases of Bud Light. *Source:* Kid Rock on Twitter, Inc.; https://Twitter, Inc.com/KidRock/status/1643090302410936323/ Last accessed August 04, 2023.

for featuring a transgender person in its April 2023 commercial. In fact, Kid Rock recorded a video of himself shooting at cases of Bud Light in response to the commercial. Kid Rock's video received over 50 million views and over 200,000 likes on Twitter alone. Early data indicate that sales of Bud Light in the United States declined with the largest decline recorded in the middle of the country (29% sales decline in the Rocky Mountain states). In addition, several bars and restaurants, including Kid Rock's steakhouse, removed Bud Light from their shelves (James, 2023).

Chapter Summary

Customers and subscribers are those who use the organization's products and services and in return provide the cash flow organizations need to operate. B2B organizations focus on business customers and subscribers, and B2C focus on retail consumers; in addition, many organizations employ both B2B and B2C strategies. The discipline that studies customer relations is marketing, which also emphasizes the need for relational marketing as opposed to transaction marketing. A key part of customer relationships is two-way communication where organizations listen to their customers and build intelligence based on their listening. Part of such intelligence is developing a better understanding of the organization's customers by placing groups of customers into market segments. Such a process of market segmentation can be based on demographics, psychographics, and behavior, or a combination of the three. Organizations must also stay abreast of changes among their customers and adjust to shifting societal expectations related to environmental, social, and governance issues as customers can reward or punish brands that do not conform to societal demands. Some organizations become active advocates for various social issues through CSA initiatives and try to lead their customers proactively rather than reactively responding to their demands.

Five Key Terms to Remember

Bussines-2-Business
Business-2-Consumer
Relationship Marketing
Customer Relationship Management
Market Segmentation

Discussion Questions and Activities

1 Discuss different strategies for relationship management in the B2B and B2C contexts. Provide examples of B2B and B2C companies.
2 Explain different approaches to market segmentation. Discuss their pluses and minuses.
3 Identify some recent examples of Corporate Social Advocacy. Discuss the reasons why the organization made the CSA stance that they did. What potential types of customers can their CSA actions attract or alienate?
4 Analyze different ways organizations can listen to their customers. Identify some good and bad examples of organizational listening from your experience and how the chance to provide feedback to the organization made you feel.

5 Think about a product or service you use (car, cell provider, university, etc.). In your opinion, does the organization behind this product or service perform well in their relationship-management efforts with you? What would you recommend to the organization to do differently?

How to Learn More

Blakeman, R. (2009). *The bare bones: Introduction to integrated marketing communication.* Rowman & Littlefield.

Fearn-Banks, K. (2011). *Crisis communications: A casebook approach*, (4th ed.). Routledge.

Kotler, P., & Armstrong, G. (2021). *Principles of marketing*, (18th ed.). Pearson.

Case Study

Victoria's Secret: Is the Secret Out?

Figure 8.3 *Source:* WestportWiki / Wikimedia Commons /

1. Summary of the Case

Victoria's Secret is a lingerie and beauty brand that from a single store in Ohio grew to over 350 stores within the United States with their annual sales approaching a billion US dollars by the 1990s. More recently, however, the company experienced a decline in sales, share price, and considerable criticism from its own customers and other publics. Its historical focus on female beauty as expressed by its Angels, the most exclusive models imaginable, put it in contrast with the societal expectations of inclusivity. The company became a representation of misogyny. As a result, Victoria's Secret, failing to expand their market share and increase revenues due to those shifting consumer trends and social changes, eliminated its Angels program and launched a new program called the "VS Collective" in the summer of 2021 to appeal to a broader audience and in an effort to adapt to their changing environment. As a result, this case highlights the importance of knowing and understanding customers for organizational reputation.

2. Organization's Background and Historical Development

Victoria's Secret is a "specialty retailer of modern, fashion-inspired collections including signature bras, panties, lingerie, casual sleepwear, athleisure and swim, as well as award-winning prestige fragrances and body care" (Victoria's Secret, 2023). The company started in 1963 as a single store, The Limited, located in Ohio's Kingsdale Shopping Center. The name The Limited referred to the limited selection of products in the store that focused only on young female clientele. Eventually, a small family store grew into a large corporation, Limited Brands and later L Brands. Among L Brands were Victoria's Secret, Bath & Body Works, Lane Bryant, Lerner, and Abercrombie & Fitch. However, on August 3, 2022, Victoria's Secret became an independent publicly traded corporation with its shares trading on the New York Stock Exchange under the symbol VSCO.

The most famous Victoria's Secret campaign over the years was the promotion of its 1997 underwear collection "Angels." Five models were selected to be the original angels – Helena Christensen, Karen Mulder, Daniela Peštová, Stephanie Seymour, and Tyra Banks. While Victoria's Secret brand employed many models to promote its products, only a select few were recognized as Angels. Angels were the most exclusive supermodels, and an Angel title became a recognition of extraordinary beauty and success. Victoria's Secret Angels were among the highest-paid models in the world in exchange for becoming full-time Victoria's Secret brand ambassadors. One of the most successful angels, Gisele Bündchen, earned $30.5 million in 2018 alone. The Angels were often viewed as unattainable beauty standards with the company itself referring to them as women with the perfect body.

3. Operational Environment and Main Publics

In 2014, Victoria's Secret launched their, "I Love My Body," campaign to promote their new bra styles in the *Body by Victoria* collection. However, their efforts were highly criticized in the media and by their own customers for portraying an unrealistic standard of beauty for women. The company used their Angels to model the new collection and plastered their images across a variety of marketing platforms. Victoria's Secret came under fire for promoting that the "perfect body" was that of a supermodel. They were viciously chastised for sending out a damaging message and playing on women's insecurities. "There is a line between aspiration and thinspiration, and this campaign clearly oversteps the mark ... As for their use of the word 'perfect,' it's not only offensive to the 99.9% of the female population who don't share the models' 'perfect' proportions, it's also deeply irresponsible, if not downright cruel" (Peterson, 2014).

To boost its sales, the company sought to expand its product line. Victoria's Secret announced the launch of the "VSX Very Sexy Sport Collection," offering a variety of workout gear. The campaign was marketed to inspire women to "... feel like they can get a runway body" (Victoria's Secret, 2011). The launch of this collection arose on the heels of the style trend dubbed as "athleisure" – clothing that can be worn for athletic activities as well as in a day-to-day setting.

(Continued)

Case Study   (Continued)

The company also launched their apparel-focused line, "PINK," which targeted high school and college-aged women. PINK was received well by consumers, quickly becoming a staple of young women's wardrobes. The subsidiary of Victoria's Secret primarily offers loungewear apparel as well as bras and panties that cater toward younger consumers. PINK introduced a younger audience to the company, creating a larger customer base.

Victoria's Secret has established a strong media presence through their digital campaigns, retail website, and social media platforms. However, one marketing strategy that catapulted Victoria's Secret's reputation as a retailer and created a name for themselves in the modeling and television industries is their iconic annual Victoria's Secret Fashion Show. This promotional event showcased the company's lingerie in a high-profile setting. The first show was in 1995, but it was not until 1999 that the event was presented as a webcast and in 2001 when it was broadcast by ABC. The fashion show featured the company's top contracted models, the Angels. The event garnered the attention of millions of viewers, peaking its viewership in 2001 at 12.4 million (Hanbury & Tayeb, 2021). The Victoria's Secret Fashion Show enabled the company to permeate into the media industry while concurrently promoting their products and dominating retailer commerce. Among the most beautiful models wearing the most beautiful lingerie, the hottest musical acts were performed during the show, including Taylor Swift, Harry Styles, Kanye West, Shawn Mendes, Rita Ora, and many more. The show also attracted celebrities from around the world (Schnurr, 2018).

However, in recent years the viewership of the fashion show experienced significant declines until in 2019 the show was canceled altogether. Along with the declining viewership, the company experienced declining sales as well. At the same time, Victoria's Secret competitors were doing well. Among them were Aerie and Savage X Fenty that prioritized body inclusivity by offering a range of sizes in their products, indicating that consumer demand had shifted, forcing Victoria's Secret to adjust its strategy. The CEO of Victoria's Secret, Martin Waters, concluded that the company must move away "from what men want to what women want" (Hanbury & Tayeb, 2021, p. 4). This became the focus of the company's repositioning strategy.

First step – the elimination of Victoria's Secret Angels programs – "It's about including most women rather than excluding most women and being grounded in real life, rather than mostly unattainable" (Hanbury & Tayeb, 2021, p. 5). To replace the Angels, Victoria's Secret launched a new program, *The Collective*, to focus the brand on DEI and celebrating women's empowerment. Instead of Angels, The Collective has Partners: "These extraordinary partners, with their unique backgrounds, interests, and passions will collaborate with us to create revolutionary product collections, compelling and inspiring content, new internal associate programs and rally support for causes vital to women" (Victoria's Secret & Co., 2022a). The new goals include the following: (1) Create revolutionary product collections, (2) create compelling and inspiring content, (3) develop new internal associate programs such as Inclusion Resource Groups with a top of line focus on DEI, and (4) rally support for causes vital to women.

The launch of the VS Collective is just one of many steps of the Victoria's Secret rebranding that focuses on becoming a more inclusive, empowered, and feminist brand. Former Victoria's Secret Angels and supermodels, Heidi Klum and Tyra Banks, have recently spoken out about their support for the rebranding efforts, stating that it is, "about time," and celebrating the new role models (Flanagan, 2021).

4. The Issue Development

November 2017: Victoria's Secret hosts their annual Victoria's Secret Fashion Show. "The show had its lowest ratings so far at just under 5 million viewers, down 32% from the previous year" (Jennings, 2018).

November 2018: Victoria's Secret hosts their annual Victoria's Secret Fashion Show. The show experiences a viewership of only 3.3 million.

May 2019: L'Brands, Victoria's Secret's parent company, announces on a quarterly earnings call that they are canceling the annual Fashion Show due to declining viewership, deteriorating business performance, and external pressures including accusations of misogyny, hyper-sexualization, and lack of inclusivity. "The brand's hypersexualized portrayal of women doesn't appear to resonate with modern customers as strongly as it once did. Shoppers today tend to look for inclusive sizing, comfort, and a brand identity rooted in female empowerment" (Nguyen, 2019).

June 16, 2021: Victoria's Secret announces via social media they are launching "The VS Collective" as their new partnership platform to replace the previous Angels program.

June 2021: Founding members announced with a focus on their accomplishments. This includes

- Adut Akech – Refugee, Wellness Supporter, Model
- Amanda De Cadenet – Journalist, Photographer, Girlgaze Founder & Equality Advocate
- Bella Hadid – Advocate, Entrepreneur, Model
- Eileen Gu – World Champion Free Skier, Youth & Women's Sports Advocate, Model
- Hailey Bieber – Model & Advocate
- Megan Rapinoe – LGBTQIA+ Activist, Pay Equity Crusader, Professional Soccer Player
- Naomi Osaka – Athlete, Equality Advocate, Designer, Entrepreneur
- Paloma Elsesser – Body Advocate, Community Creator, Model
- Priyanka Chopra Jonas – Actor, Producer, Entrepreneur
- Valentina Sampaio – LGBTQIA+ Activist, Actor, Model

Victoria's Secret's rebranding is still a work in progress but its focus is clear – to become a more inclusive brand. New Partners that replaced Angels seem to champion women's rights and equality over sexuality. Critics, however, point to the fact that this attempt at rebranding came only after Victoria's Secret's decrease in sales forced the company to act: "The brand has been criticized for selling lingerie for the male gaze rather than for the female body. It has been scrutinized for its misogynistic viewpoint of women. It failed to keep up with the times and remained

(Continued)

Case Study   (Continued)

in the padded, push-up period when the rest of the world has already moved on" (Helena, 2022). It remains to be seen whether "better late than never" will prove true in this case. It is also important to consider the reach and influence of Victoria's Secret, and a campaign championing women and inclusiveness from a company with this much reach may be quite impactful.

The company products are changing as well. The company is often accused of selling products for "the male gaze rather than for the female body" (Helena, 2022). Victoria's Secret has been hesitant to amend their offerings in the past, but now it introduced sizes above a large and extra-large and announced their first plus-size models (Prinzivalli, 2019). The company also announced that it would start selling maternity bras for the first time. Victoria's Secret also plans to display curvy mannequins in its stores and expand representation on its website to include a variety of body types modeling its products (La Jeunesse, 2021).

5. What Is Next?

Now the leadership of Victoria's Secret is left wondering, will this be enough to save the company and return it to growth? From share price almost reaching $75 in August 2021, the price continuously declined to under $25 in May 2023 – eliminating two-thirds of the Victoria's Secret valuation, despite showing profitability in the last two years. Martin Waters, CEO of Victoria's Secret, and other executives, have a long road ahead of them to maintain relationships with their traditional customers and also to build relationships with new customers that the organization so desperately needs. Will the new approach to the issues of DEI be enough to align the brand with the current societal expectations to entice new customers to the brand without losing the Victoria's Secret and PINK desirability for their traditional shoppers? While beauty may have many definitions, success on the financial bottom line has only one....

References

Afego, P. N., & Alagidede, I. P. (2021). What does corporate social advocacy signal/ evidence from boycott participation decision. *Journal of Capital Market Studies*, *5*(1), 49–68.

American Marketing Association (2017). Definition of marketing. https://www.ama.org/ the-definition-of-marketing-what-is-marketing/

Apple (2023). Apple at work. https://www.apple.com/business

Blakeman, R. (2009). *The bare bones: Introduction to integrated marketing communication*. Rowman & Littlefield.

Cha, M., Yi, Y., & Bagozzi, R. P. (2016). Effects of customer participation in corporate social responsibility (CSR) programs on the CSR-brand fit and brand loyalty. *Cornell Hospitality Quarterly*, *57*(3), 235–249.

Clayton, J. (2020). Apple to pay $113m to settle iPhone 'batterygate.' *BBC* (19 November). https://www.bbc.com/news/technology-549996601?xtor=AL-72-%5Bpartner%5D-%5Bbbc. news.twitter%5D-%5Bheadline%5D-%5Bnews%5D-%5Bbizdev%5D-%5Bisapi%5D&at_

campaign=64&at_medium=custom7&at_custom1=%5Bpost+type%5D&at_
custom3=%40BBCNews&at_custom4=F94F611E-2A07-11EB-8042-A0A74744363C&
at_custom2=twitter

Dodd, M. D., & Supa, D. W. (2014). Conceptualizing and measuring "corporate social advocacy" communication: Examining the impact on corporate financial performance. *The Public Relations Journal*, *8*(3), 2–23.

Fearn-Banks, K. (2011). *Crisis communications: A casebook approach*, (4th ed.). Routledge.

Flanagan, H. (2021). Heidi Klum says it's "good" that Victoria's Secret is rebranding: "about time." *People* (13 July). https://people.com/style/heidi-klum-talks-victorias-secret-rebranding/

Frederick, W. C. (1960). The growing concern over business responsibility. *California Management Review*, *2*(4), 54–61.

Golob, U., & Podnar, K. (2019). Researching CSR and brands in the here and now: An integrative perspective. *Journal of Brand Management*, *26*(1), 1–8.

Hanbury, M., & Tayeb, Z. (2021). Victoria's Secret ditched its Angels after a successful decades-long partnership. Take a closer look at how the concept was born — and why the lingerie chain thinks Angels are no longer relevant. *Insider* (27 June). https://www.businessinsider.com/victorias-secret-angels-rise-history-iconic-models-photos-2021-6

Helena, S. (2022). Why the new era of Victoria's Secret is just as problematic as the previous. *Medium* (6 January). https://medium.com/fearless-she-wrote/why-the-new-era-of-victorias-secret-is-just-as-problematic-as-the-previous-e932aff4832a

James, E. (2023). Bud Light's hangover from hell. *Daily Mail* (10 May). www.dailymail.co.uk/news/article-12068311/Bud-Light-sales-plunged-region-dropping-29-heartlands.html

Jennings, R. (2018). Victoria's Secret fashion show 2018: History and controversies. *Vox* (3 December). https://www.vox.com/the-goods/2018/11/8/18068148/victorias-secret-fashion-show-2018-history-controversy

Kim, J. K., Overton, H., Alharbi, K., Carter, J., & Bhalla, N. (2023). Examining the determinants of consumer support for corporate social advocacy. *Corporate Communications: An International Journal*, *28*(3), 451–468.

La Jeunesse, M. (2021). Unpacking the Victoria's Secret rebrand. *Teen Vogue* (29 December). https://www.teenvogue.com/story/unpacking-the-victorias-secret-rebrand

Laskin, A. V. (2022). *Investor relations and financial communication: Creating value Through trust and understanding*. Malden, MA: Wiley-Blackwell.

Laskin, A. V. (2018). The third-person effects in the investment decision making: A case of corporate social responsibility. *Corporate Communications: An International Journal*, *23*(3), 456–468.

Laskin, A. V., & Kresic, K. M. (2021). Inclusion as component of CSR and a brand connection strategy. In D. Pompper, Ed., *Public relations for social responsibility: Affirming DEI commitment with action*. Bingley: Emerald Publishing.

Laskin, A. V., & Nesova, N. M. (2022). The language of optimism in corporate sustainability reports: A computerized content analysis. *Business and Professional Communication Quarterly*, *85*(1), 80–98. https://doi.org/10.1177/23294906211065507

Luca, M. (2016). Reviews, reputation, and revenue: the case of Yelp.com. Harvard Business School Working Paper 12-016. https://blog.reputationx.com/are-online-reviews-reliable#:~:text=How%20important%20are%20Yelp%20reviews,percent%20increase%20in%20business%20revenue

Nguyen, T. (2019). The Victoria's Secret 2019 fashion show has been canceled. *Vox* (22 November). https://www.vox.com/the-goods/2019/11/22/20978041/victorias-secret-fashion-show-canceled

Nothhaft, C. (2022). Crisis is the new normal. *EUPRERA* (30 March). https://euprera.org/2022/03/30/crisis-is-the-new-normal/

Overton, H., Choi, M., Weatherred, J. L., & Zhang, N. (2020). Testing the viability of emotions and issue involvement as predictors of CSA response behaviors. *Journal of Applied Communication Research*, *48*(6), 695–713.

Peterson, H. (2014). Victoria's Secret sparks outrage with "perfect body" campaign. *Insider* (31 October). https://www.businessinsider.com/victorias-secret-perfect-body-campaign-2014-10?international=true&r=US&IR=T

Prinzivalli, L. (2019). Victoria's Secret announces first campaign with plus-size model. *Allure* (9 October). https://www.allure.com/story/victorias-secret-plus-size-model

Rim, H., Lee, Y., & Yoo, S. (2020). Polarized public opinion responding to corporate social advocacy: Social network analysis of boycotters and advocators. *Public Relations Review*, *46*(2), 101869.

Schnurr, S. (2018). These Victoria's Secret fashion show musical guests will have all the hits covered. *E News* (1 November). https://www.eonline.com/news/982630/these-victoria-s-secret-fashion-show-musical-guests-will-have-all-the-hits-covered

Statista (2022). Customer retention rate of business worldwide in 2018, by industry. *Statista* (6 July). https://www.statista.com/statistics/1041645/customer-retention-rates-by-industry-worldwide/

Strategic Business Insights (2020). U.S. Framework and VALS types. https://www.strategicbusinessinsights.com/vals/ustypes.shtml

Tesla (2023). Tesla owners club directory. https://engage.tesla.com/pages/clubs

Victoria's Secret (2011). Victoria's Secret announces launch of VSX Sexy Sport. Cision. https://www.prnewswire.com/news-releases/victorias-secret-announces-launch-of-vsx-sexy-sport-128389228.html

Victoria's Secret & Co. (2022a). VS collective. Victoria's Secret collective. https://www.victoriassecret.com/ca/thevscollective

Victoria's Secret (2023). About us. https://www.victoriassecretandco.com/our-company/about-us

Wood, C. (2023). How Haleon built social media intelligence in-house. *MarTech* (7 March). https://martech.org/how-haleon-built-social-media-intelligence-in-house/

Yu, X. (2009). From passive beneficiary to active stakeholder: Workers' participation in CSR movement against labor abuses. *Journal of Business Ethics*, *87*(S1), 233–249.

9

Government and Regulators: Playing by the Rules

LEARNING OBJECTIVES

1. *After reading this chapter, students will be able to define who governments and regulators are as the organizational public.*
2. *After reading this chapter, students will be able to understand the importance of managing relationships with governments and regulators.*
3. *After reading this chapter, students will be able to develop strategic plans for building and maintaining relationships with governments and regulators to enhance organizational reputation.*

Define the Public

For many organizations, an act by the government may lead to growth in profits or put it out of existence completely. As a result, building and maintaining relationships with the government is of utmost priority. However, when people say the government, they may actually refer to a variety of different governmental, quasigovernmental, intergovernmental, and supranational entities.

In most countries, governments exist at different levels. There may be *federal* government, *state* government, *city* government, and even smaller levels of *local* governments like district or municipal governments. In addition, the governmental organizations may also be classified based on their functions. For example, the United States of America has three branches of government: *executive, judicial,* and *legislative.* The United States Constitution divides the government into these three branches to ensure that no one person and no one entity can accumulate absolute power – instead, the power is split between three branches, thus introducing the system of *checks and balances.* Such checks and balances are based on the ability of different branches to affect each other's work. This is especially noticeable during the appointment of the Justices on the Supreme Court. The Supreme Court is part of the judicial branch, but its justices are nominated by the US President, part of the executive branch. The president's nominations, however, must be approved by the Senate, part of the legislative branch.

Organizational Reputation Management: A Strategic Public Relations Perspective,
First Edition. Alexander V. Laskin.
© 2024 John Wiley & Sons, Inc. Published 2024 by John Wiley & Sons, Inc.

All of the above examples represent the federal level in the United States. Different US states also have their executive, judicial, and legislative branches. For example, at the state level, the state of Connecticut has a legislative branch known as the General Assembly, which consists of two chambers: State Senate and State House of Representatives. The state of Connecticut legislative branch consists of the State Supreme Court, Superior Court, Appellate Court, and Probate Court. Finally, the executive branch is headed by the State Governor and includes a long list of various departments, commissions, and offices, such as the Department of Energy and Environmental Protection, the Commission on Human Rights and Opportunities, and the Office of Governmental Accountability (Figure 9.1).

Within the US federal regulations and within the state of CT state regulations, various municipalities also operate with their own governments. For example, the state of CT has 169 different cities and towns. One of these is the town of Cheshire. The town has its own executive branch headed by the Town Manager. The executive branch is responsible for town operations and resident services. The executive branch consists of various departments – police, animal control, fire department, recreation, public works, and so on. But, in addition to the executive branch, the town also has the Town Council, an elected legislative body for the town. The full chart of the government structure of the town of Cheshire shows many commissions, committees, and boards that ensure the town's operation and provide an opportunity for residents' interests to be taken into account when making decisions.

With so many levels of government, it is also necessary for cooperation within the government. In other words, governmental organizations need to build and maintain relationships with other governmental organizations as well. In fact, it is quite common to have governmental projects involving different levels of governments at the

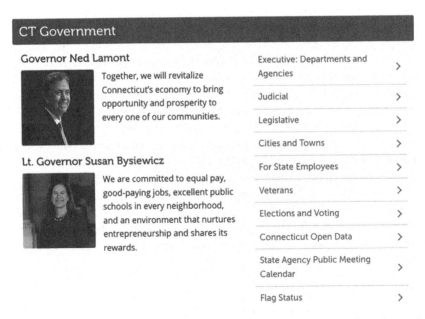

Figure 9.1 Government of the State of Connecticut. *Source:* Connecticut / https://portal.ct.gov/ last accessed August 04, 2023.

same time, sometimes even all three – federal, state, and local – in order to address shared challenges or implement joint initiatives. One of many examples of such collaborations is the National Dam Safety Program in the United States. Dams are part of the crucial infrastructure element, failure of which could lead to catastrophic events at the national level. As a result, Federal Emergency Management Agency (FEMA), a federal-level agency, works in cooperation with various agencies at state levels to ensure the safety of dams across the country; for example, Connecticut's Department of Energy and Environmental Protection is responsible for the safety of dams in the state of Connecticut (Figure 9.2).

In addition to government agencies, there are also *quasigovernment* agencies. These are entities that provide a governmental function but are organized independently of the government. One of the key reasons for such a structure is the need to avoid having their decisions be approved by the federal government, especially when it comes to the decisions that may affect that federal government directly. For example, the central bank of the United States is known as the *Federal Reserve System*. The main function of the Federal Reserve System is "conducting the nation's monetary policy, supervising and regulating banking organizations, and providing financial services to financial institutions and the government" (Federal Reserve, n.d., p. 1). But despite its governmental function, the system is organized into 12 regional banks that issue shares of stock similar to corporations, and these shares are owned by the member banks and even earn dividends for the members.

Finally, there are governmental entities that exceed the level of any one country – they are known as *supranational* entities. One of the examples of such supranational entity is the European Union (EU). EU member nations sacrifice some of their country's autonomy when it comes to legislative, judicial, and executive powers to the supranational EU – most noticeably, monetary policy with 20 EU countries sharing

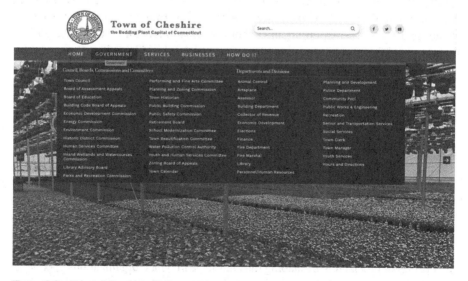

Figure 9.2   Town of Cheshire, CT Government Structure. *Source:* Intrado corporation / https://www.cheshirect.org/ last accessed August 04, 2023.

the common currency of Euro (Archick, 2023). Of course, for organizations operating within the EU borders, building and maintaining relationships with the supranational EU also becomes an important priority. While some supranational entities provide a direct opportunity for the people affected to voice their opinions and elect representatives, most of them do not provide an election mechanism, leaving people affected by their decisions without direct representation. This may lead to a negative image of such supranational among the publics affected.

Value of the Relationship

Whatever country and type of government is involved, it is important for organizations to ensure they have strong relationships with them. A single legislature may be life-changing for the organization. For example, the country of Norway proposed a plan to ban sales of all new gas-powered cars in the country by 2025. Just imagine how impactful this regulation is for many organizations and people working for them. It would, of course, affect the gas car manufacturers – the organizations that make and sell gas-powered cars. It will also affect local dealership networks in the country: if they will not be able to sell these cars after 2025, they may be forced to shut down. Then, all the car repair shops and mechanics in the country who work on gas-powered cars would either face a decline in business, as there would be less and less gas-powered cars on the roads, or would have to relearn how to service electric cars that may require less service or different types of service. Finally, the networks of gas stations throughout the country will no doubt be affected by the switch from gas cars to electric cars.

On the other hand, a government action may lead to a profit boom. When the United States and other countries introduced the vaccine requirement in a fight against the COVID-19 global pandemic, many vaccine manufacturers registered record sales and profits. Pfizer alone reported $3.5 billion in revenues from its vaccine sales just in the first three months of 2021 after its vaccine received government approval in the United States and mass vaccination began (Robbins & Goodman, 2021). Later, the government around the world issued several vaccine mandates and introduced vaccine passports, which basically made it impossible to travel, attend public events, or even work without getting a vaccine – once again, helping vaccine manufacturers record higher revenues.

Many of the regulations do not seem as life-altering, but nevertheless can have a significant impact on various organizations. A small change in the tax code can mean less or more donations to the non-profit organization, as many non-profits in the United States discovered during the tax reform under President Trump. Or a change in a minimum wage regulation may affect the ability of local restaurants to hire the staff they need as the National Restaurant Association fears would be the case in the state of CT if the state's new proposal specifically targeting the pay of restaurants' wait staff passes (Pazniokas, 2023).

As a result, the dynamic interaction between corporations, non-profits, and governments plays a crucial role in shaping the landscape in which organizations operate. In an era of increasing globalization and interdependence, close relations between these entities have become imperative.

Maintaining and Building Reputation through Relationship Management Strategies

As discussed before, governments possess the authority to establish and enforce policies and regulations such as taxation, labor laws, environmental regulations, and consumer protection measures. Failure to comply with these regulations can result in legal consequences, financial penalties, and damage to a corporation's reputation. Collaborative engagement with governments enables organizations to navigate this regulatory landscape effectively. With the increase in globalization, it is also important to note that governments hold the power to negotiate trade agreements, resolve trade disputes, and open doors to foreign markets. By building close relations, organizations can leverage government networks to expand their market reach, access international opportunities, and foster favorable trade conditions. Governments can also support corporations in addressing geopolitical challenges and navigating international business complexities.

Lobbying

For many organizations, proactive engagement with the government is also important. In other words, it is not sufficient to follow regulations and stay abreast of regulatory changes, but it is also important to contribute to policy development and influence future policy changes to the benefit of the organization. Thus, one of the key functions of government relations is *lobbying*. Lobbying is usually defined as "the stimulation and transmission of a communication, by someone other than a citizen acting on his own behalf, directed to a governmental decision-maker with the hope of influencing his decision" (Milbrath, 1963, p. 8). Lobbying spending exceeds $4 billion a year in the United States (Statista, 2023). Kurt Wise, who studies lobbying in the United States, noted that lobbying is based on relationships, and one of the key relationship management strategies lobbyists use is openness – without being truthful it is impossible to maintain the trust in the relationship (2007) (Figure 9.3).

Lobbying in the United States has a rich historical tradition. In fact, the right to petition governments is part of the US Constitution's First Amendment. US government officials also benefit from lobbying efforts as they become better informed about the needs and wants of their constituents. Association of Government Relations Professionals (AGRP), the leading professional association of lobbyists, explains that it is a misconception that only large corporations employ lobbyists to push their agendas through the legislature. Instead, lobbying is used by such organizations as non-profit animal rights advocate Humane Society of the United States, the environmental organization League of Conservation Voters, and even local apple growers represented by U.S. Apple, the voice of the apple industry. AGRP provides a framework for lobbying:

1. Researching and analyzing legislation or regulatory proposals;
2. Monitoring and reporting on developments;
3. Attending congressional or regulatory hearings;
4. Working with coalitions interested in the same issues;
5. Educating government officials but also employees and corporate officers as to the implications of various changes.

(AGRP, 2023, p. 1)

Figure 9.3 The United States Bill of Rights. *Source:* National Archives / https://www.archives.gov/milestone-documents/bill-of-rights / last accessed under August 04, 2023.

In addition to the official lobbying by registered lobbyists, lobbying or any efforts to influence governments may happen informally. It may be as simple as a CEO of a corporation chatting with a senator at a reception or be as convoluted as helping a government representative's child get a job at a company. For example, a billionaire real estate developer, Harlan Crow, reportedly purchased a house for the mother of the US Supreme Court Justice Clarence Thomas, which prompted serious discussions in Congress of whether this constitutes an act of bribery (*Wall Street Journal*, 2023). Of course, different countries around the world have different regulations when it comes to lobbying and providing presents to government officials. It is important for organizations to operate within the legal frameworks of the countries they operate in and remain true to the organization's ethical principles as well.

Public–Private Partnerships

Sometimes, organizations help governments directly and create what is known as Public–Private Partnerships (PPPs). These PPPs focus on addressing immediate needs of the people, implementing societal challenges, developing infrastructure projects, and even delivering public services. PPP allows various organizations to contribute expertise, resources, and innovation to such initiatives, fostering social responsibility, enhancing reputation, and creating new opportunities. Some PPP projects help governments provide electricity, build roads, or offer housing. For example, if government deems that a road is necessary but has no money to build and/or maintain the road, it may engage in a PPP. Under such an agreement, a private company and the government would create a company, Special Purpose Vehicle (SPV). The SPV company would build the road using private funds but rely on government's infrastructure plans and permits and then operate the road as a toll road for a certain amount of time, perhaps 30 years. During those years, the money from road users will repay the investment the private company made in the SPV; after 30 years, the road will become government property and will become free or stay as a toll road but with profits going to the government now. In general, corporations get to expand their business and serve the local community by providing a vital service such as transportation. This is beneficial for the organization's reputation and its financial bottom line.

The process of transferring assets into PPP is known as *privatization* because the assets became private property in the process, temporarily or indefinitely. According to the World Bank (2022), there are many types of PPP arrangements around the world: BOT (Build-Operate-Transfer), such as the example above where the private company builds the road, SPV operates it, and then after some time the road is transferred to the government; BTO (Build-Transfer-Operate); BOOT (Build-Own-Operate-Transfer); DBFOM (Design-Build-Finance-Operate-Maintain); DBFO (Design-Build-Finance-Operate); DCMF (Design-Construct-Manage-Finance); ROT (Rehabilitate-Operate-Transfer); PFI (Private Finance Initiative); Concession; Franchise; Affermage; and Management Contracts, when the government retains full ownership but passes day-to-day operations to a private entity.

Non-Profit Organizations and Governments

While PPPs are typically partnerships between for-profit organizations and governments, non-profit organizations help governments as well. For example, after the tornado touched down in the town of Laguna Heights in Texas on May 13, 2023, leaving one person dead and at least 10 injured and causing significant damage to the town's infrastructure, one of the first organizations on the scene was the American Red Cross, providing resources to the local government, helping people affected by the tornado, and even offering mental health services, if needed (Morales, 2023).

Countless non-profit organizations work around the world, often in the most dangerous places like Ukraine, Syria, Somalia, and Venezuela, helping various governments take care of their residents. World Central Kitchen (WCK) is a non-profit organization that strives to provide "meals in response to humanitarian, climate, and community crises" (2022, p. 1), helping after an earthquake in Haiti, hurricane in Puerto Rico, tornadoes in Kentucky, border crisis between the United States and Mexico, and so on. After devastating earthquakes in Turkey and Syria in February 2023, WCK reported serving over 20 million meals in the affected regions. WCK sees its mission as more than just providing calories to the hungry, the organization relies on local food providers and uses locals to help with cooking and deliveries, thus helping local economies recover faster and rebuild the sense of community. The founder of WCK, Jose

Andres, explains: "You see, food relief is not just a meal that keeps hunger away. It's a plate of hope. It tells you in your darkest hour that someone, somewhere, cares about you. This is the real meaning of comfort food. It's why we make the effort to cook in a crisis" (WCK, 2022, p. 1).

Crisis Management Strategies

While governments have the power to impose rules and regulations on the organizations and enforce compliance, threatening with significant consequences for failure to comply, sometimes compliance itself may lead to trouble. For example, during the 2023 elections in Turkey, the government required Twitter to censor some of the posted content. Twitter, on the one hand, had to comply as it faced potential disconnect and ban in the whole country of Turkey and hefty fines for violating the country's regulations. On the other hand, Twitter and its CEO, Elon Musk, were criticized heavily by its own users and people around the world for silencing free speech. In fact, over the years, organizations got in trouble for working with governments of countries such as South Africa, China, and Russia. Google was even a target of a US Congressional investigation for its close collaboration with the government of China (Gallagher, 2018). In other words following the laws of the government of one country may put the organization in trouble with the government of another country. It is, however, unlikely that with 193 different countries, members of the United Nations, and a few additional countries and territories that are not UN members, organizations will be able to find a middle ground between all of them and satisfy everybody. As a result, cases of Cross-National Conflict Shifting, discussed in Chapter 5, are constantly growing as the world becomes progressively smaller and enhanced global communications virtually eliminate national borders. This adds significant complexity to the issue of managing government relations, as it is not about managing relationships with a government but instead it is about managing relations with multiple governments simultaneously (Table 9.1).

This also brings into focus the issue of ethics and professionalism. The organizations are required to follow the laws of the countries they operate in, but if such laws violate the ethical beliefs and professional responsibilities of these organizations and their employees, they may be better off avoiding those countries altogether. For example, since Russia's invasion of Ukraine, hundreds of organizations shut down their operations in Russia and left the country – among them are brands such as Adidas, Danone, H&M, Ikea, Citigroup, McDonald's, Netflix, and many more (*New York Times*, 2022). Many non-profit organizations also closed their operations in Russia, sometimes forcefully by Russian authorities for failing to cooperate with the Russian government and violating Russian laws and, as a result, becoming criminal enterprises in the eyes of the Russian law. Among those non-profits were Amnesty International, MacArthur Foundation, and Freedom House.

This makes it essential for organizations to carefully evaluate the risks associated with their government associations and to make responsible decisions that align with their values and long-term objectives. No one market is worth the overall existence of the organizations and no one market is worth abandoning its mission and purpose. Engaging with governments that have questionable human rights records, corruption

Table 9.1 50 Largest Countries of the World (by Territory).

Rank	Country	Area (sq. km)	% of Earth's Area (%)
1	Russia	17.1M	11.52
2	Canada	10M	6.73
3	China	9.7M	6.54
4	United States	9.4M	6.31
5	Brazil	8.5M	5.74
6	Australia	7.7M	5.18
7	India	3.3M	2.21
8	Argentina	2.8M	1.87
9	Kazakhstan	2.7M	1.84
10	Algeria	2.4M	1.6
11	DR Congo	2.3M	1.58
12	Greenland	2.2M	1.46
13	Saudi Arabia	2.1M	1.45
14	Mexico	2M	1.32
15	Indonesia	1.9M	1.28
16	Sudan	1.9M	1.27
17	Libya	1.8M	1.19
18	Iran	1.6M	1.11
19	Mongolia	1.6M	1.05
20	Peru	1.3M	0.87
21	Chad	1.3M	0.86
22	Niger	1.3M	0.85
23	Angola	1.2M	0.84
24	Mali	1.2M	0.84
25	South Africa	1.2M	0.82
26	Colombia	1.1M	0.77
27	Ethiopia	1.1M	0.74
28	Bolivia	1.1M	0.74
29	Mauritania	1M	0.69
30	Egypt	1M	0.68
31	Tanzania	945.1K	0.64
32	Nigeria	923.8K	0.62
33	Venezuela	916.4K	0.62
34	Pakistan	881.9K	0.59
35	Namibia	825.6K	0.56
36	Mozambique	801.6K	0.54
37	Turkey	783.6K	0.53

(Continued)

Table 9.1 (Continued)

Rank	Country	Area (sq. km)	% of Earth's Area (%)
38	Chile	756.1K	0.51
39	Zambia	752.6K	0.51
40	Myanmar	676.6K	0.46
41	Afghanistan	652.2K	0.44
42	Somalia	637.7K	0.43
43	Central African Republic	623K	0.42
44	South Sudan	619.7K	0.42
45	Ukraine	603.5K	0.41
46	Madagascar	587K	0.4
47	Botswana	582K	0.39
48	Kenya	580.4K	0.39
49	France	551.7K	0.37
50	Yemen	528K	0.36

Source: World Population Review. https://worldpopulationreview.com/country-rankings/largest-countries-in-the-world

issues, or controversial policies can negatively impact an organization's reputation and stakeholders' perceptions of such organizations. Mitigating these risks requires careful consideration and ethical decision-making. For Danone, for example, the Russian market represented 5% of global sales, and while it was painful to lose those sales the company preserved and protected from risk 95% of its sales by leaving Russia.

Sometimes, the crisis in government relations may come from just a single individual in the government. Donald Trump, the 45th president of the United States, for example, sent shockwaves through the airline industry when he blamed the chaos at airports, after the introduction of the US travel ban in January 2017, on airline companies and specifically on Delta Airlines (Trump, 2017a). Another time, President Trump on Twitter announced that ESPN rankings are tanking and that people are dumping the network in record numbers (Trump, 2017b). Of course, organizations that have significant business interests in the United States must take the words of the US president seriously and commit resources for properly managing their communications and behavior in response to such statements.

Future Proofing Your Strategies

The future of government relations is shaped by two contradictory trends that affect governments around the world: first, people expect less government interference in their lives with more individual freedoms and less taxes, but, second, people also expect governments to take better care of them in terms of pensions, healthcare, social, and other services. For example, France in 2018 saw violent protests that lasted for weeks after the country's government announced a fuel tax increase in order to fund infrastructure improvements. Then, in 2023, in the same country of France, violent protests erupted again when the government proposed to increase the retirement age from 62 to 64 in an effort to save money. In this contradictory environment, it is reasonable to expect governments to turn to corporate and non-profit sectors for help.

PPPs can be expected to be on the rise, and these may be lucrative opportunities for private businesses in terms of making a profit and at the same time growing their reputations among local communities. After all, if such PPP is providing the only road in and out of a village, or this PPP is the only provider of fresh clean water, electricity, or education, it is delivering the vital service people need to survive and prosper. In fact, the 2023 Edelman Trust Barometer showed the business sector of the economy is the only sector that is seen as competent and ethical. People believe in business's abilities to solve societal problems and do it the right way more than they believe in governments, non-profits, or media (Edelman, 2023).

This solution is not without risks, however. In the United States of America, for example, several prisons and detention centers were privatized, yet the companies that ran them were caught exploiting their inmates, trying to squeeze as much money out of them as possible. In one case known as *kids-for-cash*, two judges in the state of Pennsylvania received bribes from private juvenile detention centers to send them more prisoners. One of the judges instituted a zero-tolerance policy and "ordered children as young as 8 to detention, many of them first-time offenders convicted of petty theft and other minor crimes . . . often ordered youths he had found delinquent to be immediately shackled, handcuffed and taken away without giving them a chance to say goodbye to their families" (*Associated Press*, 2022). PPPs highlight the responsibility of the organization to the society and the added trust that the society places on the businesses by making them a provider of vital services to the communities.

Another important trend in government relations is globalization. Already today, private organizations may struggle with competing and even directly opposite requests from various governments in the countries they operate (see, for example, the case of Twitter discussed earlier in the chapter). On top of 193 different countries, organizations need to manage relations with supranational entities that may also impose significant challenges on trade, capital movement, and even labor practices.

Even within any single country, the societal expectations are evolving and societies are expecting more from organizations, corporations, and non-profits alike, in terms of work hours, benefits, vacations, social responsibility, environment sustainability, and governance. Governments serve to codify and enforce society's expectations and thus it is reasonable to expect the evolution in the regulatory landscape to follow the changing societal expectations. This will require even closer collaboration between governments, corporations, and non-profits as many of the current problems are too complex to be solved by any one sector of the economy. For example, the issue of climate change requires everyone to get involved in order to understand and deal with the problem at hand.

This may also lead to an increased role of non-profits. Non-profits traditionally stepped in where governments failed. If the government shrinks its services and PPPs will not be able to adequately assist communities, non-profits will become the last straw of hope. Already today we see a consistent growth of charitable donations year after year, with private donations reaching about $485 billion in the United States (NPT Trust, 2023). This trend is likely to continue and the non-profit sector is likely to grow in volume and importance.

Chapter Summary

Building and maintaining relationships with the government is vital for organizations as a change in the regulatory landscape may mean significant profits or significant losses or even put the organization out of existence completely. Such a process of governmental relationship management is known as lobbying. Lobbying involves reactive and proactive strategies and is aimed at helping various organizations and governments adjust to each other. An important challenge in government relations is a variety of different governmental organizations that have different functions – executive, judicial, and legislative, and operate at different levels – supranational, federal, state/provincial, city/town, and local municipalities. In addition, there are quasigovernmental entities that function like a government. Sometimes, organizations may have to deal with competing pressures from governments of different countries – and with 193 countries, members of the United Nations, it may become quite difficult to find a middle ground. Governments also often rely on corporations and form Public–Private Partnerships. Non-profits often work in cooperation with government entities or step up when governments fail to act.

Five Key Terms to Remember

Lobbying
Public–Private Partnership
Privatization
Supranational
Branches of Government

Discussion Questions and Activities

1 Explain why lobbying is part of the US Constitution.
2 Discuss why governments are typically split into different branches and operate at different levels.
3 Discuss the benefits and drawbacks of engaging in Public–Private Partnerships for governments, for businesses, and for people.
4 Identify a recently passed legislature. Discuss how this legislature may affect various organizations. Identify organizations that may be affected positively and organizations that may be affected negatively.
5 Think of a supranational entity that affects the country you live in or the country you are from. Discuss how such supranational government affects corporations, non-profits, and government within the country. What is your opinion about this supranational?

How to Learn More

Baumgartner, F. R., Berry, J. M., Hojnacki, M., Leech, B. L., & Kimball, D. C. (2009). *Lobbying and policy change: Who wins, who loses, and why.* University of Chicago Press.
Scott, J. C. (2018). *Lobbying and society: A political sociology of interest groups.* Wiley.
Zetter, L. (2014). *Lobbying 3e: The art of political persuasion.* Harriman House Limited.

Case Study

Tesla: Can Tesla Follow the (Yellow Brick) Road?

Figure 9.4

1. Summary of the Case

Tesla, an American automaker and technology company, released one of the first test models of the driverless car in 2014. While many consumer concerns regarding safety and efficiency surrounded the production of the vehicle, Tesla was confident that testing the product out on the roads of California would provide consumers with the evidence they needed to trust the software. Despite over 130 million miles of accident-free autopilot use in Tesla vehicles, a Tesla car utilizing the driverless software was involved in a fatal accident where the driver was killed, causing widespread concern over safety, and multiple investigations and lawsuits. With the release of the autopilot software in every car produced by Tesla, the company needs to find a way to address the situation, especially as more accidents are happening with the increase in usage of Tesla cars around the world. Tesla must go beyond just calming the fears of their consumers so that their reputation is not tarnished and their sales are not affected, but also proactively work with various governmental entities to avoid potentially embarrassing bans on their vehicles as well as expensive recalls and modifications. As a result, this case highlights the importance of government relations for organizational reputation.

2. Organization's Background and Historical Development

Tesla, Inc. is a multinational corporation that was founded in 2003–2004 by Martin Eberhard and Marc Tarpenning. They realized that a high-performance electric vehicle did not exist yet and saw this as a business opportunity. After researching the ins and outs of electrically powered cars, the pair stumbled upon the company AC Propulsion, which produced a small, yellow electric car called

(Continued)

Case Study   (Continued)

tzero, the predecessor of all Tesla cars. This car drove smoothly, easily, and could reach very high speeds. Eberhard and Tarpenning knew that there was a niche in the market this car could occupy, and quickly decided that it was time to start the electric-car company. The pair invited Malcom Smith, future vice president of vehicle engineering at Tesla, to come try out the car. After one ride in the car, Smith realized that he was sitting in the car of the future. He concluded that the pair were onto something bigger than anyone could imagine at the time, and by combining technologies that were barely available to the public yet, they had present a technological breakthrough that society was longing for (Baer, 2014).

After inviting Elon Musk to invest and join forces in order to implement the idea of the *electric vehicle* (EV), Tesla announced their "Signature 100" plan in which they would sell 100 electric cars for $100,000 each. At this announcement party, guests were given a short ride in the prototype. Production of the Roadster officially started in March 2008, and the first batch of cars was delivered to their owners on October 31, 2008. The company would produce 2,450 Roadsters before it moved on to newer models. While the company was initially focused on developing a high-performance electric sports car that could compete with gasoline-powered vehicles, Tesla shifted its focus on developing more affordable electric cars for the mass market. The Tesla Model S was released in 2012. This model was a more affordable vehicle and more family-friendly, as it could seat up to seven passengers. With the release of the new model came a new charging system that shortened recharging time. The company has since introduced several additional models, including the Model X, Model 3, and Model Y, which have helped to reinforce Tesla's position as a leading producer of electric cars.

Today Tesla's mission is: "We're building a world powered by solar energy, running on batteries and transported by electric vehicles" (Tesla, 2023). In addition to being a leader in the electric car market, Tesla is also involved in the production of renewable energy solutions. The company's solar panels and energy storage and distribution products are designed to allow homeowners and businesses to generate their own electricity and reduce their reliance on the traditional power grid (IANS, 2023; Tabora, 2022).

A revolutionary aspect of Tesla is its ability to manufacture parts more efficiently than anyone else in the industry. Elon Musk, CEO of Tesla, continually emphasizes the impact of manufacturing (Nambiar, 2021). Tesla's manufacturing "utilizes a combination of traditional manufacturing techniques, advanced robotics, and state-of-the-art ERP systems to create its vehicles at a high rate of speed and with a high level of precision" (Tesla's advanced manufacturing, 2023, para. 1). Additionally, as an eco-friendly brand, the company strives to minimize waste and reduce production time. To accomplish this, "Tesla uses a just-in-time manufacturing approach, ensuring that parts and components are delivered to the assembly line only when needed … which helps reduce inventory levels and allows the company to adapt to changes in demand quickly" (Tesla's advanced manufacturing, 2023, para. 3). Musk presents a shift from the focus of improving the machine to improving the machine that makes the machines (Nambiar, 2021, para. 11). This focal point is backed by the creation of Gigafactory, Tesla's manufacturing plant. With several of these Gigafactories already in operation and more planned, production rates are set to increase exponentially, with Musk's goal of reaching "a production volume of 20 million vehicles per year probably by 2030" (Nambiar, 2021, para. 14).

3. Operational Environment and Main Publics

One of the key societal trends that guide Tesla cars is the focus on achieving autonomous driving. Car companies such as Ford, GM, Audi, BMW, Tesla, Nissan, Mercedes-Benz, and others have all promised to produce self-driving cars within the next few years. These companies are partnering up with tech companies such as Microsoft and Nvidia, to deliver on these promises. Not only are established automakers paving the way for this new industry, but other companies such as Google and Uber have joined in as well. Google was among the first to announce its interest and entrance into the autonomous vehicles market. These tech companies are partnering with automakers to collaborate their technologies with existing vehicles to create an autonomous car that appeals to consumers.

Elon Musk, Tesla CEO, announced that by the end of 2017 the company would "produce a car that would drive itself from Los Angeles to New York City" (Stewart, 2016). This announcement left many critics with the question if consumers would be able to trust a computer being behind the wheel and if the governments around the world would even let this experiment happen on their roads. While Google may have been the first to announce its idea of releasing an autonomous car, Tesla has pulled ahead of the company in regard to production and success of the product. Google has begun to pull away from the idea while both Tesla and Uber are racing ahead (Yu, 2016). Tesla's ability to almost flawlessly integrate all aspects of a vehicle into one company, with the addition of technology, gave Tesla the upper hand in autonomous vehicles.

In late 2016, Tesla began testing four driverless vehicles on the roads in California. These vehicles traveled a combined total of 550 miles and reported 182 disengagements, or points at which human intervention was required to either avoid an accident or resolve a technological issue. The company even allows you to watch videos with the point of view from the driver's seat to see what it is like to be sitting in an autonomous car. In October, Musk announced that all vehicles produced by Tesla will have full self-driving hardware installed in them, including the Model S and Model X.

Tesla's customers are a crucial public for the company, as they provide the revenue that sustains the company's operations. Tesla's customers are typically environmentally conscious individuals who are looking for sustainable and high-performance transportation solutions. Tesla must continue to provide high-quality products and services that meet the needs and expectations of its customers to maintain their loyalty and satisfaction. As the public's desire for more sustainable products grows, so does Tesla's popularity. Studies show that 77% of consumers are motivated to purchase from companies committed to making the world a better place, as well as 73% of investors say that a company's CSR has an

(Continued)

Case Study (Continued)

impact on whether they invest with them (Stobierski, 2021). Additional reports show that "electric vehicles have picked up 2.4 percentage points of U.S. market share this year, growing to 5.2% of all light vehicle registrations" (Krisher, 2022, para. 5). These statistics and trends provide ample opportunities for Tesla to gain customers, investors, and continue to grow. Many Tesla customers are also early adopters of technology. This makes them quite receptive to trying out the self-driving cars and makes them supporters of Tesla's vision.

Tesla's investors are another important public for the company, as they provide the capital needed to finance Tesla's growth and expansion plans. Tesla's investors are typically interested in the company's financial performance, growth prospects, and innovation capabilities. Tesla must continue to deliver strong financial results and showcase its innovative products to attract and retain investors. Investors are fascinated by Musk's vision of the future where cars drive themselves and pick up passengers along the way. This may change the way people buy and use cars, and investing in a company like Tesla that is at the forefront of such revolution promises good returns.

Tesla's relationship with regulators and governments is critical to its success, as it operates in a highly regulated industry and relies on government incentives and subsidies to promote the adoption of EVs. Tesla must comply with the regulatory requirements and standards in each country where it operates and maintain positive relationships with governments to continue to receive the support and incentives needed to sustain its operations and growth. Unfortunately, out of all key publics, relationship with the government is probably Tesla's weakest link. Tesla is no stranger to government probes as it was involved in multiple governmental investigations: from stock manipulation to exploding battery fires. The governmental agencies also remain quite skeptical about Tesla's claims regarding its self-driving cars, leading to several investigations around the world already in progress and several more expected.

4. The Issue Development

On May 7, 2017, a man was killed in a motor vehicle accident in Williston, Florida. This was not any regular car accident, however, as the driver was operating a Tesla Model S electric sedan that was in the self-driving mode. The incident quickly hit the news as this was the first fatal accident involving an autonomous vehicle. Officials say that the accident occurred when a tractor-trailer made a left turn in front of the Tesla vehicle and the car failed to apply the brakes. The driver of the vehicle, later identified as Joshua Brown, had posted videos of himself driving in the autonomous vehicle prior to the crash. In one video, he praised the self-driving software for saving both him and his car from an accident.

Already prior to this accident, many consumers and critics worried about the deaths caused – or possibly not prevented – by the self-driving software. This accident further supported these concerns as the software was not able to prevent the collusion. After the crash, the National Highway Traffic Safety Administration (NHTSA) opened an investigation into how autonomous vehicles actually work and their role in the accident. Since then, additional Tesla self-driving issues were investigated by NHTSA, including a highly publicized crash on the San Francisco Bay Bridge (Kloppenstein, 2023).

While the investigations launched by NHTSA generally concluded that the auto-pilot software was not at fault in the accidents and the director of the agency said "We want to promote these technologies . . . they will save lives and cut crashes dramatically, but innovation is a bumpy road" (Stewart, 2017), Tesla had to issue a recall affecting over 360,000 of its cars and included certain Model S, Model X, Model 3, and Model Y vehicles with Full Self-Driving Beta software. The recall bulletin stated: "The FSD Beta system may allow the vehicle to act unsafe around intersections, such as traveling straight through an intersection while in a turn-only lane, entering a stop sign-controlled intersection without coming to a complete stop, or proceeding into an intersection during a steady yellow traffic signal without due caution . . . may respond insufficiently to changes in posted speed limits . . . exceed speed limits or travel through intersections in an unlawful or unpredictable manner increases the risk of a crash" (KBB, 2023). This was not a great endorsement for Tesla's self-driving software and further damaged the relationship between Tesla and government agencies.

Tesla's recalls, however, look differently from recalls of other car brands. Since Tesla's cars are internet-enabled, Tesla sends an over-the-air (OTA) software update to all their cars, free of charge, and the update remedies the issue without the need for the car to travel to a service center or any Tesla mechanic to work on a Tesla vehicle. Nevertheless, while this approach may save Tesla money, this recall practice may be confusing to consumers and government officials.

In April 2023, NHTSA launched its 40th investigation into Tesla's self-driving software causing another Tesla car crash, this time in North Carolina. While many Tesla crashes attract a lot of media attention, this particular crash involved a student and a stopped school bus that Tesla failed to stop for despite the bus displaying the stop sign and the flashing lights (Johnson, 2023). While Tesla cars may have driven millions of miles in the autonomous mode, even a few high-profile crashes may hurt the car's reputation among government officials and customers (Alvarez, 2022).

United States is not the only country concerned with Tesla's self-driving software. Germany, Netherlands, and Euro NCAP also have official probes into Tesla's self-driving software (McFarland, 2022; Rodriquez, 2022). All these investigations, combined with well-publicized crashes, and misleading names for the software, such as "Full Self-Driving," may hurt Tesla's reputation as a trustworthy producer of autonomous vehicles and may hinder the company's ability to receive official governmental approvals to utilize their autonomous technology even after such technology is, in fact, capable of reliably and safely delivering the fully autonomous self-driving experience.

5. What Is Next?

Tesla usually reacts defensively to any public attacks on its self-driving technology and to government interventions, denying any wrong-doing. Yet, Tesla still faces lawsuits from customers, investors, and regulatory agencies over its self-driving

(Continued)

Case Study (Continued)

cars. Despite being right and not at fault, Tesla's reputation can still be damaged. In fact, Tesla won its first Autopilot lawsuit against a customer who blamed Tesla's software for a car crash in April 2023 (Peters, 2023). While an important legal victory, more challenges are heading Tesla's way. The court of public opinion does not always follow the court of law. In addition, the company remains under criminal investigation by the US Department of Justice. The state of California recently banned Tesla from calling its software Full Self-Driving, as the state saw it as false advertising practices (Crider, 2022). Without government's approval and support, it would be impossible for Tesla to actually have autonomous vehicles that could travel from point to point without any driver intervention or even without a driver altogether (Alvarez, 2022). As the CEO of Tesla Elon Musk thinks about his vision of autonomous vehicles, he realizes that the road to this autonomous future would actually require meticulous steering, especially when it comes to government relations. Will Tesla be able to get there?

References

AGRP (2023). What is government relations? https://grprofessionals.org/resources/what-is-government-relations

Alvarez, S. (2022). Elon Musk still estimates 6 billion Tesla FSD miles for global regulatory approval. Teslarati (12 September). https://www.teslarati.com/elon-musk-6-billion-tesla-fsd-miles-global-regulatory-approval

Archick, K. (2023). The European Union: questions and answers. *Congressional Research Service* (6 February). https://fas.org/sgp/crs/row/RS21372.pdf

Associated Press. (2022). Judges who sent children to for-profit jails for kickbacks ordered to pay more than $200 million in damages. *NBC News* (17 April). https://www.nbcnews.com/news/us-news/judges-sent-children-profit-jails-kickbacks-ordered-pay-200-million-da-rcna43538

Baer, D. (2014). The making of Tesla: Invention, betrayal, and the birth of the roadster. *Business Insider* (11 November). http://www.businessinsider.com/tesla-the-origin-story-2014-10

Crider, J. (2022). California passes law banning Tesla from calling software FSD. Teslarati (22 December). https://www.teslarati.com/califonia-banning-tesla-fsd

Edelman (2023). 2023 Edelman trust barometer. https://www.edelman.com/trust/2023/trust-barometer

Federal Reserve (n.d.). Federal reserve Q&A. https://www.okhistory.org/historycenter/federalreserve/bankingfaq.html#:~:text=The%20Federal%20Reserve%20is%20a,and%20control%20the%20Reserve%20Banks

Gallagher, R. (2018). Google CEO hammered by members of Congress on China censorship. *The Intercept* (11 December). https://theintercept.com/2018/12/11/google-congressional-hearing

IANS (2023). Tesla remains EV market leader in US with over 50% share. *The Times of India* (25 April). https://timesofindia.indiatimes.com/auto/news/tesla-remains-ev-market-leader-in-us-with-over-50-share/articleshow/99268175.cms

Johnson, W. (2023). Tesla hit with 40th NHTSA probe into autonomous driving system. Teslarati (8 April). https://www.teslarati.com/tesla-nhtsa-probe-autonomous-driving-2023

KBB (2023). Tesla recalls 2016-2023 Model S, X, 2017-2023 Model 3, and 2020-2023 Model Y. Tesla Recalls. https://www.kbb.com/tesla/recall/

Kloppenstein, K. (2023). Exclusive: Surveillance footage of Tesla crash on SF's Bat bridge hours after Elon Musk announces "self-driving" feature. *The Intercept*. https://theintercept.com/2023/01/10/tesla-crash-footage-autopilot/#:~:text=Since%20 2016%2C%20the%20federal%20agency,accidents%20have%20killed%2019%20people

Krisher, T. (2022). Competitors chip away at Tesla's US Electric Vehicle Share. *AP NEWS* (29 November). https://apnews.com/article/technology-business-electric-vehicles-climate-and-environment-9e6f2f773a5ed00f95debc87b15d17d1

McFarland, M. (2022). A tweet launched an investigation into Tesla's Autopilot software. *CNN* (12 October). https://www.cnn.com/2022/10/12/business/tesla-euro-ncap-investigation/index.html

Milbrath, L. W. (1963). *The Washington lobbyists*. Chicago: Rand McNally.

Morales, M. (2023). Red Cross brings disaster assessments in Laguna Heights. *Valleycentral* (15 May). https://www.valleycentral.com/news/local-news/red-cross-brings-disaster-assessments-in-laguna-heights

Nambiar, K. (2021). The manufacturing revolution of Tesla. *Analytics Steps* (9 July). https://www.analyticssteps.com/blogs/manufacturing-revolution-tesla

New York Times. (2022). Companies are getting out of Russia, sometimes at a cost. *New York Times* (14 October). https://www.nytimes.com/article/russia-invasion-companies.html

NPT Trust. (2023). Charitable giving statistics. https://www.nptrust.org/philanthropic-resources/charitable-giving-statistics/#:~:text=General%20Philanthropy,a%204%25%20 increase%20from%202020.&text=Corporate%20giving%20in%202021%20increased,a%20 23.8%25%20increase%20from%202020.&text=Foundation%20giving%20in%202021%20 increased,a%203.4%25%20increase%20from%202020

Pazniokas, M. (2023). CT now a battleground in fight over minimum wage at restaurants. *CT Mirror* (9 March). https://ctmirror.org/2023/03/09/ct-restaurant-wages-minimum-wage-bill/

Peters, J. (2023). Tesla wins lawsuit that blamed Autopilot for crash. *The Verge* (21 April). https://www.theverge.com/2023/4/21/23693482/tesla-lawsuit-blamed-autopilot-crash

Robbins, R., & Goodman, P. S. (2021). Pfizer reaps hundreds of millions in profits from Covid vaccine. *The New York Times* (5 May). https://www.nytimes.com/2021/05/04/business/pfizer-covid-vaccine-profits.html

Rodriquez, J. (2022). Germany is the latest country investigating the safety of Tesla's autopilot. *Gizmodo* (23 February). www.gizmodo.com.au/2022/02/germany-is-the-latest-country-investigating-the-safety-of-teslas-autopilot/

Statista (2023). Total lobbying spending in the United States 1998 to 2022. https://www.statista.com/statistics/257337/total-lobbying-spending-in-the-us/

Stewart, J. (2016). Tesla's self-driving car plan seems insane, but it just might work. *Wired* (24 October). https://www.wired.com/2016/10/teslas-self-driving-car-plan-seems-insane-just-might-work/

Stewart, J. (2017). As self-driving cars approach, the auto industry races to rebuild. *Wired* (15 January). https://www.wired.com/2017/01/self-driving-cars-approach-auto-industry-races-rebuild/

Stobierski, T. (2021). 15 eye-opening corporate social responsibility statistics. *Business Insights Blog* (15 June). https://online.hbs.edu/blog/post/corporate-social-responsibility-statistics

Tabora, V. (2022). Why Tesla is still the leader in EV. *Medium* (23 March). https://medium.com/0xmachina/why-tesla-is-still-the-leader-in-ev-375a30fd3055

Tesla (2023). Our impact. https://www.tesla.com/impact

Trump, D. (2017a). Only 109 people out of 325,000 were detained and held for questioning. Twitter (30 January). https://twitter.com/realdonaldtrump/status/826041397232943104

Trump, D. (2017b). ESPN is paying a really big price for its politics (and bad programming). Twitter (15 September). https://twitter.com/realDonaldTrump/status/908651641943003136

Wall Street Journal. (2023). Opinion: Potomac watch. *WSJ Podcasts* (21 April). https://www.wsj.com/podcasts/opinion-potomac-watch/the-billionaire-who-bought-justice-thomas-mothers-house/9efa40a6-8a56-4836-ae31-717e824c9833

Wise, K. (2007). Lobbying and relationship management: The K street connection. *Journal of Public Relations Research*, *19*(4), 357–376 https://doi.org/10.1080/10627260701402457

World Bank. (2022). PPP contract types and terminology. https://ppp.worldbank.org/public-private-partnership/ppp-contract-types-and-terminology

World Central Kitchen. (2022). Our story. https://wck.org/story

Yu, H. (2016). Google fumbles while Tesla sprints toward a driverless future. *Forbes* (15 December). https://www.forbes.com/sites/howardhyu/2016/12/14/why-google-is-fumbling-while-tesla-is-sprinting-toward-driverless-cars/#3675e5d06a02

10

Media and Influencers: Any Publicity Is Good Publicity?

LEARNING OBJECTIVES

1. *After reading this chapter, students will be able to define who media and influencers are as the organizational public.*
2. *After reading this chapter, students will be able to understand the importance of managing relationships with media and influencers.*
3. *After reading this chapter, students will be able to develop strategic plans for building and maintaining relationships with media and influencers to enhance organizational reputation.*

Define the Public

An important public for building and maintaining organizational reputation is media. Sometimes, media are called an *intermediary* public. The term intermediary refers to the fact that the role of media is often to help organizations reach some other publics – in other words, organizations communicate through the media and build relationships through the media with publics such as customers, investors, governments, and so on. In fact, if Apple wants to inform their customers about releasing a new model of their iPhone, the best way to reach customers may be through news media outlets – for example, by sending a news release about the new phone or inviting media to a presentation of a new iPhone model. Chances are the story about a new iPhone release will be featured in the news on television, radio, newspapers, and online. Such messages through the media can reach millions of customers effectively and efficiently.

Print media are among the oldest forms of news media. This includes newspapers, magazines, and other printed publications. Some of them have a broad focus and some may focus on a particular region or particular issue. Many industries have publications dedicated exclusively to that industry. For example, the advertising industry's leading publication is *Adweek*, published since 1979. Such industry-specific media are called *trade publications*. Radio and television media are often called *broadcast media*. While traditionally print media was printed on paper and broadcast media was broadcast via airwaves, today both print and broadcast media have a presence in the digital form with websites on the internet and apps on phones. This became known as *digital*

Organizational Reputation Management: A Strategic Public Relations Perspective, First Edition. Alexander V. Laskin.
© 2024 John Wiley & Sons, Inc. Published 2024 by John Wiley & Sons, Inc.

media. Some media outlets are reaching their audiences through a variety of ways. For example, *NBC Connecticut* news can be seen via over-the-air broadcast, via cable or satellite subscriptions, at http://nbcconnecictut.com website, through the *NBC CT News* mobile app on the phone, through the *NBC CT News* app on Roku, and even on social media such as Facebook or Twitter. This trend is known as the *digitization of media*, when traditional media outlets move into the digital space (Figure 10.1).

Of course, in addition to the traditional media moving into digital space, brand-new purely digital media appear as well. One of the most famous examples of digital native news media is *HuffPost* (also known as HuffPo and The Huffington Post) that launched as an independent news site on the internet in 2005. In addition to digitization of traditional media, when traditional media develops a presence in the digital realm, sometimes the opposite happens: digital media can go into the traditional media landscape. For example, leading Russian digital media outlet RBC (also known as RosBusinessConsulting), which started as a website on the internet, over time launched its own TV broadcast, newspaper, magazine, and even acquired an event space to host in-person forums and conferences.

A unique type of media is *social media*. Social media platforms enable users to create, share, and interact with content. Examples include Facebook, Twitter, Instagram, TikTok, and Snapchat. Social media platforms facilitate communication, networking, content sharing, and online communities. Social media also serve as great intermediaries to reach the publics important for organizations as they allow for specific

Figure 10.1 *NBC CT News* Website. *Source:* NBCUniversal Media, LLC / https://www.nbcconnecticut. com/news/ last accessed August 04, 2023.

targeting and segmentation of their users. For example, on LinkedIn, it is possible to identify people who work for a specific company or who went to a specific university or who are employed in a specific industry.

Reaching certain publics may require relying on some unique intermediaries. For example, in investor relations, reaching the buy-side may involve using the sell-side as an intermediary or, more specifically, using the sell-side's financial analysts. A positive report by a financial analyst with a strong buy recommendation may do more to attract investors than positive stories in news media or cheerful posts on social media. If a company is looking to hire new employees, its reviews on Glassdoor, an important intermediary for employee publics, may be the key deciding factors for prospective hires.

And, of course, an important intermediary is influencers, creators, and celebrities. In fact, one of the communication theories explains that information often travels from the organization to the public not directly but through an intermediary. This theory, *two-step flow theory*, calls such intermediaries *opinion leaders*. Customers may not be persuaded directly by an ad for a new iPhone but if they see that somebody whose opinion they value highly starts using this phone, then they may consider buying it for themselves as well. Organizations know about the importance of these opinion leaders and often develop special programs for those whose opinions may help them influence the opinions of others. As a result, today these opinion leaders are often called *influencers*.

Sneakers endorsed by a celebrity may sell more pairs, and the organization may be able to charge more for them as well. Nike, for example, was able to sell US$ 70 million worth of Air Jordan sneakers in just two months after releasing these sneakers endorsed by basketball star Michael Jordan who was paid just US$ 2.5 million for his endorsement (Baum, 2023). More than just products, celebrities may help win elections, promote a particular lifestyle, or direct tourists to a specific destination. Kim Kardashian, one of the most famous influencers, over the years promoted traveling to California, eating at Carl's Jr., removing body hair with laser, investing in several crypto assets, buying countless products, visiting various stores, as well as getting on diets and dietary supplements (Mulshine, 2014) (Figure 10.2).

Value of the Relationship

The relationships between organizations and the media are quite valuable for everyone involved. Since media are intermediaries between organizations and other publics, they depend on organizations to plan on using the media in their role as intermediaries. Many media outlets rely on advertising revenues that organizations pay in order to have a message in the media. The same is true for social media – without advertising dollars Facebook or Twitter are unlikely to survive for long.

On the other hand, media can provide a quick and cost-effective way for organizations to reach their publics. For example, to reach 100 million customers, an organization may have to mail 100 million letters to their homes or complete 100 million phone calls. Instead, the organization can buy one commercial during the Super Bowl, a premier sporting event in the United States that in 2023 was watched by 115 million people. Of course, a standard 30-second commercial during the Super

Figure 10.2 Nike Air Jordan Sneakers on Sale.

Bowl is expensive – the costs reached US$ 7 million per commercial – however, it can still be quite an effective investment.

One of the key metrics the media industry uses to measure advertising effectiveness is *Cost-Per-Mille* (CPM) – which divides the overall cost of the commercial by the number of people watching and expresses the result as dollars spent for 1,000 viewers. The CPM of a Super Bowl commercial, as a result, can be calculated as US$ 7 million cost divided by 115 million viewers and multiplied by 1,000. The end result: CPM of about US$ 60. For US media markets, the CPM of US$ 60 is on the cheaper side as the CPM of an average television commercial in the country is over US$ 73 (Cassidy, 2023). And, it is important to consider the alternative – it is unlikely the organization will be able to reach 1,000 people for US$ 60 if they instead try mailing them letters. The postage alone will cost more than US$ 60 and this is not counting the cost of paper and envelopes.

The figure, however, is less cost-effective than advertising on streaming platforms, such as Netflix, which estimates its CPM to be about US$ 55. With that CPM, the same US$ 7 million investment can reach over 127 million people, or *impressions* – the term used in the media industry to indicate an exposure of one person to one advertisement. Social media CPM is even less and ranges from one to three dollars. Thus, the same US$ 7 million investment can be stretched to 2 billion impressions on TikTok or Instagram or Twitter. Such cost-effectiveness is the reason digital advertising is growing at a very high pace (Monllos, 2023). In 2022, social media advertising exceeded US$ 230 billion worldwide (Dencheva, 2023).

In addition to advertising, many organizations invest significant efforts in media relations to earn editorial content – what is known as *earned media* as previously discussed in Chapter 3, Managing Reputation. In fact, many believe that earned media is more trustworthy than advertising and, as a result, more valuable for the organization. Imagine, for example, a local pizza shop buying an ad on social media in which they claim to have an amazingly great pizza. People who would see the ad, however, are not likely to immediately believe that to be true because we would expect an ad to overexaggerate the reality in favor of the business being promoted. But then imagine if instead of an ad a local pizza shop invited a famous pizza critic, perhaps David Portnoy – El Presidente of Barstool Pizza Reviews – to try and conclude that they have a great pizza. Most people would be more likely to believe an independent third-party claim than advertising directly from the business. This phenomenon is known as a *third-party endorsement.*

When Barstool Pizza Review posts a positive testimonial about a pizza, they provide that restaurant with a third-party endorsement. This earned media is also often measured using similar approaches to advertising, such as impressions, but it is a mistake to think that their values are comparable. While it is possible to report that Barstool Pizza review of New York Pizza Co. in Danielson, CT, had 454,000 impressions, it is not the same as 454,000 impressions of an ad. When we see an ad on Facebook, on TV, or anywhere else we are more than likely to ignore it – however, when we consume the content we are actually interested in, we are more likely to pay attention. In addition, and especially on social media, people can interact with the content but not with advertising – people can like, comment, share, or repost the content they are interested in. That same New York Pizza Co. review in addition to 454,000 views also had almost 8,000 likes and over 1,000 comments, indicating a pretty significant level of engagement unattainable for a typical advertisement. As a result, the International Association for Measurement and Evaluation of Communication (AMEC) cautions against using advertising as a measuring stick for editorial content and does not recommend *advertising value equivalency* (AVE) as a measure for earned media (Figure 10.3).

In recent years, there has been an increase in sponsored content and native advertising, where corporations pay for content that resembles editorial content but promotes their products or services. In other words, it is a *paid media* disguised as an *earned media*. This blurring of boundaries between advertising and journalism can affect the objectivity and credibility of media outlets. The same is happening on social media. While we expect Barstool Pizza Review to provide their objective opinion on the pizzas they eat, what if some other pizza reviewer would just offer pizza places to provide great reviews in exchange for the payment? If customers discover that celebrities, influencers, journalists, and any other intermediaries, just say whatever the client pays

Figure 10.3 Barstool Pizza Review. *Source:* Barstool Facebook page.

them to say, it destroys any credibility we may have in those third-party endorsers. What is worse, this can affect not just the unethical influencers but hurt the overall trust of the society in the media. As a result, many media organizations adhere to ethical standards and codes of conduct, aiming to maintain integrity, independence, and impartiality. Conflicts of interest, disclosure of relationships with corporations, and avoiding biased reporting are essential considerations in maintaining the credibility of a specific media outlet and the credibility of media as an institution.

Maintaining and Building Reputation through Relationship Management Strategies

Many corporations have dedicated media relations professionals who are responsible for managing relationships with journalists and editors. Various government organizations have press secretaries and public affairs professionals. Nonprofit organizations have staff dedicated to media relations as well. These professionals act as the primary points of contact for media inquiries and work to build and maintain relationships with media over time. While advertising professionals can just buy an ad in a media outlet, earning coverage from a journalist is a more complex task. Many in the media see their job as watchdogs who must hold organizations accountable by investigating and reporting on their actions, practices, and controversies. The media's job is to inform the publics about relevant news: media organizations strive to provide objective, balanced, and accurate information to the public, ensuring transparency and accountability in corporate behavior.

This would suggest that media would write about an organization when this organization has something that can be considered news. It becomes the job of the media relations team to package the information they want to see in the media as newsworthy. Previous research identified eight criteria of *newsworthiness* that organizations can use to help them frame the stories they want to see in the media as news:

1. *Timeliness* – for something to be considered newsworthy it should be current. We would not consider an event to be news if it happened last year.
2. *Prominence* talks about the importance of the story for the audience. For example, a person dining out at a local restaurant would not be considered newsworthy, but a celebrity dining out at a local restaurant may make local news coverage and help the restaurant promote its food and service.
3. *Proximity* – a news event should have a local connection. *NBC Connecticut News* will be more likely to report on a house fire in Connecticut than on a house fire in Arizona.
4. *Significance* refers to the potential effect on the audience. If there is an epidemic of a disease, media outlets want to warn their audiences about this as this knowledge may be the difference between life and death. As a result, many organizations try to frame the stories they want to see featured on the news as a life-or-death scenario – whether it is actually the case or not.
5. *Unusualness*, or uniqueness of the event. This is something organizations can also try to emulate to get on the news. For example, when the state of Oregon wanted to promote its lottery they created a 75-ft. statue of King Kong and placed it on the side

of a building in Portland to make it look like a famous scene from a movie. It captured the attention of passers-by but also made it on the local news, as it was quite an usual site.

6. *Human interest*, also called *soft stories*, are stories focused on emotions, on what may make people laugh or cry. Those would include stories about a company's product that could help a three-legged dog walk, or a hotel that helped a homeless veteran, or a university that graduated triplets.

7. *Conflict* is usually newsworthy as it provides drama even for ordinary issues. A state agency removing a river dam may not make it on the news, but a group of local citizens protesting a dam removal, because they would lose a pond they have been swimming in for years, is likely to make it on the evening news. Controversy tends to lead to newsworthiness.

8. *Newness* as a component of newsworthiness refers to the fact that whatever product or an event organization wants to see on the news must be new: a new model of a truck, a new type of a phone, a new intersection opening, and so on. When it is new it is news! (Wilcox, 2005).

Media relations professionals also employ specific tools to build and maintain relationships with the media. For example, organizations often distribute *media releases* (sometimes called *press releases*) and *media kits* to journalists and editors in order to provide them with relevant and timely information about the company, its products, services, initiatives, or events. These materials are designed to make it easier for journalists to gather accurate information for their stories. Media also often rely on organizations to provide expertise for different stories. For example, Quinnipiac University's media relations teams assist journalists in finding a relevant expert for their stories among many faculty members available on campus. One of the Quinnipiac professors, Rich Hanley, is a football expert and, as a result, often comments in the media on sports-related stories. This helps organizations have their name in the media even when the stories are not about them, but also helps maintain good relationships with journalists.

Organizations understand the importance of building personal relationships with journalists and editors and that is why they also may invite them to special events, product launches, or press conferences to facilitate face-to-face interactions and foster a better understanding of the organizations' values, goals, and offerings. Organizations may also share exclusive content with an editor or a journalist or provide early samples of products or services to ensure the publication of positive stories. For government organizations, this may be giving exclusive access to a prominent political figure for an interview or behind-the-scenes story on their family life or personal hobby.

Organizations may also share exclusive information or provide early access to products or services for social media influencers. Influencers are online accounts that develop significant audiences and may also be viewed as experts on certain subjects or carry a unique perspective. In the past, it was common to define influencers as people, but today influencers can also be animals, plants, and even AI software. For example, an Instagram influencer, @lilmiquela, describes itself as a 19-year-old robot living in LA. In reality, it is a computer-generated image, created just to grow following and produce revenues. With 2.8 million followers, @lilmiquela worked with brands such as Calvin Klein, Samsung, and Prada, earning millions of dollars (Qureshi, 2021). The

Figure 10.4 Miquella Instagram Page. *Source:* Instagram.

process of working with influencers is called *influencer marketing* and is often done through partnerships between organizations and influencers; it is similar to *celebrity endorsement* when the partnership is between the organization and the celebrity (Figure 10.4).

What makes influencer marketing and celebrity endorsements successful is usually the connection between the product and the influencer. For instance, if a new bass guitar is endorsed by a person known as a great bass player, for example, Robert Trujillo, who played for Metallica, Infectious Grooves, Suicidal Tendencies, and Ozzy Osbourne, it makes the endorsement more valuable than any other third-party endorsement. Experts in influencer marketing explain that such successful partnerships must be based on four key criteria:

1. *Expertise.* The influencer should be an expert in what they are talking about.
2. *Authenticity.* The influencer must be viewed as true to who they are and be perceived as honest and trustworthy.

3. *Engagement.* The influencer should interact with their community but also with the products or services they promote.
4. *Passion.* The influencer should love what they are doing
   (Freberg, 2022; Luoma-aho et al., 2019).

In the case of Robert Trujillo, an expert in bass guitars, endorsing a specific brand of bass guitar will certainly be seen as authentic and within his expertise, and if he would actually play that brand of guitar on stage, it would add a dimension of passion and engagement with the product (Table 10.1).

Hootsuite identifies key criteria for analyzing influencers and deciding what influencer the organization should partner with for reputation-building and maintaining activities. First, it is the *total number of followers*. Organizations want to reach a lot of people through the influencer partnership and thus the sheer number of followers may be a deciding factor. Second is the engagement metrics. Identifying an influencer with lots of followers is important, but it is also important to see if these followers actually pay attention to the influencer's posts. Are they actively engaging in the conversation by liking, sharing, or commenting on the posts? An influencer with higher engagement may be a better investment than an influencer with more followers who do not pay attention to the posts at all. Third is the *brand status*. Does the influencer already work with other brands? This is really a double-edged sword. On the one hand, it is great to work with an influencer who works with a lot of prestigious and famous brands. It can prove to the organization that the influencer is professional and dependable to work with – at the very least, they have experience and know and understand the requirements. On the other hand, the brand the organization wants such an influencer to promote may be lost among all other brands they are working with. Even worse, they may be already involved with your competitor – then, it is a no-go. Nike cannot work with an influencer who already promoted Adidas and, thus, it is important to analyze the influencer's other brand connections. Fourth is the *frequency of postings*. Do they post a lot or once a month; will the branded post stand out or will it be buried among hundreds of posts per day? These points are important to discuss with the influencers as the partnership is being developed. The fifth point is the *type of partnership*. When deciding on an influencer partnership, the organization should set clear expectations – will the influencer just do one post or will they actually become a brand ambassador? Michael Jordan saying Nikes are great is one thing, but it is a very different thing when he actually played in those shoes during his NBA career. The sixth component of developing an influencer partnership is analyzing how strong the *connection* is between the influencer and their audience. Does the audience admire and aspire to be like the influencer or are they on the page just for the memes or gossip? The distinction may be important for the brand's decision. The seventh point is the *communication style* of the influencer – simply speaking, can they sell the product or service without the audience feeling that this is just a sales pitch? The eighth point to consider is the influencer's personal *values*. Will these values be compatible with the values of the brand? Even if everything else is perfect, organizations may want to stay clear from controversial figures, because associating with them may hurt the organization and their number of followers, and high-engagement metrics can actually work against the organization. For example, in 2023, Adidas reportedly lost US\$ 540 million after Ye's (formerly known as Kanye West) controversial remarks forced Adidas to revoke their brand partnership (*Associated Press*, 2023).

Table 10.1 The World's Top 50 Influencers across Social Media Platforms.

Rank	Influencer	Category	Followers	Biggest Platform
#1	Cristiano Ronaldo	Sports	517M	Instagram
#2	Justin Bieber	Music	455M	Instagram
#3	Ariana Grande	Music	429M	Instagram
#4	Selena Gomez	Music	425M	Instagram
#5	Taylor Swift	Music	361M	Instagram
#6	Dwayne Johnson	Film & TV	342M	Instagram
#7	Katy Perry	Music	338M	Instagram
#8	Kylie Jenner	Other	333M	Instagram
#9	Rihanna	Music	332M	Twitter
#10	Kim Kardashian	Other	319M	Instagram
#11	Lionel Messi	Sports	298M	Instagram
#12	Neymar	Sports	283M	Instagram
#13	Shakira	Music	282M	Facebook
#14	Jennifer Lopez	Music	277M	Instagram
#15	Beyoncé	Music	267M	Instagram
#16	Ellen DeGeneres	Film & TV	260M	Instagram
#17	Miley Cyrus	Music	235M	Instagram
#18	Nicki Minaj	Music	232M	Instagram
#19	Barack Obama	Politics	221M	Twitter
#20	Will Smith	Film & TV	217M	Facebook
#21	Kendall Jenner	Other	212M	Instagram
#22	Demi Lovato	Music	211M	Instagram
#23	Lady Gaga	Music	210M	Twitter
#24	Kevin Hart	Film & TV	201M	Instagram
#25	Virat Kohli	Sports	195M	Instagram
#26	Eminem	Music	194M	Facebook
#27	Drake	Music	192M	Instagram
#28	Khloé Kardashian	Other	191M	Instagram
#29	Bruno Mars	Music	191M	Facebook
#30	Chris Brown	Music	187M	Instagram
#31	Vin Diesel	Film & TV	177M	Facebook
#32	Narendra Modi	Politics	175M	Twitter
#33	Justin Timberlake	Music	175M	Twitter
#34	Billie Eilish	Music	171M	Instagram
#35	Charli D'Amelio	Other	169M	TikTok
#36	Kourtney Kardashian	Other	165M	Instagram
#37	Cardi B	Music	160M	Instagram
#38	LeBron James	Sports	157M	Instagram

Table 10.1   (Continued)

Rank	Influencer	Category	Followers	Biggest Platform
#39	Adele	Music	156M	Facebook
#40	Priyanka Chopra	Film & TV	144M	Instagram
#41	Germán Garmendia	Gaming	143M	YouTube
#42	Wiz Khalifa	Music	142M	Facebook
#43	Felix "PewDiePie" Kjellberg	Gaming	141M	YouTube
#44	Akshay Kumar	Film & TV	140M	Instagram
#45	Snoop Dogg	Music	138M	Instagram
#46	Deepika Padukone	Film & TV	138M	Instagram
#47	Britney Spears	Music	137M	Twitter
#48	Shawn Mendes	Music	136M	Instagram
#49	Whindersson Nunes Batista	Other	135M	Instagram
#50	Salman Khan	Film & TV	134M	Facebook

Source: Wallach (2021). https://www.visualcapitalist.com/worlds-top-50-influencers-across-social-media-platforms/

Crisis Management Strategies

The importance of media relations is never as high as during a crisis. This is the reason why many organizations practice how to conduct media relations during a crisis. As discussed in Chapter 5, preparing for a crisis response is an essential step in the crisis management process. For media relations, it means designating a spokesperson who will handle media inquiries during a crisis. It is important to select a spokesperson who is knowledgeable, calm, and skilled in media relations. This person should be media-trained and able to deliver messages effectively under pressure. In addition, maintaining a consistent spokesperson throughout the crisis can help avoid confusion. The choice of a spokesperson may also depend on the crisis: for example, a security breach at a university may point to the head of security as a spokesperson, but an electrical outage may call for a director of facilities. Of course, a highly significant event would usually require the top leader, the CEO or the president, to speak on behalf of the organization. Whoever the spokesperson is, they will need to respond to the crisis promptly and transparently. Delays in addressing the situation can lead to speculations and further damages.

One of the tactics of crisis media relations is known as *go ugly early*. While the natural reaction in crisis is to minimize and downplay the extent of the problem, this tactic encourages speaking about worst-case scenarios. When the audience is in shock from the crisis already, it is important to draw a picture of potential damages the crisis may cause. As the situation develops, the real damages are likely to be less than the worst-case scenarios and the publics' perception would be improving from the worst-case expectations. This is better than minimizing the crisis at first and then having to admit worse-than-expected damages.

It will also be important to provide timely updates and communicate with the media as the crisis continues. Actively sharing information with the media may also help the organization control and shape the narrative about the crisis. Of course, such communications must be honest and transparent. Failure to provide accurate information may cost the organization more in reputational damages than a crisis event itself. While legal experts generally advice against it, admitting mistakes or shortcomings, if applicable, may demonstrate accountability and can help regain public trust and restore reputation.

On the other hand, avoiding the media altogether is unlikely to help the organization during a crisis event. Media's job is to inform the public – if the organization is not available to share their side of the story, media will use other sources and present the story without the organization's perspective. In fact, organizations are encouraged to utilize social media and other communication channels to reach a broader audience or specific publics, such as employees or local community, directly in addition to working through intermediaries such as news media. These publics may become important organizational allies during the crisis.

Once again, listening is important during crisis media relations. Organizations should keep track of media coverage to stay informed about public sentiment and address any inaccuracies or misinterpretations promptly, if needed. It is recommended to engage with the media to provide clarifications or additional information as needed. Organizations should also continuously monitor social media platforms to identify mentions, discussions, and sentiments related to the crisis and use social listening tools to track conversations and gather insights about public perception and concerns.

Future Proofing Your Strategies

Building and maintaining relationships with mass media and influencers is likely to continue to grow in importance in the future. In fact, experts predict that more and more influencers will pop up. These new influencers, though, may have a rather small following and lack a celebrity status. These *nano influencers* are perceived as regular people, and advice from them is seen as advice from a friend, making their endorsements seem highly authentic. On the other hand, these nano influencers do not require big investments from the organization – they may be happy to praise the product simply in exchange for free samples (Freberg, 2022; Maheshwari, 2018). As the role of nano influencers increases, organizations may have to reevaluate their partnerships with larger mega influencers and mass media to better understand the most effective use of their marketing dollars.

Media landscape is constantly changing and this affects organizations. For example, the virtual reality (VR) media market is expected to grow at a rate of 13.8% every year till 2030. Just in the United States, the VR market was already reaching US$ 30 billion in 2022, and every year it is expected to continue expanding (Grand View Research, 2023). While for many, VR is just about gaming, but it is in fact used in a variety of industries, including medicine, education, and manufacturing. In VR worlds, new influencers and media types are developing and will continue to do so. This will create new challenges for organizations but also provide additional opportunities. In addition to VR, augmented reality (AR) and mixed reality (MR) create opportunities for organizations to communicate with media and influencers.

Many organizations are becoming their own media organizations. In the past, if the organization wanted to speak about an issue, they had to rely on a few publications that may or may not give them their platforms to speak on. Today, however, organizations have their own pages on Facebook, Twitter, YouTube, TikTok, in addition to their organizational websites, where they may speak freely without any editorial control. Some organizational leaders even write their blogs to share their perspectives on the organization, industry, politics, world, or anything else. For example, Mark Cuban, a business leader who runs several organizations, has his own blog, Blog Maverick (he is a former majority owner of the Dallas Mavericks NBA team), where he talks about NBA, gives advice to small businesses, proposes infrastructure spending plans to the US president, and shares his experience with VR. Thus, organizations can develop their own influencers by encouraging their CEOs or other employees to blog or use other forms of social media consistently.

Chapter Summary

Media and influencers are often referred to as intermediary publics, as the organization uses them to reach a larger audience. Some of these intermediaries are also considered opinion leaders who, through a two-step flow of information, may make the organizational messaging more persuasive for the target publics than direct communications from the organization. An important component of the media's and influencer's appeal is the third-party endorsement, if the endorser is seen as an expert on the subject or just an honest and trustworthy source. While the focus has traditionally been on mega-influencers and celebrities with millions of followers, a rise of nano influencers may change organizational priorities. Mass media is also experiencing significant changes, including digitization of media where many traditional media outlets become digital, offering websites, social media presence, and mobile apps. Some digital-first media are moving in the opposite direction, adding traditional media to their digital presence. Technological changes will continue to affect how people and organizations communicate as new platforms are appearing, including in virtual reality, augmented reality, and mixed reality.

Five Key Terms to Remember

Intermediary
Two-Step Flow
Third-Party Endorsement
Influencer
Cost-per-Mille

Discussion Questions and Activities

1 Explain how organizations can justify spending millions of dollars to advertise during key sporting events. Discuss the benefits and drawbacks of such advertisements.
2 Analyze the concept of newsworthiness. Then, look at the home page of the university's news media or local news media outlet. What components of newsworthiness can you identify in the news stories you see? What components are missing?
3 Scroll through social media of any influencer of your choice. Identify what products and services they endorse. Do you think there is a good connection between the influencer and what they promote?

4 Pick any organization you are familiar with. Propose an influencer this organization should partner with; develop three strategies for this partnership.

5 If an organization would approach you to promote their products on your social media, how would you respond? What considerations would you have in making this decision?

How to Learn More

Wilcox, D. L., & Reber, B. H. (2021). *Public relations: Writing and media techniques*, (8th ed.). Pearson.

Fitch, B. (2012). *Media relations handbook for government, associations, nonprofits, and elected officials, 2e*. The Capitol Net Inc.

Freberg, K. (2022). *Social media for strategic communication: Creative strategies and research-based applications*, (2nd ed.). Sage Publications.

Case Study

Peloton: How Bumpy Is the Trail Ahead?

Figure 10.5 *Source:* Michael Vi / shutterstock.

1. Summary of the Case

Peloton's holiday season commercial for its highly regarded exercise bike led to a public outcry and ridicule the organization had not anticipated. The exercise company became a topic of conversation not just online but also on every major media network and social media outlet with its reputation turned into a meme. The repercussions of the advertisement that media dubbed dystopian and sexist soon became financially detrimental causing the largest crisis the organization had ever experienced. An ad designed to generate sales unleashed a public outcry that took aim at Peloton's reputation and created a media firestorm that Peloton was not ready for. As the media pressed on, Peloton decided to stand its ground and fight the waves of media criticism. This decision already cost the company US$ 1.5 billion in valuation and the memes just keep coming. As a result, this case highlights the importance of proactively managing media relations for organizational reputation.

2. Organization's Background and Historical Development

Peloton is the largest interactive fitness platform in the world with millions of members and revenues in the billions. It was founded in 2012 by John Foley, a former Barnes & Noble executive, who realized that his instructor-led workouts were much more rewarding than his self-led workouts at the gym. After years of struggling to get to in-person classes while balancing work and family, the idea of Peloton was born. Foley wanted to bring the experience of his exercise classes home "in a more accessible, affordable and efficient way" (Frieswick, 2016). A new concept in fitness was introduced using technology and world-class instructors to enable users to reach their goals at home, on their own time (Peloton, 2023).

It took some time for the concept to gain momentum. In 2013, a prototype bike was designed and produced, which was used to generate awareness and capital via a Kickstarter crowdfunding campaign. Foley opened a small store in a luxury mall in Millburn, New Jersey, where he hoped to sell a minimum of one bike per day. To his surprise, initial sales for this 2,000-dollar bike exceeded all expectations. Venture capital investments followed and allowed the company to expand its reach.

Sales were growing and the first Peloton studio opened in New York City that allowed instructors to record their classes. Peloton began to charge US$ 39 a month for streaming classes as they continued to open showrooms across the country (Griffith, 2019). Peloton's unlimited live and on-demand classes' monthly subscriptions were growing in popularity as well. This represented the second piece to the company's value proposition – not only was the consumer receiving a robust piece of equipment, but they would be able to experience the camaraderie of being a part of group classes from the comfort of their home.

By integrating themselves into their customers' lives, Peloton created a "cult community" where users could watch themselves competing against others in the class and then chat on social media pages or comment on their favorite instructors' photos. Peloton brought the experience outside of the workout and gave their instructors and customers a place to engage worldwide and feel a sense of

(Continued)

Case Study   (Continued)

community. Peloton started being compared with another corporation with a cult following as media referred to it as the "Apple of Fitness" (Huddleston, 2019). In 2018, the company expanded its product lineup to offer a US$ 4,000 treadmill to combat consumers who were experiencing "spin fatigue." Over the next five years, it was clear that Peloton was delivering a superior product and experience to its growing customer base. In 2019, Peloton described the scope of their operations: "we are a technology, media, software, product, experience, fitness, design, retail, apparel, logistics company" (Schleifer, 2019).

In October 2019, Peloton went public but struggled to convince investors of its financial merits with trading down 11% from its IPO price (O'Brien, 2019). Despite this less-than-stellar start, the newly public organization was valued at US$ 8 billion, which was a far cry from its early days operating as a pop-up store in a mall. As a publicly traded organization, Peloton recognized the need to increase profits as it entered the 2019 holiday season, taking into account that, in its focus on growth, the company was still unprofitable.

3. Operational Environment and Main Publics

Peloton's mission statement is more than just about exercise: "Peloton uses technology and design to connect the world through fitness, empowering people to be the best version of themselves anywhere, anytime" (Peloton, 2023). The focus on connection makes it similar to various social media platforms, and its community features are the key components of what makes Peloton a highly valuable company. Peloton also lists its core values:

1. Put Members First
2. Operate with a Bias for Action
3. Empower Teams of Smart Creatives
4. Together We Go Far

Over the years, Peloton added the fifth one: Be the Best Place to Work (Peloton, 2023).

Despite the lack of profitability that worried investors and financial analysts, customers loved Peloton. The Apple of Fitness truly garnered an avid following that resulted in over 400,000 bikes sold as of early 2019 (Huddleston, 2019). One of the company's leaders, Tom Cortese, focused his efforts on creating the consumer experience as satisfactory as the best technology companies like Netflix and Amazon provide.

But the main reason consumers seemingly cannot get enough of the exercise company is centered around their fitness instructors. In fact, industry experts conclude that Peloton enjoys a distinct competitive advantage due to how Peloton "built their instructors into their brand, with many of their instructors achieving a sort of cult status among the Peloton following" (Huddleston, 2019).

Terms like *cult* and *gang* became common in the media when talking about Peloton's customers and reflected fervent support by the fans of the organization. Peloton became more than a bike, treadmill, and classes – it became a dedicated community with a strong feeling of exclusivity due to the high price tag of equipment and subscription. Peloton became a status symbol for its consumers and prospective buyers.

The company took special pride in how riders who virtually participated in live classes soon began to develop genuine relationships with one another after months of partaking in the same virtual classes. *Peloton meet-ups* became commonplace with riders traveling across the country to connect in-person with one another and with the instructors (Mull, 2019a). Aside from the company's public social media page, loyal customers soon developed subgroups online to connect with one another in their local regions. Reddit's r/Pelotoncycle has over 400,000 members, making it one of the largest communities on the platform. Ultimately, this organically created fanbase only fueled the organization's reputation of reliability, positivity, and community.

4. The Issue Development

External momentum was reaching a fever pitch for Peloton in late 2019. The company was building a cult-like following for its renowned exercise bike, treadmill, and online classes. The relatively new organization found a sweet spot in the market by converging the aesthetic simplicity of Apple products while taking cues from in-person exercise experiences such as SoulCycle to deliver a refined and inspirational health experience for consumers.

In this environment, Peloton was launching a holiday ad hoping to capitalize on the season of gift giving. The 30-second advertisement centers around a young and fit woman. She wakes up on Christmas morning surprised to see that her husband presented her with a new Peloton bike as a holiday gift. The commercial then chronicles the wife's journey over the course of the next year. She documents her experience with the exercise bike through a series of self-filmed vignettes, which include her coming home from work to ride the bike, waking up early to partake in a live class, and exercising while her daughter plays nearby. The commercial culminates a year later with the family watching the video the wife created that follows her tear-log Peloton journey. She remarks in the video how much the bike has changed her and thanks her husband.

Once the ad aired, however, the reaction was not what the company expected: "An internet that rarely agrees on anything was seemingly united on this one thing: The Peloton ad was downright dystopian" (Shammas, 2019, p. 1). Many in the mass media and on social media seemed outraged about the notion of a man suggesting to his wife she needed to exercise: people felt it was tone deaf for the husband to provide his wife with a piece of exercise equipment, as if she did not conform to his expectations of health and beauty. Others took issue with the actress portraying the wife due to her already slim physicality. They found the notion that this seemingly fit woman finds emotional strength from an exercise bike when she is already very slender. On top of it, the end scene of the commercial looked like the wife was providing a report to her husband on how much she worked out on the bike over the course of the year. In addition, throughout the commercial, almost every time we saw the woman's face

(Continued)

Case Study   (Continued)

exercising, it looked painful and even terrified – as if she was forced to exercise or resorted to it in a "desperate effort to please her spouse" (Mull, 2019b). *USA Today* asked the country to save the woman from the Peloton commercial (Shammas, 2019).

Overall the reactions ranged from outraged to amused, with some ridiculing the commercial as sexist (Abad-Santos, 2019).

The specific timeline of the case is below:

- November 4, 2019. Peloton's new commercial "The Gift That Gives Back" goes into the market on TV ads (Graham, 2019).
- November 12, 2019. Peloton amplifies the new commercial on their social channels (Peloton, 2019).
- Late November. Media erupts with criticism as the commercial begins to gain traction.
- December 4, 2019. Peloton releases an official statement to CNBC and shares words of support it received from its consumers in an attempt to counter the negative backlash in the media (Graham, 2019).
- December 6, 2019. Peloton actress parodies herself on Ryan Reynolds' Gin Commercial "The Gift That Doesn't Give Back" (Reynolds, 2019).
- Dec. 12, 2019. Peloton actress "Monica Ruiz" does an exclusive interview at *The Today Show* alongside Ryan Reynolds (*Today Show*, 2019).
- December 12, 2019. Over a week, Peloton's stock price tumbles following negative publicity (Fineman, 2019).

Monica Ruiz of Hermosa Beach, CA, who starred in Peloton's commercial as the young wife also became a media phenomenon. Prior to her engagement with Peloton, Ruiz starred in other commercials and modeled for Target, Gap, Old Navy, and Speedo (Spencer, 2019). During the height of the public outcry, many ridiculed her facial expressions throughout the advertisement, which were turned into memes and parodies across various social media platforms. She also became the star of a new commercial for Aviation American Gin. The commercial was a lighthearted play on the original character Ruiz portrayed in the original Peloton commercial. The advertisement was aimed to put a comedic spin on the stressed young wife following the public debacle of the commercial. In the ad, Ruiz's character is out for drinks with two of her girlfriends following what is clearly a volatile experience given she appears close to tears and begins to quickly drink the Aviation Gin excessively and toasts to "new beginnings" (Reynolds, 2019).

On December 12, 2019, Ruiz appeared on *The Today Show* with Ryan Reynolds. Both Ruiz and Reynolds acknowledged how the advertisement played off the Peloton commercial in a comedic sense and was meant to be a lighthearted way to poke fun at the series of events (*Today Show*, 2019). Shortly after the gin ad aired, the commercial received over 9 million views on Twitter (Spencer, 2019). Ruiz goes on to say in her interview with *The Today Show* how she takes a degree of accountability for the situation. "Honestly, I think it's my face . . . that was the problem. I want to let everyone know that I am okay, I am fine" (*Today Show*, 2019).

Thus, the ad itself became a media phenomenon. It resulted in numerous parodies in addition to the Ryan Reynolds famous take and received coverage all over the media outlets. But there was more to the commercial woes – viewers noted that the commercial featured multi-million-dollar homes, healthy families, and even zen gardens outside – Peloton was accused of being a privileged brand for privileged consumers. The fact that the CEO of the company called Peloton's US$ 2,245 bike "crazy affordable" did not help either (Andrew, 2019).

5. Peloton's Response

Peloton from the very beginning did not handle the media criticism well and focused on attacking the media back. The company blamed its critics for producing an engineered outrage over topics that were benign in nature and expressed their dissatisfaction with the media (Cerullo, 2019). Peloton, in fact, released an official statement to CNBC over its holiday ad. According to the statement, the company expressed that "while we are disappointed in how some have misinterpreted this commercial, we are encouraged by – and grateful for – the outpouring of support we've received from those who understand what we were trying to communicate" (Graham, 2019).

In addition to the statement, Peloton's team provided CNBC with a PDF of several customer emails and social media posts expressing their continued support for the exercise company amid the increased public scrutiny (Graham, 2019). One of the PDFs reads: "When I see that ad, I see a woman who is lovingly gifted a Peloton bike because it is something just for her . . . I love this ad, because, in it, I see me" (as cited in Graham, 2019). The company also promoted the hashtag *#Iamthepelotonwoman* but it did not gain much traction.

This response, however, did not help deter the media coverage. As media backlash reached a peak during the first week of December, the fitness company's stock began to slide. On Tuesday, December 4, shares for the company fell more than 9%, resulting in a loss just shy of 1 billion dollars for the organization (Reinicke, 2019). This was the single largest day drop for the company since October 2019. In the weeks following the stock slump, the company continued to lose value. Wall Street analysts released a report in mid-December indicating more bad news for the company. Andrew Left, from Citron Research, articulated that investors are increasingly worried about the company. The research predicted that "investors will soon tire on the exercise bike and streaming workout video producer" (CBS News, 2019).

While Peloton did have its supporters over the commercial, its response was harder to defend. While the commercial was a great target of ridicule, many took great offense to Peloton's response itself when the company announced their disappointment in essentially anybody who would disagree with them. In particular, the company's phrase that they were "disappointed in how some have misinterpreted this commercial" (Graham, 2019) seemed quite dismissive. Jason Aten analyzed Peloton's response and concluded: "Peloton's response to criticism

(*Continued*)

Case Study   (Continued)

demonstrates that it not only doesn't believe it has a brand issue but that the company is sorry if you feel it does ... Rather than fix it, that ends up feeling like a slap in the face" (Aten, 2019).

Aten was not the only one to weigh in on the company's response. In fact, other media relations wrote several thought leadership pieces on the fitness company's communications response. Amy Rosenberg from PR News Online offered her perspective that the fallout could have been avoided if the company had more women represented on its communications team. She wrote, "To the Peloton CEO: Where are the women on your team? PR is full of your core audience – smart women who could tell you that your actress looks like she's starring in a hostage video instead of a fitness ad. They'd also remove the gas-lighting tone of your statement" (Rosenberg, 2019). For the longest time, the company championed positivity and inclusivity, but now, its reputation was being maligned by the very ideals that run counter to its core values – leaving them in a precarious position.

What Is Next?

Overall, Peloton encountered a very bumpy road during a rather volatile period of its existence – both financially and reputationally. The company had several challenges to overcome as it looked to repair its reputation with consumers and gain some positive coverage in the media. Peloton's CEO John Foley was entering the new year trying to convince everyone that the Apple of Fitness can continue to grow its sales while remaining a premium brand, just like the actual Apple, Inc. does. For Foley, however, Peloton was his baby – it was always more than a job, it was personal. In this situation, facing criticism from investors, analysts, and colleagues also seemed personal. But nothing could be more personal than the public ridicule of Peloton in the media – as Foley was looking at the memes that followed the ad, he could not avoid feeling personally under attack....

References

Abad-Santos, A. (2019). Peloton's terrifying new ad is the best horror movie in recent memory. *The Vox* (3 December). https://www.vox.com/culture/2019/12/3/20993432/peloton-new-commercial-horror-movie

Andrew, S. (2019, December 3). Peloton's perplexing new holiday ad has incensed the internet. CNN. https://edition.cnn.com/2019/12/03/us/peloton-ad-controversy-trnd/index.html

Associated Press (2023). Adidas reports a $540M loss as it struggles with unsold Yeezy products. NPR (8 March). https://www.npr.org/2023/03/08/1161905306/adidas-ye-kanye-west-yeezy-loss#:~:text=Adidas%20reports%20a%20%24540M,of%20unsold%20Yeezy%20products%20%3A%20NPR&text=Press-,Adidas%20reports%20a%20%24540M%20loss%2C%20in%20part%20because%20of,over%20the%20rapper's%20antisemitic%20remarks

Aten, J. (2019). Peloton's latest ad was bad, but its response to the criticism was far worse. *Inc.* (5 December). https://www.inc.com/jason-aten/pelotons-latest-ad-was-bad-but-its-response-to-criticism-was-far-worse.html

Baum, B. (2023). How Michael Jordan revolutionized the sneaker industry – and our relationship to shoes. *Temple Now* (3 April). https://news.temple.edu/news/2023-04-03/how-michael-jordan-revolutionized-sneaker-industry-and-our-relationship-shoes

Cassidy, K. (2023). Big game, big bucks: The value of advertising during the Super Bowl. CCF (7 February). https://ccf-ideas.com/2023/02/big-game-big-bucks-the-value-of-advertising-during-the-super-bowl/

CBS News (2019). Peloton shares drop as critic claims he's found something "worse than the commercial." CBS News (11 December). https://www.cbsnews.com/news/peloton-shares-drop-as-short-seller-flags-something-worse-than-the-commercial-2019-12-11/

Cerullo, M. (2019). Peloton holiday ad sparks heated debate on social media over body imagery. CBS News (4 December). https://www.cbsnews.com/news/peloton-bike-ad-internet-divided-over-peloton-holiday-ad-today-2019-12-03/

Dencheva, V. (2023). Social media advertising and marketing. *Statista* (17 February). https://www.statista.com/topics/1538/social-media-marketing/#topicOverview

Fineman, J. (2019). Peloton stock is pummeled on backlash from 'gift that gives' ad. *Bloomberg* (3 December). https://www.bloomberg.com/news/articles/2019-12-03/peloton-backlash-over-gift-that-gives-ad-pummels-stock

Freberg, K. (2022). *Social media for strategic communication: Creative strategies and research-based applications* (2nd ed.). Sage Publications.

Frieswick, K. (2016). This startup will keep you from ever going to the gym again. *Inc.* (28 April). https://www.inc.com/magazine/201605/kris-frieswick/peloton-studio-cycling-home-fitness.html

Graham, M. (2019). Peloton responds to ad criticism, says it's 'disappointed in how some have misinterpreted' the spot. CNBC (4 December). https://www.cnbc.com/2019/12/04/peloton-says-its-disappointed-in-how-some-have-misinterpreted-ad.html

Grand View Research (2023). Virtual reality market size, share & trends analysis report by technology (semi & fully immersive, non-immersive), by device (HMD, GTD), by component (Hardware, Software), by application, by region, and segment forecasts, 2023 – 2030. https://www.grandviewresearch.com/industry-analysis/virtual-reality-vr-market#:~:text=Report%20Overview,environment%20in%20the%20real%20world

Griffith, E. (2019). Peloton is a phenomenon. Can it last? *New York Times* (28 August). https://www.nytimes.com/2019/08/28/technology/peloton-ipo.html

Huddleston, T. Jr. (2019). How Peloton exercise bikes became a $4 billion fitness start-up with a cult following. CNBC (12 February). https://www.cnbc.com/2019/02/12/how-peloton-exercise-bikes-and-streaming-gained-a-cult-following.html

Luoma-aho, V., Pirttimäki, T., Maity, D., Munnukka, J., & Reinikainen, H. (2019). Primed authenticity: How priming impacts authenticity perception of social media influencers. *International Journal of Strategic Communication*, *13*(4), 352–365.

Maheshwari, S. (2018). Are you ready for the nanoinfluencers? *New York Times* (11 November). https://www.nytimes.com/2018/11/11/business/media/nanoinfluencers-instagram-influencers.html

Monllos, K. (2023). Here's what a $7M, 30-second Super Bowl ad can purchase in digital media in 2023. *Digiday* (10 February). https://digiday.com/marketing/what-a-7m-super-bowl-ad-buy-can-purchase-in-digital-media-in-2023/

Mull, A. (2019a). I joined a stationary-biker gang. *The Atlantic* (4 November). https://www.theatlantic.com/magazine/archive/2019/12/the-tribe-of-peloton/600748/

Mull, A. (2019b). Peloton doesn't understand the people who love it most. *The Atlantic* (5 December). https://www.theatlantic.com/health/archive/2019/12/peloton-christmas-gift-controversy/603148/

Mulshine, M. (2014). A brief history of Kim Kardashian's endorsement deals. *Observer* (22 October). https://observer.com/2014/10/a-brief-history-of-kim-kardashians-endorsement-deals/

O'Brien, S. (2019). Peloton falls below IPO price in Wall Street debut. CNN (7 October). https://www.cnn.com/2019/09/26/tech/peloton-ipo/index.html

Peloton (2019). A gift like no other. Twitter (12 November). https://twitter.com/onepeloton/status/1194389524203343873?ref_src=twsrc%5Etfw%7Ctwcamp%5Etweetembed%7Ctwterm%5E1194389524203343873%7Ctwgr%5E

Peloton (2023). The Peloton story. https://www.onepeloton.com/company

Qureshi, A. (2021). Lil Miquela and the dawn of the CGI influencer, explained. *34th Street* (1 February). https://www.34st.com/article/2021/02/cgi-influencer-youtuber-instagram-bella-hadid-lil-miquela-insta-model-digital-ai-artificial-intelligence-shudu-gram-calvin-klein-social-media#:~:text=Meet%20Lil%20Miquela%2C%20or%20Miquela,influencer%20created%20using%20motion%20graphics

Reinicke, C. (2019). Peloton saw $942 million in market value wiped out in a single day amid backlash to its controversial holiday ad (PTON). *Insider* (4 December). https://markets.businessinsider.com/news/stocks/pelotons-stock-price-plummet-wiped-942-million-market-value-holiday-ad-2019-12-1028737428

Reynolds, R. (2019). Exercise bike not included. #AviationGin. Twitter (7 December). https://twitter.com/vancityreynolds/status/1203118775815622664?lang=en

Rosenberg, A. (2019). A PR Pro's takeaways from the Peloton controversy. *PR News* (17 December). https://www.prnewsonline.com/a-pr-pros-takeaways-from-the-peloton-controversy/

Schleifer, T. (2019, August 27). Peloton, a bike company, claims it "sells happiness" and is 'so much more than a bike.' Vox. https://www.vox.com/recode/2019/8/27/20835839/peloton-ipo-filing-messaging-happiness

Shammas, B. (2019). The worst Christmas advert of 2019? Peloton creates dystopian fitness inspo hellscape. *Stuff* (5 December). www.stuff.co.nz/life-style/well-good/117952633/the-worst-christmas-advert-of-2019-peloton-creates-dystopian-fitness-inspo-hellscape

Spencer, A. (2019). Peloton girl, aka Monica Ruiz, stars in a hilarious new ad for Aviation Gin. *Prevention* (9 December). https://www.prevention.com/fitness/a30169191/peloton-ad-controversy-explained-monica-ruiz/

Today Show (2019). Peloton ad actress Monica Ruiz tells her story. *Today Show* (12 December). https://www.today.com/video/peloton-ad-actress-monica-ruiz-tells-her-story-74963525915

Wallach, O. (2021). The world's top 50 influencers across social media platforms. *Visual Capitalist* (14 May). https://www.visualcapitalist.com/worlds-top-50-influencers-across-social-media-platforms/

Wilcox, D. L. (2005). *Public relations: Writing and media techniques*, (5th ed.). Allyn and Bacon.

Index